The New
ASTROLOGY

The New ASTROLOGY

Sun Signs

Taina Ketola

BOOKS
A Division of Shapolsky Publishers

The New Astrology

S.P.I. BOOKS
A division of Shapolsky Publishers, Inc.

Copyright © 1994 by SPI Books

ISBN 1-56171-326-0

For any additional information, contact:

S.P.I. BOOKS/Shapolsky Publishers, Inc.
136 West 22nd Street
New York, NY 10011
212/633-2022/FAX 212/633-2123

Manufactured in Canada

10 9 8 7 6 5 4 3 2 1

For my Mother,
Tophe, Steve and Tyler.
Together they form a cardinal cross,
which it is my privilege
to carry.

Acknowledgments

The following people have been instrumental in helping me to acquire the knowledge, experience and opportunities that have made this book possible: First of all I would like to thank my mother who always believed her children should be free to do whatever they really wanted to do. She encouraged me, and paid for my astrology lessons. Secondly, H. Eugene Adams, whose astrology lessons she paid for. These gave me a good, solid traditional basis to branch out from.

Astrology today is a vast and growing field. There are many excellent astrologers out there, and many forms of "new astrology" other than my own. We all learn from each other, and whether or not it is immediately apparent, I have been strongly influenced by the following authors: Stephen Arroyo, Maurice B. Cooke, Fred Gettings, Liz Greene, Myrna Lofthus, Betty Lundsted and Martin Schulman.

I would like to acknowledge what I have learned from my clients in the process of working with them. I have had the privilege of meeting some incredible people doing the work I do. Special thanks also to my dear friend Eutonnah V. Olsen-Dunn for the shared inspiration that has contributed greatly to my theories.

I would also like to thank Ann Emerson, Valanne Ridgeway, Marie Matte D.C., Anita Levin, Michael Morrison and many others for helping to promote my career and providing the referrals which have helped me to hone my knowledge even further, and Pamela Hammond for unfailing support, inspiration and the use of her computer skills before I was able to acquire my faithful dinosaur. Thank you, Steven, for your constant support, and for providing the necessary childcare that allowed this book to see completion. And finally, I would like to thank John McCabe Bell at S.P.I. Books for helping this volume to see print. Many happy Solar Returns, Johnnie. You will one day be a famous third-stage Libra!

Introduction

This book is the first in a series of guides designed to introduce you to a revolutionary new approach to emotional, psychological and spiritual development through astrology. It is designed for use by everyone, whatever their present level of astrological knowledge. Even if you have no previous experience of astrology, this series will enable you to walk step-by-step through your own birth chart in order to discover the riches that may be found within. On the other hand, even the experienced practitioner will find new and fascinating theories to explore.

This volume describes the development of the natal Sun sign.* Just as the physical Sun is the vital center of our solar system, so is the Sun sign in the birthchart the central theme of the soul's development. All other aspects of the birth chart must be referred to this central theme before they can be fully understood — and this is exactly what we will do in future volumes. Because the Sun sign is the most basic foundation of any chart, it is important enough to merit a book of its own.

I have studied both astrology and reincarnation for the last 20 years, and have discovered some interesting ways in which the two appear to be related. It seems that we are not victims of our stars. Instead, we select them before we are born to achieve a specific purpose. As we progress, we all ultimately learn to view our lives from the spiritual level at which our first selections were made. One of the most important discoveries I have made is that each Sun sign represents a universal archetype that each individual may choose to perfect over an entire series of lifetimes. We choose one sign to govern our overall life purpose, and we keep trying until we get it right. If this is Earth school, the birth chart is our curriculum, and the Sun sign

*This is astrological jargon for your birth sign. When people ask, "What's your star sign?" this is what we mean by the natal Sun sign. Because we are dealing only with the Sun sign in this guide, I will try to avoid the use of too many traditional astrological terms. They will be described in detail in future volumes.

is the subject in which we are majoring. (I'm majoring in Aries, what Sun sign are you majoring in?)

In addition, our courses of study seem to be divided into "semesters" which I have named the Three Stages, complete with periods of relative ease, and times of test or crisis. (Are you going through your 'exams' right now?) Each of these stages takes most individuals several lifetimes to complete. Each stage has a totally different personality from the one that precedes it. Each has a completely different set of priorities and experiences. In fact there are not simply 12 different types of people — there are at least 36.

This can go a long way towards explaining why you can meet someone who has the same Sun sign as you do, and yet find that you are radically different from one another. In fact you may find certain individuals to be quite irritating at times who are at an earlier stage than yourself, but one you have not yet fully come to terms with.

An individual at a certain stage of development often seems to have more in common with other individuals at the same stage of development in other signs than he or she may have with those at a different stage of development in the same Sun sign. This is because each phase has common needs and goals. There seems to be an archetypical process of soul progression shared by all signs.

Everybody selects a Sun sign to represent the specific goals towards which their souls are striving. In first stage they will attempt on an innocent level to develop the basic characteristics upon which future development will be founded. For most signs (Pisces being the notable exception) the first stage represents a kind of spiritual childhood when the winds of fate blow easily in one's favor. First stage is a necessary subjective building process. We cover the basics in a sort of 'user-friendly' manner. Each stage lasts several lifetimes.

By the end of first stage, life and the character of the individual are becoming more complex. Before one even realizes what is happening, certain questions must be faced for which there seem to be no answer. The first crisis is now encountered. Most souls will respond in fear or denial, passing or, so it seems, falling into the second stage, where they undergo what appears to be a process of self-undoing.

When the soul can no longer cope with the neuroses born of the second stage of development, it passes into the transition to third stage, where it must take conscious responsibility for its own soul development. Ultimately each of us achieves the seemingly impossible transition into the third stage, where the full potentials of the sign are made manifest.

This theory may seem somewhat abstract, but once you have read concrete examples of the signs themselves, you will be able to understand this theory in greater depth. More will be said in the conclusion (see page 304).

I used to believe that the three stages represented an inevitable progression through which all must pass. However my work often allows me to see the previous lifetimes of many of my clients, and I began to encounter individuals who seemed to have bypassed second stage and all of its discomforts. I learned that a kind of doorway opens to all of us at the end of first stage, offering a crossroads where we may choose to develop ourselves to the point where we can move directly into the third stage and bypass the illusions and struggles lying ahead in second stage. Each individual has the opportunity to pass directly into third stage, rather than being doomed to make the long and difficult journey along what appears to be a path of least resistance through the second stage of his development.

From a spiritual level, I cannot say which choice may be the better one. I only know that I have seen the crossroads, and that each soul must be free to make its own choice. It is my suspicion that, all appearances to the contrary, each will also make the personal best decision.

Many older writings dating from the early part of this century, the middle ages and beyond, speak of members of the various signs as being 'evolved' or 'unevolved' and seem to speak of these as being completely different personality types -- as though there were really more than just 12 character types found among humanity. In addition there is evidence from some of the earlier writings of an astrological system that used more than one symbolic image for each of the 12 signs of the zodiac. Linda Goodman records a good example of this in her Sun Signs book. She mentions that Scorpio is represented symbolically by the

Scorpion, the Grey Lizard and the Eagle—each of these symbols referring to a different form of personality type characteristic of the sign in question. Other ancient symbols include the Wolf for Aries (usually the Ram), the Cat and the Scarab for Cancer (usually the Crab), and the Whale for Pisces (normally the Fishes).

These apparent remnants have always fascinated me, and as my study of astrology progressed, they remained in the back of my mind. It has always seemed to me that these symbols contained a wealth of hidden knowledge. To me they have always indicated that there is more than one possible blueprint or character type for each sign of the zodiac. With time, and through observation, I came to realize there are indeed several different astrological types to be found within each sign and that these types do seem to be aligned in some form of evolutionary order. The results of this discovery form the theory upon which this book is based.

Although some systems which attempt to integrate astrology and reincarnation teach that we reincarnate in an orderly progression from the first sign of the zodiac to the last (from Aries to Pisces), or that certain signs are more spiritually evolved than others, in my own experience I have not found this to be the case. No sign is spiritually superior to any other sign, and everybody chooses the path through the zodiac best for them as they pursue their completely unique path of personal development.

In this chapter I will consider the pattern of evolution through these three distinct stages of development as they commonly occur in every sign. To make best use of the material in this book, I would recommend that you read this chapter first, followed by the chapter that relates to your natal Sun sign. Then return to this chapter and read it again to better understand the theories presented here. You will be able to apply this information to yourself and others in the most beneficial manner.

Before I begin giving a more detailed description of the characteristics of each of the three stages, I would like to spend some time discussing the theories of reincarnation. Reincarnation seems like a new and startling theory to the average Westerner, but it is an ancient doctrine which is still firmly respected by a vast portion of the world's population. Recent public opinion polls indicate that this number includes fifty million Americans, so perhaps it is not such a foreign idea after all. Reincarnation is a part of the doctrine of most of the world's religions. It was not rejected by the Christian church until the middle of the first millennium, and it still forms part of the teachings of certain branches of esoteric Christianity, and is taught by the Sufis and the Kabbalists.

Many records exist of people who have been hypnotized and who have recalled details of previous lives that were later verified through the study of ancient records. There are also many cases on record of children who have remembered their previous lives and were able to lead investigators back to where they had once lived, identifying relatives and recalling intimate details of their previous lifestyles, sometimes even uncovering hidden money and other valuables no one else had known about.

Because my own most recent previous lifetime was unusually traumatic, the nightmares, phobias and health problems that plagued me eventually led me to investigate reincarnation. When I was able to completely recall my past experience, all of the problems with which I had struggled disappeared, practically overnight. This is not uncommon. While the memory remains submerged, the subconscious seems to believe that the traumatic event is still happening or could repeat itself at any time.

Once one set of memories is accessed, it seems to make it much easier for the mind to recall other lifetimes and, at times, perceive the past experiences of others. I have experienced shared memories with friends and relatives, where we were able to compare notes concerning shared past experiences. I remember one time when I was discussing a wonderful past-life love with the object of my former affection, only to discover it really hadn't meant very much to him as he'd had "women all over Europe." In another situation I remembered a specific past event and, years later, a friend of mine, who had not known the details of my situation, phoned to apologize for what he had done to me in that lifetime as he had just remembered these events.

According to the theory of reincarnation, it takes far more than just a single lifetime to reach maturity as an individual. With each passing incarnation, we develop in our quest for perfection as individuals. This process is subject to several laws. Many people have heard of the idea that we choose our own parents. I have heard people jokingly say, ``If that's the case what was I thinking?'' The truth of the matter is that we choose all our experiences. But we are not always in control of the part of us that does the choosing.

Esoteric tradition teaches that we consist of three separate or apparently separate aspects. We are aware of our conscious self, and are able to recognize when that part of us makes a life decision. At other times we choose less consciously, and the subconscious mind seems to be in control. An obvious example of this is when we sleepwalk. Sometimes we sleepwalk through life. But a part of spiritual evolution involves learning how to properly utilize the conscious and subconscious aspects of ourselves, so that we can consciously be in control of all of our life experiences.

The third aspect of consciousness is the eternal spiritual self, often called the Higher Self. This part of us often makes decisions for us that we are not aware of, but which are always in the best interests of our soul's development. Another important part of our spiritual development involves becoming consciously aware of this part of ourselves as well, and learning to work in harmony with this Higher Self, which is also our true Self, so that we can learn to completely master our lives. It is through the Higher Self that all miracles are accomplished and all spiritual power and understanding is achieved.

When all three aspects of the self have found their proper function, they work in unison, and our most important basic quest is complete. All of life's challenges and experiences lead to this ultimate goal. An esoteric astrologer can look at your birth chart and see there the plans that your Higher Self has made for you. It is also possible to use the birthchart as a key to understanding the subconscious motivations that have drawn your past and present life experiences to you. The birthchart, like a map or travel log, shows where you are in life's spiritual journey at the present time. In this book we are discussing the 12 main travel packages from which we all choose our own personal itineraries.

There is a lot more which could be said, but for the purposes of this book, there is only one more topic that I would like to discuss. Most people cannot think of reincarnation without thinking of the law of karma. Usually they think it means we will receive from life exactly what we have given out. You kick the dog—the dog kicks you. While karma can function in this manner, that is not its only definition, nor is it the only way of dealing with the results of one's actions. Karma is very much related to the subconscious. The subconscious carries a perfect record of our experience. It is as if, wherever we go, we carry an enormous bag of video tapes describing everything that we have ever done, thought or experienced. Imagine the load. Imagine what a heavy load our negative thoughts, actions and experiences must be. This is what is meant by instant karma. All of our karma affects us now, as we carry it around with us.

Surprisingly, the greatest 'karmic debt' which we 'owe' to anyone is to ourselves. The way in which we have treated ourselves, the definition that we have of ourselves as individuals, and our most basic beliefs concerning life itself—all of these represent forms of karma that determine our very destiny. Whatever the subconscious stores away forms our own personal karmic pattern. Great sorrow, love, guilt and anger carried from one lifetime to the next is a karmic pattern.

Ultimately karma represents responsibility. It is the karma—the destiny or responsibility—of humanity to learn to master all aspects of self, and to learn to be the most constructive force that this world has yet seen. Therefore we do have karmic patterns that involve others—from 'the dog' to the very planet itself. If we have caused harm to others, the best way to atone may be to suffer in a similar manner if that is what we need in order to learn better. But, if we have already learned the necessary lessons, only our guilt and the negative beliefs that we have about ourselves can cause us to undergo what is often unnecessary pain and suffering. Karma works to the greater good of all, and may instead prompt an individual to act in a positive manner which will more than make up for any of the simple mistakes that we all inevitably must make as younger souls.

Each of the chapters that follow begins with a description of the nature or purpose of the sign in question. There seem to be a certain set of motives, a common urge that draws each individual to select a specific astrological sign. Each sign has its own individual perspective on life, its own set of goals that it seeks to perfect through its own life experience. Each sign begins in simplicity, develops almost impossible complexity, and ends in completion and fulfillment. Once the individual enters upon his or her chosen life path, his first step is to develop a personal ego that forms the basic personality through which everyone eventually perfects themselves. This is the goal of the first stage of development in every sign.

Everyone knows those people who seem to get "all the breaks," regardless of whether or not they seem to have earned them as a result of their basic efforts or abilities. This is not to imply that first-stage individuals are necessarily lacking in ambition, integrity or intelligence. It simply means at this stage they are involved in a process that I call the subjective development of self. They are innocently involved in building the basic foundations of their long-term response to life — and life is cooperating with them in the process. In the beginning of first stage they usually have some sort of spiritual awareness and knowledge of the purpose of their soul's evolution, but as they progress this knowledge generally tends to fade.

First-stage individuals tend to have a secure, if limited, life environment. At least until they are nearing the end of first stage, the early home environment tends to be a positive influence. Pisces is the only exception to this general rule — their lives are exceedingly difficult almost from day one. They may make up for the difficulties they experience in first stage once they reach second stage, as many second-stage Pisceans construct safe and bountiful lives for themselves at some point during this time. Eventually, in all signs, as first stage progresses life becomes increasingly more complex, and the ego, as its foundation nears completion, begins to show certain cracks or flaws. Conflict enters the picture, as it must in order for a deeper perspective of any kind to be developed. As the individual approaches the second stage of development, the soul's evolution seems to be progressing more rapidly than one feels able to cope with. The force of this forward momentum, seems to produce only conflict and confusion, and threatens to dissolve the ego and its secure, if limited, foundation.

Each stage represents not just another level of development, but quite literally a change in the basic world view and life perspective of the individual. In each stage of our Sun sign's development, we enter a new world that represents a completely unknown experience. Not only is each stage radically different from the one which preceded it, it also represents a level of reality that is invisible to those who exist in the previous stage. As far as first-stage individuals are concerned, the world is populated by nothing but other first-stage individuals. To those in second stage, the Earth is populated only by those experiencing the first and second stage of their development. Only those passing through the third stage are able to see the complete picture. (Only your hairdresser knows for sure — but only if he's in the third stage.)

As the first stage nears its completion, there is mounting anxiety. While the individual once absorbed what life had to offer without question, he now becomes aware of nagging feelings of self-doubt. Life suddenly seems about to overwhelm him, and his self-worth begins to come into question. If the first stage is an experience of innocent subjective self-development, the second stage threatens to become an experience of blind self-destruction or personal dissolution of one form or another. The transition between first and second stage confronts the individual with the first experience of true pain, as the opportunity to deepen personal understanding presents itself.

This transition is a spiritual crossroads, as the soul's desire to grow begins to disrupt the smooth and tranquil world the individual created for himself. Because his development literally threatens to overwhelm him, he has two choices. He must either find some way to make direct contact with a spiritual source of guidance to assist him in his process of self-development, or he must learn to cope in whatever way he can. Since, in this culture, most first-stage individuals receive no external guidance concerning spiritual principles, and because the surrender which spiritual development requires is often viewed as a threat to one's individuality, most souls will choose to continue to go on coping as best they can. This decision marks the entrance into second stage.

In second stage the ego develops greater complexity. While first stage is innocent and may be unaware of certain spiritual and philosophical truths, individuals at the second stage of their development are not yet capable of assimilating all the truths that they are able to perceive. They live a tumultuous existence stranded in a realm halfway between innocence and self-realization.

Some signs may live their lives on the basis of personal feelings of guilt concerning actions in their first stage of development, not realizing that their own innocence at the time prevented them from being anything other than what they were. Other signs experience a constant struggle to keep their lives or minds from disintegrating under the pressures of greater and greater personal challenges, perhaps longing for a lost glory or a lost innocence.

Second-stage individuals tend to be born into more complex cultures and living situations than in their first-stage lifetimes. In addition, their early childhood experience tends to become increasingly conflict-ridden and dysfunctional. Most individuals, through most of their first-stage existences, lead simple and protected lives, but by second stage it seems as if life is determined to throw the book at them. In essence this is quite true, for it is only through experience that the book of life comes to be known and mastered.

As second stage progresses, the crisis reaches a fever-pitch. The opportunity to achieve spiritual understanding that knocked on the door at the beginning of second stage continues to subtly make its presence known. Since the ego has come to view it as a threat, it continues to be strenuously resisted. This is why first-stage individuals encountering some form of mystical ideology are inclined to be rather uninterested, whereas second-stage individuals are often secretly or openly hostile to such concepts. On a more subtle level they may appear to accept the tenets of mystical thought, only to transform such ideas into some sort of dogma, unconsciously using it to serve their own ends, rather than truly opening themselves to a process of personal transformation.

Eventually the pressure becomes too much, the soul cries "uncle," and the transition into the third stage begins. The transition between the second and third stage is the most difficult period in soul development, but it is also the most interesting. At this point the individual must face everything that he or she has buried or suppressed, not only in the present life, but also for the entire series of lifetimes spent in the sign in question. While first and second stage represent periods of unconscious and subjective development of the individual, to enter the third stage the personality must be consciously and deliberately reconstructed. The foundations are built during first stage, they are tested and all their weak points discovered during the second stage, and the entire structure is rebuilt in time to enter the third stage.

At third stage the soul once again enters a new reality. The first taste of real suffering occurs as the individual prepares to enter the second stage; the first taste of true wisdom, as he or she begins the transition into the third stage. Each sign presents the individual with certain riddles to solve—an impossible task without the ability to approach life from a more spiritual level, and to work productively with existing subconscious patterns.

In resolving the difficulties of the second/third-stage transition the soul achieves a greater ability to integrate the three levels of being (the conscious self, the subconscious self and the Higher Self, as indicated above), and with each new sign the individual makes greater progress in achieving his or her final goal. It could be said that in each stage a different one of the three selves dominates. In first stage the conscious self is dominant. In the second stage the individual is usually swept along by subconscious defense mechanisms. This is what makes some second-stage individuals such poor listeners. In third stage the Higher Self becomes dominant, giving the individual an opportunity to develop tremendous breadth of vision, as the full soul purpose of the sign is finally expressed. See figure 1 for a more simplified explanation of the three stages and how they function.

For years I assumed that everyone passed through all three stages as they went about the process of perfecting the sign under which they were born. Then I began to encounter people who seemed to have passed into third stage without undergoing the trials of second stage.

The majority of my clients come to me during the

Figure One

	To serve the life force.	To become the embodiment of unconditional love.	To develop skills, knowledge and understanding with which to serve human evolution.	To nurture what is most precious in life.
PURPOSE				
FIRST STAGE	Builds ego. Innocently self centered. Develops talents. The Peacock.	Loves those who do not return his love. Innocently optimistic. Earthy or creative.	Spends time alone developing skills and knowledge. Fails to mature emotionally.	Creates a family to whom he is dedicated. Develops nurturing skills.
1ST/2ND STAGE TRANSITION	Frantic, insecure. Ego is crumbling. Demanding. May unwittingly harm others, causing great regret.	Wonders why no one loves him. Confidence crumbles. Pain and insecurity result.	Shares discoveries. Ahead of his time. May be worshipped, but still feels isolated. May be rejected or traumatically persecuted.	Wonders if there will be time for him. Develops ambivalence towards family.
SECOND STAGE	Generosity returns. Gives compulsively. Easily manipulated. The doormat.	Frantic search for love and for a means to compensate for its absence. Seeks security through money pleasure or addictions. May demand unconditional love.	Feels rejected by society. Hides emotional self. Controlled by childlike emotions. May become 'good child', selling self short, bad manipulative child, or noble persecuted rebel.	Family is disrupted. Inner upheaval may occur, or outer events may destroy family. Cancer feels guilty. May become fearful or defensive.
KEYS TO MASTER 2ND/3RD STAGE TRANSITION	Learns to say "no". Develops self-discipline. Accepting his altruism, he chooses a specific goal.	Focuses inward to develop talents. Learns to love self unconditionally. Receives Universal Love. Avoids addictive relationships.	Nurtures and supports child self. Becomes own best friend. Accepts controversial nature of his purpose. Learns vulnerability can be a strength. Finds supportive relationships.	Discovers spiritual contact through nature and the creative process. Learns the purpose of death and suffering. Becomes socially active.
THIRD STAGE	A Master specialist. Nurtures self for the sake of his purpose. Balanced attitude towards self.	Loving Being. Glories in self, giving towards others. Fulfilling partnership. Socially conscious.	Leads with vulnerable, joyful child self. Total self-acceptance. Knows how to be in right place at right time. Sees humor in his position. Supportive personal life.	Invokes spiritual power to nurture and protect what is really important in life. Social impact—"My children cannot be happy unless your children are happy." Positive detachment.

second/third or third stage of their development, because in the earlier stages most have little interest in looking at their lives in any depth. From time to time, however, I would see individuals in the first/second-stage transition, and some of them seemed to acquire certain third-stage traits and to develop the ability to avoid falling into the tendencies of second stage.

I soon realized that there was a kind of crossroads that occurs at the end of the first stage. The path of least resistance will always lead the individual into the second stage of his development. But if he can succeed in becoming objectively aware of his or her life patterns, and act from that awareness, then he can avoid the suffering which is an inevitable part of the second stage. From the point of view of saving oneself a lot of pain, it would seem to be better to do so. What is really best for the development of the soul is often difficult to determine. I cannot say that it is a mistake to refuse to take the high road from first to third stage, for a great deal of personal depth and compassion for others can be acquired by passing through the second stage. It would seem to be better for the younger soul, who may not have the strength to move directly from first into third stage, to pass through the second stage in order to deepen his or her response to life. For the older soul, it might be valuable to achieve the transition between first and third stage. Because this individual is ready to begin work on overall life mastery, and second stage represents a state of spiritual ignorance which may no longer be conducive to his or her larger purpose, the challenge of the crossroads becomes an important one.

In the chapters which follow, the first/third-stage transition is described after the usual pattern of the first, second and third stages has been discussed. Figure 2 shows some key words and phrases describing the three transitions between the stages. It is important to realize that our lifetimes do not end with the completion of just one sign.

When one sign has been mastered, the individual usually moves on to another sign of choice. Each sign represents a year spent in Earth School, while each of the stages represents a different semester of study. Younger souls will respond differently to each sign and stage than older souls. Younger souls tend to take a gentler journey. Second stage is not as difficult. Old souls are far more

Figure Two

	To be a vehicle for the expression of Divine Will on Earth.	To achieve and demonstrate right relationship.	To heal and realign the Earth and its peoples.	Inspired leadership.
PURPOSE				
FIRST STAGE	Born with strong sense of purpose. Feels he has come to a Godless world. Purpose more important than his own or others' well being. Not wishing to cause harm, may hurt others while achieving goals	Lives in harmonious, usually natural environment. Finds compatible partner(s) and lives in conjugal bliss.	New to the world and vulnerable. Lives in a protected environment, developing talents. Assistance leads to easy success. Feels alienated.	Great benefits in early life, bestowing strength and vision. Leads people out of a negative situation and into a better world.
1ST/2ND STAGE TRANSITION	Purpose not fully achieved, he feels inadequate. May become self-centered opponent of God. Eventually collapses in guilt over harm caused to others.	Wishes greater sophistication. Wants to share his knowledge of relationship. Is attracted to troubled partners, who promise greater sophistication.	Time to enter the real world without assistance. Feels abandoned by caretakers. May be attacked by enemies who are jealous or threatened by his differences.	Has tried to conquer greater and greater worlds. Finds a challenge he cannot meet. Crippling failure destroys confidence.
SECOND STAGE	Subconsciously punishes self for past wrongs. Attracts rejection and destructive experiences. Sabotages career and life purpose to prevent himself from hurting anyone.	Chooses incompatible partners and attempts to win them over. Is at first successful, but chooses greater challenges until relationships become impossible. Becomes bitter, cynical.	Traumatized, reacts by closing down parts of himself. Looses contact with emotions, body, sexuality and/or inner voice. May seek dependency and/or fear intimacy.	Reaction to previous failure. May seek glory for its own sake. Compulsive conformity or Nonconformity. Sets impossible goals or fails to achieve. Gives or takes too much.
KEYS TO MASTER 2ND/3RD STAGE TRANSITION	Learns to forgive and develop compassion for self. Develops the capacity to live according to faith. Realizes original error was 'going it alone'.	Recognizes and defuses subconscious motivations for choosing difficult relationships. Attracts positive partnership. Resurrects personal strengths. Begins social involvement.	"Physician heal self." Trapped in self-created repressions, pain beginning to surface. Must learn to listen to inner voice as a guide to self-healing.	Stops putting pressure on self to achieve external success. Begins discovery of inner self. Enjoys creative process for its own sake. Discovers true self.
THIRD STAGE	Lives by the power of his faith. Teaches others how to do so. Penetrating insight. Follows Higher Will.	Supported by nurturing mate he teaches right relationship on a larger social level. Is a vehicle for Divine Justice.	Unconditionally accepts himself and others. In powerful contact with inner voice and physical self. Heals others. "If I have done it, you can too."	Joyfully plays to an audience of one. May once again achieve great things, but is more involved in the process, less concerned about outcomes.

creative in the process of getting themselves into much bigger messes. (And you thought it was better to be an older soul!)

Younger souls may occasionally enter third stage without developing the usual amount of introspection or spiritual understanding. In this case they will express many of the traits of third stage without having the underlying knowledge of the process which has brought them to where they are for the present. Most of my descriptions of third stage lean more towards the manner in which an older soul would express the third stage. Although my descriptions of third stage may seem to give an unrealistic image of personal perfection, please remember that third stage only represents perfection in terms of one basic phase of human expression. A third-stage Libra may not be a perfect parent; a third-stage Aries or Capricorn may not make the most attentive partner; a third-stage Leo may not always have complete consideration for others. This is not to say that individuals in the third stage of these three signs will inevitably have these character flaws, only that they will seldom be perfect in every way. An individual in the early part of third stage will still often have a few of the traits of second stage.

At the end of each chapter I give a brief list of famous people and fictional characters for each of the three stages. This list may help you to understand the different forms of soul expression which come about at different soul ages. It is difficult to find examples of some stages of certain signs. In some cases this is because some stages do not lend themselves to public life in any way. In other cases it is difficult to find examples of famous people for certain stages because the most important experiences of that stage take place in the private life of the individual, and it is difficult to obtain accurate details of the private lives of most well-known individuals. I may also be mistaken in some cases concerning the stage of development of a given individual. I have not met any of the people listed. See what you think. You may disagree with me in certain cases and may be able to add to my lists.

Each chapter also includes a section describing the early childhood experiences and types of intimate relationships which are common to each stage. These have to be rather general, as these circumstances are strongly influenced by the chart as a whole. They will not be applicable to everyone, because other influences in the individual birth chart may disrupt the usual pattern. However, you may still find this information insightful and informative.

At this point I must mention that the ideas presented above can easily be misinterpreted and could, if we are not careful, form the foundation of a new form of spiritual elitism. The important thing to remember is that no stage is inherently superior to any other stage, any more than adults are superior to children. To think that being at the third stage of your Sun sign's development makes you somehow better than those who are not, is a certain indication that you are not at that third stage of development! Another interesting point is that an individual progressing through the third stage of his or her astrological sign may not necessarily be more spiritually evolved than another individual who is presently experiencing the first level. This is because, as most of us are aware, there are 12 signs in the zodiac, and most individuals will experience many signs before completing the mosaic of self. More will be said about this later, but for now it is important to realize that one soul may be at the third stage of his or her first sign, while another may be at the first stage of his or her final series of incarnations. It would be difficult to say in this case who would have one up on whom, and it would be unimportant. Our evolution is not a race, and we have far more important things to do here than to compete with one another in such a manner.

Lastly, in describing the characteristics of each sign, I often use the word 'he' as a neutral term which can apply to either gender. In the chapters relating to Aries, Gemini, Leo, Libra, Sagittarius, and Aquarius, which are the traditionally masculine signs of the zodiac, I use the word "he" as a neutral term, and without connotation of gender. In the chapters relating to Taurus, Cancer, Virgo, Scorpio, Capricorn, and Pisces, the traditionally female signs, I use the word "she" similarly for convenience.

The Law of Three

Imagine that you are seated at an oval table in a spacious, modern conference room. All around the room are large windows looking out onto blue sky. You are too far above the ground to be able to see anything but clouds. Seated at the head of the table is the Source of All Being. Everybody present perceives the speaker in their own individual manner. This God-Source may be male and/or female. You may see a blinding flash of light, or a mysterious hooded figure. Perhaps the chair at the head of the table appears vacant, though imbued with an undeniable presence, which seems to speak silently within the minds and hearts of all present. The occupant of this chair may look exactly as you yourself do.

When all are seated and settled, the silent speaker speaks, "Your inner being has called you here today in preparation. You will soon be ready to embark once again, or perhaps for the very first time, upon a series of lifetimes upon the Earth below. Your mission will be to solve the riddles which you shall be presented with. Each riddle contains a perfect divine idea which you shall learn to express and embody in your own individual manner.

In the process of solving this riddle you will be subject to the law of three. Each of your riddles is like a program or a play in three acts. I must warn you that once you have begun, you must continue on until you reach the end, regardless of how difficult the process may seem to become, or how many lifetimes you require in order to reach your final destination.

For most individuals present, the first act of the play will be relatively smooth and simple. Like a caterpillar you will feast upon the lushness of life. One of you shall find in this stage that food is rather scarce, and that fulfillment eventually eludes you. Another will seem constant prey to every predator, and will shudder as the wind blows all about. In the end you will all taste some form of suffering. The purpose of this first stage is to build the beginnings of a personal self within the earthly world. You shall begin the first act of the play you are about to experience by putting down your roots, and end with the enormity of your task facing you in all of its splendor.

For most of you the challenge of this vision will appear too great. You will most likely have forgotten your true home within yourself, and this briefing which we undertake today. If you are able to remember your true relationship to life, there will be no need for the second phase, as this memory will assist you in becoming the perfect expression of the archetype which you have chosen, and you will then take wing. However, if you have forgotten, and must pass into the second stage of your journey, you should realize that ultimately there is no real harm in doing so.

If you choose to continue into the next phase, you will find that the pace grows sluggish, and that enemies seem to throng all about you. You will grow heavy with the weight of your experience, as life seems constantly prepared to feast upon you. Though the voice within quietly whispers that you will miss the sunshine, it is with great relief that you spin a grey cocoon about yourself and step further into the web of illusion. And yet there is no complete security. The cold wind blows outside, and you may be visited by nightmares. In time the cocoon grows horribly restricting, yet it seems by now to be the only world there is.

The quiet voice within shall speak once again, prompting you to seek a way beyond your present difficulties, telling tales of a bright world outside of your present bounds. By this time it will have been many lifetimes since we last spoke, and perhaps several since you entered the cocoon which has become your prison. You will have forgotten the world outside, and that it was you who first spun the web which now entangles you. The purpose of this stage is to become fully entangled in the riddle, so that you shall empower yourself through the search for a solution, completing the process of achieving personal liberation.

At first you will not believe this inner voice, and you will return to the world of your dreams. But the nightmares will return, with ever-increasing and overwhelming intensity, until you feel that you would do almost anything in order to be free. Most of you will desire to end your physical lives at some point in this process, but few of you actually will. Instead you will struggle to the point where you tear a small hole in the cocoon which surrounds you, allowing a tiny ray of light to give you the inspiration to make the commitment to awaken fully and achieve your liberation.

As time passes, you will begin at last to truly heed the

inner voice, and in so doing, will attract the attention of those who live beyond the walls of your chrysalis. These individuals, physical and non-physical, will aid you in your quest. And yet only you will be able to destroy the walls which surround you. In time you will find the keys which will allow you to solve the riddle, and achieve the seemingly impossible.

The final phase of the journey will begin as you emerge from your limitations and begin to express your full potential through the archetype which you have chosen. You will be able to fly above the concerns of the world, and see all life from the vantage point of eternal truth. You will serve the cause of freedom, and reach complete fulfillment. The older souls among you will leave your seed behind in the service of future generations.

Your mission accomplished, you shall return here once again to receive yet another riddle to be solved. Or, having completed your larger course of study upon the great wheel of life, you shall choose the path of immortality, and so we shall meet again in some greater hall of being. "

All is quiet in the great hall for a few moments as the speaker pauses. When next he speaks it is to inform each participant of the archetype which he or she has selected. "There are 12 archetypes which exist as opportunities for personal soul development upon the Earth below. The archetype you have chosen will determine your season of birth, for the Sun appears to pass through a specific sign of the zodiac once each month, as time is measured on Earth."

As the briefing continues, you are directed to a private viewing room where you will receive more individualized information concerning the natal Sun sign you have chosen. . .

ARIES
the hero

The ancient astrologers called Aries a cardinal fire sign. Cardinal means goal-oriented and fire is associated with the life force: the warmth of life which lends its strength to all beings. This means that it is Aries' goal to serve the life force; to give his all to serve the All. Fire signs are traditionally considered to be masculine in nature. This does not mean that they are lacking in femininity, though it does indicate that their father is likely to have a profound effect on their development as individuals. Because Aries is one of the masculine signs, I have used the words "he" "him" and "his" as neutral terms in this chapter, though they refer to either gender.

No one loves life in all of its forms more than Aries. In his or her natural state this individual sees all life as equal to, if not even more important than, himself. His purpose is to serve life; to give his all to some very important aspect of life which he has chosen to serve. He knows the mystical secret that all of life is one. In many stages of his development, Aries is the sort of person who would rush into a burning building in order to rescue someone he does not even know. Even in his more self-centered phases, this individual will often surprise those who know him best with sudden acts of courage which are undertaken impulsively and with no thought of the self.

First Stage

A spontaneous desire to be of service to life is a tall order. The soul seems young and innocent as it enters its first stage, and it becomes immediately apparent that nothing can be accomplished without first developing the self. In addition, the Arian feels such a spontaneous sense of unity with all of life, that it would be easy for him to simply disappear into this state of oneness and accomplish nothing. His natural state of being is to focus on the whole rather than on the one aspect of the whole which must be developed if he is ever to be worthy of his greater purpose.

Knowing that he does not yet seem to possess the power to make good on his highest dreams and aspirations, his sense of self seems fragile. He feels the need to hold himself together so that he does not disappear. Even though he is by nature idealistic and generous, in order to make the most of his potential and purpose, his goal in first stage must be to develop the ego.

Developing the ego means putting Aries first. To do this he must often suppress the feeling of oneness with life which is his natural inheritance. This is a great sacrifice to make. The first-stage Aries has two conflicting desires. On the one hand he longs to develop himself as a separate and unique individual. This means that he must harden his heart to much of the outside world while honing his skills and building his own personal self-image. On the other hand he longs for the old feeling of simple unity with life, and the ability to live in the moment without any concern for himself, which he suppressed in order to achieve personal prominence. Secretly he longs to simply lose himself in the joy of life and feeling of innocent love for all beings.

Because, at this stage, they cannot do both, many Arians in the first or second stage of their development tend to possess a strong addictive streak. They may be addicted to food, drugs, alcohol, sex, work, television — anything which they can use to experience a false sense of unity to remind them of, or allow them to blot from their memory the state of innocent oneness with life which they still somewhere in the back of their minds recall. Aries never does anything by half measures, and therefore is inclined to be the most addictive sign of the zodiac.

Everyone, Aries included, is aware that he possesses great potential. He quickly learns that if he is to be worthy of his highest ideals, he must first focus primarily upon himself, feeding and developing his sense of identity and developing all of the strengths and talents which he possesses. The paradox of first-stage Aries is this: if he is to ready himself for selfless service, he must at first be self-centered almost to the point of self-indulgence. To give, he first must take.

Not for nothing is he called the infant of the zodiac. First-stage Aries needs a lot of attention, and the positive input of others. He holds a dream of himself as some sort of hero or person of beauty and importance. He puffs himself up like a peacock, and seems blustery and self-involved. Some of his confidence is real, as he is learning to develop the best of his potential. But beneath his colorful exterior he is often invisible to himself and secretly wonders if he is indeed worthy. These feelings he tries to hide from himself as well as from others.

When he feels insecure he will generally turn to one of his supporting cast. He is normally born into an environment where he will be rather spoilt by at least one of his parents (usually Mom). To those who are not put off by his outward show of arrogance, he can be incredibly charming and charismatic. He generally charms or bullies his parents into giving him whatever he may need or want. When he feels insecure he turns to them for reassurance and some form of concrete evidence that he will always be loved — simply for being himself. As an adult, he may still rely upon some form of parental support, and will often marry or befriend those who will continue to play such a role in his life.

Beneath the surface lies an unconscious pressure to perform far beyond the capacity of his merely human capabilities. His dreams out distance him. In the hidden depths of his soul, he would truly rather give than take, and is impatient to be able to actually do so. In order to reconcile himself with spending his initial lifetimes being "fed" so to speak, he must see himself as being somehow special or perhaps even superior to others. He knows he must be demanding, and that few would recognize his true motives for being so, and so he worries about being accepted.

He can be deeply hurt when he is criticized for being selfish, for in his heart he actually has the best of intentions. He may be so innocent that he does not even realize when he is taking up more space than may seem to be his due. When he realizes this is what he is doing, he does not fail to feel regret; and yet he instinctively feels that he is working within a larger purpose. It is hard for him to explain to others, or sometimes even to himself, that he is actually being selfish for an unselfish reason.

At his best, he is spontaneous, generous and highly creative. Every aspect of himself which he seeks to develop is expressed with great drama; all of his strengths and beauties are exaggerated. Those who know who he truly is cannot fail to love him for being so innocently and completely himself. He will spend several lifetimes joyfully exploring and expressing his potential, never failing to believe in the dream image which he has of himself.

Those who misunderstand and oppose him, or who simply refuse to go along with his designs and desires are often treated with ruthless disdain. He tends to feel that life exists to support him, and that those who fail to do so simply serve no function. Because at this stage he is basically egocentric, he often finds it easy to take offense, usually interpreting opposition or lack of interest as a form of attack upon himself as an individual.

He is also very difficult, if not impossible to criticize, even constructively; for he is secretly afraid that he does not measure up to his inner expectations of himself, or that he may be condemned without a trial for his self-centered approach to life. Remember that when it comes right down to it, he does not *want* to be selfish, he *has* to be selfish. And yet the paradox of it all is that there are still some areas and situations in life where this behavior cannot be justified.

Very child-like, he is capable of caring about things which others are too " sophisticated " to consider — such as the welfare of plants and animals, or the feelings of a child in a moment when everyone else is busy with more "important" considerations. From time to time his true soul's essence shines through and he is spontaneously very giving and truly selfless in his concern. Yet he can also be very childish, and is prone to tantrums and rages, especially as he nears the end of first stage, and the tension begins to build.

Every first-stage Aries dreams of becoming a great hero. They wish to accomplish something which will be seen as evidence for themselves and the outside world that they are truly as great as they long to be. As the first stage nears its completion this hunger for self becomes almost totally overwhelming. Inwardly he still feels weak and childlike, and begins to search frantically for a way to find or redeem himself. At this stage he is incapable of looking at himself in a truly responsible manner, and instead may seek external success through any means possible. Alternatively, he may become morbidly introspective, obsessed with himself and the contents of his inner world, yet incapable of looking at himself realistically because of the great sensitivity of his ego and the inner panic which is mounting steadily.

He feels himself careening towards the edge of a cliff and does everything in his power to reverse the direction of this flow. Second stage is looming, and he tries with all of his might to remain in first stage. He feels out of control and fears that his ego, with all of its apparent strength and power, is nonetheless crumbling. He feels acute frustration, since he never has completely found or actualized himself, and now senses that he may be about to lose all opportunity to do so.

At this point he will most likely become extremely demanding of those closest to him. At the best of times, he is often a hungry child. Now, as first stage nears its completion, his inner sense of personal need eclipses all consideration of the personal welfare of others. He needs help, and this realization is very hard on his ego. To placate himself, he decides that the others in question owe it to him to do everything in their power to assist him to achieve his ends, avoid his pain and relieve his insecurities. He is frantic and angry and lashes out at those who cannot or will not help him.

To take responsibility for his own pain would, he feels, be seen as a weakness, so he blames others. He may become abusive towards them just for the sense of personal power which it gives him, all the while telling himself that he does so because he is superior or knows better and that it is for their own good. In reality, sometimes rage is the only outlet for the mounting tensions which become, at times, completely unbearable. He may succeed in prolonging his stay in the first stage of Aries by becoming increasingly destructive and self-deluded, but the bell is sounding for him at the soul level. It is time for him to move forward. The second stage of his journey approaches and cannot be denied.

First/Second-Stage Transition

Beneath the surface, no matter how angry or frightened, no matter how resentful and deluded he may become,

Aries remains an idealist. Every time he lashes out in the name of self, he only wounds himself all the more. His actions continue to erode his sense of self-worth. In every frantic struggle to find himself, he loses himself all the more.

Should he seek external success, the imbalances of his character are likely to deny it. He may continue struggling for many years, collapsing only when he is completely bereft of all resources, causing his failure to be total and dramatic. Should he manage to win himself external acclaim, he will ultimately be forced to undergo the terrifying realization that such achievements provide not one ounce of relief from the inner demons which plague him. In both of these cases the complete breakdown of self is a strong likelihood.

Those who search within for the source of their misery, will only find the fountain from which it flows, and not any way to stem its tide until they can acknowledge their soul's ultimate need to give true selfless service. This the first/second-stage Aries is unlikely to do, for they are so involved in their own pain that they are incapable of perceiving much of anything else, including the promptings of their own soul's purpose. To give to others may seem to take them away from their quest for self. They may also be so personally insecure, that they secretly fear they will not have what it takes to ever contribute to the welfare of any other being.

And so, they will most likely become increasingly morbid and involved with their own thoughts and feelings, endlessly analyzing themselves and getting nowhere, until they collapse in complete personal exhaustion and despair. This kind of first/second-stage Aries is often inclined to be a gentler soul and may choose to refrain from acting in an abusive way towards those in his or her immediate environment. Instead, all the anxiety may be internalized and exercised upon the self in frantic self-destructive attempts to end the pain and discomfort which the individual may be experiencing.

Stampeding about in the quest for self is likely to create quite a large shambles out of this individual's life. Before he collapses personally, he may do grave damage to others. It is not that he does not care. He does—deeply and innocently. But he simply cannot help himself; or at least that is how he feels. And how he feels is now the order of the day. Most individuals in the first/second-stage transition of Aries will have at least one experience of willfully, or more often unwittingly, causing lasting harm to another much-loved individual. Their self-centered behavior often leads to the experience of personal tragedy.

Eventually when his or her quest for self has come to nothing, a tremendous sense of regret for time wasted sweeps over him. He pauses at last in the search for self, finally hearing the voices on the wind. The personal conscience which he has denied for so long now speaks to him of those he has loved, yet ignored, abandoned or abused. He comes to the crushing realization that he has unwittingly betrayed his deepest values. Suddenly he longs with all of his being to be able to go back and undo the results of his past actions, to somehow save those whom he has wronged. Great and powerful as he may have once believed himself to be, this is the one thing that he cannot do.

He can only renounce his claim upon the self, and having realized how many past years were spent living an illusion, he attempts to purge himself of all personal desire. His overwhelming drive to give to life returns in full force, inspiring and uplifting him. If he can maintain his hold upon the highest aspects of his ideals, he will pass through the crossroads and enter into his third stage. But if he allows the often overwhelming emotions of guilt and regret to consume him, he will pass, along the line of least resistance, into the second stage of Aries.

Consciously he feels that he has somehow gone against the deepest promptings of his own soul. He will feel that he has come here to give to life, and to all of the beautiful things of nature and of this world. How could he possibly have become so self-absorbed? How could he possibly have caused harm when he deeply willed it that he bring only good? He feels guilty, he feels ugly, imperfect and unworthy. He has forgotten that there was a purpose to the stage which he has now completed. He has built a simple framework of ego and personal identity to use as a foundation for the tasks which lie ahead of him. The return of his natural generosity and love of life feels like a revelation of a truth he never should have forgotten.

Consumed with regret, he passes into Aries' second-stage, where he will frantically attempt to make amends, instinctively battling or begging to redeem himself. He has no plan, merely intention. In his subjective haste to end all pain, his own as well as that of others, he threatens to perhaps be just as dangerous as he was in the first stage of his development. True innocent that he is, however, he is as yet incapable of realizing that this might be the case.

Second Stage

In early second stage, there are essentially three basic types of personality which one is likely to encounter, whether singly or in combination. The first is a gentle, good-hearted soul, peacefully going about the business of serving and giving to all who surround him. He has little sense of self, and possesses no real concern for his own personal needs and desires. He does a poor job of caring for himself, but will care for all souls around him in need, both great or small, to the limit, and sometimes beyond the limit of his personal ability to do so. He serves the original and ultimate goal of the Arian archetype, but without full awareness or efficiency in doing so. He has willingly renounced the self, no longer aware that he is still necessary to life's great plan. Selflessness is his only ideal. In time he will lose his innocence and simplicity, as ultimately the need to manage his life, and to find a place for his own dreams and ideals becomes too overwhelming to suppress.

By far the most common response to the second stage of Aries is one of sheer panic. The individual feels on some conscious or unconscious level that he has committed a wrong from which there can be no redemption. He feels deeply unworthy of love and imagines that others will inevitably find him ugly or hateful. He possesses the same level of generosity as his more placid brother, and yet often gives more out of fear than he does out of generosity. He is inclined to give to others whatever they ask of him, for unconsciously he feels that they are all sufferers whom he may in some way have wronged. Their pleading is edged with pain, and he cannot abandon them to the suffering which he feels must be his responsibility alone.

Even when he does not feel guilt, he realizes that there may be no one else present who could or would give aid, and so he feels that he is obliged to do so. He often possesses a great fear of disapproval, subconsciously believing that the justified or unjustified anger of others would expose once again the reality of his own shortcomings. As lifetimes progress, he may become more and more of a compulsive giver, hardly aware of what he is doing, certainly possessing no knowledge of the source of the fear which leads him to his acts of self-abnegation.

For some natives of the second stage of Aries, the glory of first stage can never be forgotten. This kind of Aries may be servile and self-abnegating, but often experiences bouts of resentment and rebellion towards the role he feels he is being placed in. He is not always aware that he himself has set in motion the series of circumstances which oppress him. He still secretly wishes to be the shining hero, longing for the beauty of the self which he has left behind, or perhaps never quite managed to realize. Regardless of his physical appearance, he tends to feel ugly and insecure. He desperately needs others to acknowledge a worth in him which he fears is not present.

Often it is very difficult for him to reach out directly on his own behalf, so he gives instead, hoping that someday, when they have a moment, someone will notice that he has needs too. When no one does, he tends to feel this confirms his basic lack of worth. He has not done enough, he has not been enough, and is not beautiful enough either. He may quietly slink away in defeat or lose his temper and create a fuss or respond in a manipulative manner, feeling that having given so much he is owed something in return. This kind of response tends to confuse others, for there has usually been no stated agreement. When the Aries individual gave initially, he or she seemed to do so with no strings attached. Now it seems that this was actually not the case at all.

This stage of Aries may be subtly difficult to get close to. They may be afraid to share themselves with others because they feel so inferior and ugly. It is hard on their pride. To love them requires sensitivity and of patience, because they often do not appear to be as vulnerable as they actually are. They need a lot of time to allow themselves to open up and learn that others might truly be interested in them as individuals. Some barricade themselves to the point where they cannot get close to others at all.

Usually this form of second-stage Aries will attract only those who seek to use him in some manner, for those who are well balanced will sense that achieving a true exchange may not be possible with this individual. Seeking a true intimacy, and not wishing to take more than they receive, many will be inclined to pass him by. And so he remains lonely, only really comfortable when he is giving more than he receives, and yet remaining unfulfilled, wondering what could possibly be so wrong with him.

While the second stage may seem in many ways to be a complete waste of time, the individual is certainly learning how to care selflessly for others, even if he or she is doing so in a completely unaware, often self-destructive and undisciplined manner. He may give compulsively and for the wrong reasons, but he can also give generously in the true spirit of unconditional love. It is not uncommon for a second-stage Aries to dedicate an entire lifetime to the sole purpose of helping or saving other individuals regardless of the cost to self. They may choose to be terribly victimized by someone whose soul they ultimately manage to touch in a way which changes the course of that individual's development forever. They may place themselves in appalling situations or circumstances with a purpose known only to their soul, a purpose which will not bear fruit for centuries to come, and yet, which may be somehow crucial to the welfare of those they have chosen to serve. Yet they do not feel like heroes.

Of course the difficulty here is that Aries' heart is so large, that it tends to lack discretion. For every soul he saves at great cost to himself, there are countless others who refuse to be affected by the aid which he seeks to give. Still he bears the scars they leave. Because he has no sense of his limitations, and often finds it impossible to say no, he does not carry responsibility well (despite having great potential to do so, once he has reached his full development). He usually chooses to bite off more than he can chew, wishing to respond to all that interests him or touches his heart, and often accepting additional burdens which others know they can foist on him. He is inclined to give to others what they want, rather than what they need, and so may weaken them and create a dependency; while simultaneously he succeeds only in exhausting and depleting himself.

Secretly this individual still wishes to be the beautiful hero which he or she dreamed of becoming during his sojourn in his first stage. Although he never quite feels beautiful enough, this secret dream may ultimately be one of the keys which helps lead him out of the labyrinth of the second stage. The part of him which still secretly cherishes this dream eventually begins to scream for help, while all the other aspects of his personality seem to conspire to drown him. It frightens him that he is becoming so exhausted. No matter how much he pleases others, or attempts to please those who can never be fulfilled, he finds that he still aches with loneliness.

As he nears the end of second-stage, he may fail to save some individual in his personal life for whom he has sacrificed himself. This may be a child or other family member, a mate, lover or close personal friend. He may be subjected to considerable amounts of abuse at the hands of this individual, experiencing both the resulting sense of rejection and the feeling of personal failure as a crushing blow to all that is left of his self-esteem. It is quite possible that this experience may repeat itself in more than one form through his or her overall life time. He may see the ways in which his tendency to give according to demand rather than actual need has contributed to the downfall of other individuals. His desire to avoid repeating such a painful experience may give him pause, as he begins to realize that he must set certain limits in his life in order to assist not only himself, but also those for whom he is truly responsible. This realization must however wait until the second/third stage in order to be fully absorbed. Seeing how wasted his efforts have been may also prompt him to consider whether his excessive generosity really has the value he once felt it did.

He grows weary of the constant sense of insecurity which, if it was not a part of his nature in early second-stage, has certainly entered the picture by now, due to the fact that he has exhausted and weakened himself to such a grave extent. In addition, many individuals reaching the end of second-stage Aries will experience some form of health breakdown, caused by their tendency to give too much, bite off more than they can chew, and by the many lifetimes of addictive behavior that many first and second-stage Arians tend to indulge in.

Finally it all just becomes too much, and Aries must begin once again to seriously think of himself. He seeks to resurrect himself, to find the true being which he always was, hidden beneath the fears, insecurities and unbalanced sense of responsibility he has carried for so long. He goes looking for the truth, and so enters the transition between the second and third stages of Aries.

Second/Third-Stage Transition

His ego is still fragile, and initially it is difficult to look at himself as he truly is, or more accurately, as he has become at this stage of his development. Second/third-stage transition Arians must begin to see what they have been doing to themselves. They must learn how to accept their faults and shortcomings. Only once they have done so, will they be ready to tackle the even more difficult task of recognizing, accepting and cultivating the greatness of their true essential selves.

To reach third-stage, the Arian individual must learn how to balance his or her life. He must learn to care for himself without becoming overly self-centered, and to give to others without giving away his essence. In short he must learn self-discipline. And before self-discipline can be mastered, he must understand the value and purpose of this mastery.

It is important for Arians to acknowledge to themselves that it is in their most basic nature to be a servant of life. They must accept this as their natural role in life. One would think that by this point they would be consciously aware of this fact, but many are not. They often tend to believe that they have a good relationship with themselves and that they are number one in their own lives. It may take them some time to actually recognize their unconscious habits of self-abnegation and unbalanced giving. They may be threatened by the conscious thought of service, because they instinctively rebel against the concept of giving away any more of themselves than they already have.

And yet, if they try to become more self-centered and more self-nurturing merely for the sake of self, they will find that they will fail again and again. At this stage it is still far too easy for them to be manipulated by those who tell them subtly or blatantly that they are being too selfish. They need only hear someone say something like, "How could you be so selfish as to take an entire day off to do those foolish things only for yourself, when our company is about to go bankrupt. . ."; or, "your poor husband has nothing to wear to work on Monday"; or, "I have no one else to talk to, and I feel so lonely and abandoned," etc., etc., etc. If their guilt doesn't get to them, their compassion is bound to.

Only when the Aries individual is able to accept that it will always be in his nature to give, will he be able to choose that which he loves above all else to dedicate his life to. If it is Aries' purpose to serve the life force, then he must acknowledge his own finite capabilities, and determine what he believes to be the most important contribution which he could possibly make. He must choose a cause, a goal, an ideal, a purpose! And from that moment on he must dedicate himself to learning the art of saying "no" to all else which might interfere with the fulfillment of that purpose.

To enter the third stage, this individual must learn to be constructively self-centered for unselfish reasons. The more dedicated he becomes to his chosen purpose, the more important it is for him to learn how to take good care of himself in order to enable himself to take proper care of his true responsibilities. As he moves toward third-stage, he will become more and more of a specialist, refining his particular interest and path of service to a fine art. There will be no room in his life for inefficiency or the waste of his precious time and energy. He must learn to serve and conserve himself in order to care for that which is most precious to him.

Because of his second-stage tendency to give away almost his very essence at the request of others, his often extreme addictive tendencies, his inability to understand his personal limitations, and his tendency to bite off more than he can chew in the process of pursuing his goals and ideals, the Arian usually enters second/third stage in a state of serious exhaustion. It is important for him to learn to avoid burn-out at almost any cost. He needs to deal with his personal energy level the same way that the wise among us deal with their financial affairs. In other words, he must save more than he spends. He must even learn to do this with regard to his chosen life purpose also for, if he does, in the long run he will have far more to contribute than he might have ever imagined.

It is not uncommon for individuals entering the transition into the third stage of any sign to experience serious health problems as a result of the past and present lifetime's stresses and imbalances. Aries is one of the signs most likely to experience this. Therefore looking after their physical health and well-being becomes paramount to them. Many lifetimes' worth of addictive behavior may have taken their toll. Now the disciplines of health and simplicity may be required in order to right the balance. Their entire system must be cleaned, honed and re-aligned.

Aries has a greater spontaneous capacity to feel the oneness of life than any other sign, but in order to develop his or her individuality this awareness had to be suppressed. Addictive tendencies arose as a substitute for the original feeling of unity which is Aries' true nature. As second/third stage progresses, this experience of unity with life returns. There are several factors which allow this to take place. The first is the quest for self-knowledge, which eventually leads to an awakening of the deeper centers of the mind. Then as the life purpose begins to fully assert itself, the individual begins to feel as though he were participating in a much larger purpose than he might have previously imagined. A more healthy lifestyle also helps balance the inner mind, liberating all of its original faculties. Self-discipline helps to bridge the final gap, for it becomes for a time the new addiction, allowing the old habits to gradually dissolve, clearing the way for the spiritual experience of reunion with the greater whole.

A second/third stage or early third-stage Aries may appear to be excessively self-disciplined, but this form of behavior is necessary to his or her survival. Sometimes the pendulum must swing in the opposite direction before balance and center can be found. The old habits of the soul are still very close to the surface, and many lifetimes' worth of chaotic, addictive and self-abnegating behavior need to be overcome. Aries at this stage may seem too emphatic with their no's, but few people understand how hard won their quest for self-assertion really was. Their lifestyles may seem too Spartan, their character too driven or goal-oriented. But no one can deny the value of their ultimate contribution, for the third-stage Arian is destined to provide the world with some very valuable and necessary services and discoveries.

However, before this individual is completely free to fulfill his chosen purpose, his self-worth must be resurrected in a balanced manner. Aries could easily be said to be the most idealistic sign of the zodiac, and it is this tendency, when allowed to get out of hand, which causes him no end of trouble. He holds many ideal images of himself. In first stage he may succeed in deluding himself that he is the fully formed manifestation of all of his ideals. By second stage he may feel that he knows better, but he will still fall into the trap of berating himself for not measuring up to his own impossible standards.

To reach third stage he must learn to credit himself on the basis of his intentions, coming to learn the value of his natural sincerity of heart. As he regains his sense of oneness with life, he will come to understand himself (as well as others) as agents of evolution, and begin to realize that he has lifetimes in which to fulfill his ultimate purpose. While this realization will not slow him down, it will make him realize that his value ultimately rests in the potential that he holds, and in his responsible, honorable and patient discharge of his true life-obligations.

Retaining his natural idealism, and innate love of tackling the impossible dream, he also comes to learn the practical and efficient means of tackling it. He is tirelessly active, and yet calm and at peace. Knowing that he is firmly in partnership with life, he comes to understand that he need no longer be the foolish hero who believes that he must always go it alone, nor does he believe that it must all be done now. Finally able to enlist in active service to the aspect of life which he most deeply reveres, he passes into the third stage.

Third Stage

The third-stage Arian is almost invariably a specialist. He is an expert and an innovator. No one (except perhaps another third-stage Aries with a similar purpose who is certain to become a lifelong friend) knows his subject like he does. Aries is ruled by the planet Mars, the God of War, and in third stage the Arian goes to war for whatever he or she may have chosen to serve. Always the noble warrior, he will almost certainly be as ethical as possible in his undertakings. Nor will his purpose be likely to entail any form of destructive activity, unless the need to go to battle (on whatever plane) is deemed to be truly necessary. The older soul in third stage will know that there are truly no enemies, and so will use disciplined ingenuity to fulfill his or her purpose and triumph over any apparent opposition.

This individual can be found in almost any walk of life — science, engineering, biology, psychology. Whatever he or she does will be made into a science; new discoveries will be made, and expertise will be sought in order to serve the cause with maximum efficiency. Whether he seeks involvement in athletics, mysticism, philosophy, politics or the arts, whatever this individual chooses to pursue will also be his art form, for he is lost in the beauty of whatever he has chosen to serve. It is quite possible for the third-stage Aries to be multi-talented, serving several different life-disciplines during the span of a single lifetime. (No, Superman is not a third-stage Aries; he is a first-stage Leo.) Everything he does, however is designed to fit into the higher context of one single-life purpose.

He may remain unknown outside of a very small circle, or he may have an enduring international impact. It is also possible that he will be unknown or largely unappreciated during the course of his lifetime, yet will leave behind a legacy which is of great value to the world once society at large develops the ability to comprehend the contribution which he or she has made. A third-stage Aries need not necessarily make an earth-shattering contribution to the future of humanity, but whatever he or she does will be done well, with greater efficiency and greater knowledge or understanding than most would be able to provide.

In third-stage, Aries loses much, though perhaps not all, of his inherent impatience. As long as he knows that he is doing the sort of work which fulfills him and is giving it his best effort, he is content to take the long view. If he sees life through the eyes of a mystic, he is able to understand consciously that it may require several lifetimes to fully achieve his chosen purpose. Other third-stage Arians are not the least bit mystically inclined, but are still able to achieve great feats of self-discipline and demonstrate tremendous patience with life and those who surround them.

He usually prefers to lead a simple existence and can achieve great personal fulfillment while living in the midst of exceedingly humble circumstances, but will spare no expense of time, money or energy in the pursuit of the goals which he has chosen. Some third-stage Arians may appear overly serious to the outside observer, but they are usually unaware that they leave this impression, being so engrossed in their chosen activities that they give little thought as to how they may be seen by others.

Honesty and loyalty are personal characteristics which third-stage Aries tends to possess in great measure. Those who are not so serious are tremendously optimistic and approach life with playful joy as they go about exploring the world around them. Through personal discipline and a balanced attitude towards the self, Aries ultimately rediscovers his original oneness with life. Many Arians have a great love for small children and animals, who can share with them the positive simplicity of their basic approach to life.

After all the struggles which he has gone through in order to find himself, the third-stage Aries has finally achieved true self-esteem. He is able to say quietly to the world, "Yes I have done a good job, haven't I!". At the same time he is a good listener who is genuinely interested in the lives of others and knows that he is no more important than anyone else. The secret which he has possessed all along, and has finally fully discovered, is that we are all enormously important. The realization of this truth fills him with a kind of quiet reverence for the privilege which the life experience offers to us all.

Aries at the Crossroads
First/Third-Stage Transition

The first opportunity to take the high road at life's crossroads comes when Aries nears the end of the first stage and can no longer deny the realization that his ego is starting to crumble. He often responds to this crisis by becoming frantic and compulsive in the pursuit of the imaginary perfect self-image which he has carried with him for so long. He becomes frightened that he will never achieve his personal goals and that he may also lose much of what he has already attained. Addictive tendencies are also commonly a problem at this stage, and their presence may threaten to undo him.

Things at this point are really not as bad as they seem. The challenge lies in acquiring enough objectivity to realize the simple steps which need to be taken in order to avoid getting lost in a downward spiral. First of all Aries needs to be honest with himself. If he can do this, and if he can calm down long enough to glimpse the larger view, this individual usually possesses enough intelligence to understand what must be done in order to avoid the catastrophe which is looming before him.

Some questions to consider at this point are: What truly makes a hero? Is it glory and fame, a shining outward appearance? Is it the adulation of others, even if this adulation comes only from one fair maiden or one noble knight? Will you really die if you do not achieve your goals? Have you forgotten the bigger picture, lost touch with your highest ideals? Can the Aries at the end of first stage understand how valuable his good intentions really are?

A rebirth is required. The Aries at the end of second stage needs to become inspired by something greater than himself. Somehow the opportunity will present itself which will allow him to become involved in something so awe inspiring that his soul will be humbled and feel a great sense of honor at being allowed to contribute in even the smallest measure.

But the path of least resistance will constantly beckon. "Yes that is a wonderful ideal and I will pursue it as soon as I have the time. Look, I am doing so even now . . . sort of. " Instead he is busy chasing the smaller ideals of the self, which seem to him to be the greater. Serving a larger cause, no matter how beautiful, may also threaten his ego at this point. I can't give myself up to something that has nothing to do with my own personal potential, which I know I must now jealously guard." Loss of the ego is highly threatening to most Arians; they seldom go in for Eastern religion. At this point they may be incapable of realizing that losing themselves in an important cause or undertaking will actually strengthen the self, which they are otherwise ultimately destined to lose by holding onto it too tightly for far too long.

At this stage Aries is inclined to suffer from a tendency towards procrastination. It is easy for him to let the days slide by, never quite getting around to making the changes which he or she intuitively understands are necessary. Another danger at this point is excessive dependence on others. First-stage Aries is used to being taken care of. It is easy for him to believe that he must persuade others to somehow make the necessary changes for him. He can be very impatient with others and with the slow pace at which his life seems to be proceeding, when in fact the key to mastering the first/third-stage transition is the development of self-discipline and personal responsibility. If he has acquired an addictive tendency, as many Arians have by the end of first-stage, a self-discipline supported by the perspective of a higher goal may be the only possible salvation at this stage of development.

For some signs it may be of greater value to achieve a successful transition between the first and third stages than it is for others. Aries is not one of those signs. If the individual at this stage begins to master self-discipline and finds himself successfully achieving some sort of idealistic goal, the danger exists that he or she may remain somewhat smug and superior. Individuals who have successfully navigated the first/third-stage transition at this early point in their development often struggle later on to develop humility and compassion and to overcome a certain sense of elitism and intellectual superiority.

The crossroads between the first and third stage of Aries lasts for quite some time however. It can last from before the first/second-stage transition begins until well into second-stage. A crucial point of opportunity occurs after the first traumatic results of one's own self-centeredness have begun to make themselves felt. When the Arian individual begins to deeply regret his compulsive tendency to always place himself before others, he then has a brief opportunity to forgive himself and attempt to determine rationally what must have gone wrong. If he reacts to this experience on a purely emotional level, he will become too self-deprecating and begin to give compulsively, slipping into the second stage.

If he can learn to make good use of his feeling of regret rather than be consumed by it, he may become inspired to take certain larger steps which will allow him to serve those aspects of life which most deeply concern him. Lost in his purpose, he will acquire self-discipline and self-respect. He will eventually be able to look back upon his earlier experiences and realize that he was able to draw wisdom from them. The regret may remain, but the guilt is gone, replaced by a higher wisdom and a dedication to the present moment. If he is unable to make the transition at this point, he will receive one final opportunity in early second stage when memories of his past glories remind him that he is destroying himself in his compulsive selflessness. If Aries does not serve on a larger level, he or she will be doomed to serve in his or her personal life, and this always leads to destructive life-patterns and experiences.

My great-grandfather mastered the first/third-stage transition in a rather dramatic way. He was an alcoholic who lived with his wife and children in an isolated rural area. When one of his twins sons became ill with pneumonia, his wife sent him into town to get the doctor. He drank for several days, finally returning with the doctor after the child had died. When the other son became ill, his wife sent him back into town again. Once again he drank himself into a stupor, returning with the doctor after the second child had died.

At midnight, January 1st, 1900 his daughter was born. When she too became ill with pneumonia, her mother once again sent him into town to summon the doctor. At this point in the story I always used to wonder why she didn't go herself. Of course, he became drunk once again and lost an entire week. When he sobered up, instead of running straight for the doctor, he went into the church. He prayed, "God, if you will save the life of my daughter, I promise that I will give the rest of my life to you." He then returned home with the doctor, who saved my grandmother's life. My great grandfather became a minister. He never drank again, and was known as the "children's minister", who always spent extra time with the little ones. He always carried candies with him to give to the children to whom he had dedicated his life.

Childhood Conditions and Relationship Patterns

In traditional astrology each of the signs of the zodiac is assigned to one of the four elements of the ancient world: earth, water, air or fire. Each element symbolizes a different kind of basic human psychology and a different means of approaching life. Aries is considered to be a fire sign. Fire is a masculine element and is associated with spirituality, creativity and idealism. For a fire sign the father is extremely important subconsciously. He is associated with the ideals of the soul and with the spiritual urges of the individual. In early childhood the father of an Aries is viewed as a very powerful individual. He tends to be seen in a very black or white manner. He is either a hero or a tyrant. At different points in the same childhood he may be seen as either.

Those born into early first stage or into the third-stage of Aries tend to see their father as a knight in shining armor. In other stages he is inclined to appear the tyrant. The relationship to the father, for Aries, symbolizes or promotes the relationship of the individual to his or her own ideals and personal standards. Aries, do your ideals encourage you or do they tyrannize you? The Arian tendency to be to hard on oneself or to be overly rebellious toward or fearful of authority figures is directly related to this childhood relationship. More perhaps than certain other signs, Aries needs the support and encouragement of fathers and will suffer in some way if they do not receive it. An excessively demanding father figure can cause Aries to doubt themselves the rest of their lives.

Many Arians in late first or second stage will have a father who is given to irrational fits of anger. Aries doesn't know what his father wants, he only knows that the man is dissatisfied, and finds his father's behavior very wounding to his pride. The hurts involved may cause him to personally reject his father. On a subconscious or spiritual level this may correspond to a rejection of his own idealism and a lack of understanding of his own spiritual urges. He may choose instead to retreat into a fantasy world, making it difficult for him to act upon his true inclinations in the world as it really is.

If the Arian has had a difficult relationship with his or her father, it is important for him to let go of and forgive this individual. He may need to build a new image of a positive masculine father figure within his or her own imagination, symbolically becoming his own father as a means of overcoming those inner demons which may limit further development.

The mother of an Arian is often sensitive and empathic. Only when second-stage tendencies dominate to the extreme will she share in the tyranny of the father. She is good hearted and generous and expresses or contributes to the formative development of the best parts of Aries' emotional nature. In first and second stage she is inclined to be rather victimized. In third stage she expresses a unique form of emotionally oriented wisdom. Aries may be protective of his often fragile mother, but at the same time he often disdains her for her apparent weakness and may dominate or manipulate her to achieve the fulfillment of his desires.

The mother of an Aries usually spoils her child, especially in first stage, leading him to believe that the world owes him the same sort of indulgent care he experienced at home. A second-stage Aries often grows up feeling guilty for the sacrifices his mother made, feeling that the only way to make up for her suffering is to be just as self-abnegating as she was. Aries' mothers often end up trying to protect their child from the tyrant who is their father, and the indulgences of the mother tend to anger the father, causing him to be harder on the child than he otherwise might be.

An Aries male will grow up looking for a woman who is as utterly dedicated to him as his mother was. The Aries woman grows up vowing never to become like her mother. If she is in first stage she may emulate her father, looking for someone she can dominate who has a similar nature to her mother. In second stage she may attempt to be different from her mother, but may end up emulating her tendencies in many ways.

An Aries woman who has a hero for a father may seek a

man who can be her idealized hero once again. But Aries are usually closer emotionally to their mothers than they are to their fathers, and although she may have shared a bond of common ideals with her father, he may have been too busy being a hero to have time to forge an intimate relationship with his daughter. This might make it difficult for an Aries woman to find a man, as her ideals may tend to be so high that no man can fill them. She may also subconsciously believe that her mate will not be able to be close to her, because she had little experience of intimate sharing with her father during her childhood.

If her father was a tyrant, she may still attempt to seek a heroic father figure as a mate in order to fill the gap, but because she experienced a destructive relationship with her father, she may unconsciously attempt to love the same type of person in hopes of magically healing the wound. He may look like a hero and end up acting just like the tyrant she left behind.

An Aries woman who has completely rejected the example which her father has set for her may find herself attracted to individuals whose lifestyles and interests are in direct opposition to the values of her father. She may seek a less powerful and more gentle man who can never dominate her. She rejects the father archetype and instead is attracted to the image of the eternal youth, who represents to her an opportunity for her ideals to live in freedom, beyond the restrictions and limitations of overwhelming external authority. She may choose for a mate a man frustrated in his attempts at expressing his own masculinity, whose expression of anger is suppressed or distorted. He may become overly dependent upon her or sabotage her in subtle ways, or be unable to handle the responsibility of the relationship and therefore abandon her. Once the relationship with the father has been laid to rest, the Aries woman can go on to achieve a healthy intimate relationship.

The Aries male tends to put his mother on a pedestal. He seeks a woman who is as sweet and pure, and perhaps as good a servant as Mom was. Mom was, of course, only human, and may have used subtle techniques of manipulation in her attempt to keep from being totally subjugated by her family. The Aries male may therefore be attracted to very subtle and manipulative women without even realizing it. If his father was a hero, he may admire and wish to emulate the man and may seek a fair maiden to rescue. This may translate into a woman who has many emotional problems and is inclined to be volcanic and devious in her relationships with men. He needs to overcome his innocence and seek a partner to share in his life's quest, rather than seeking a servant or a woman who will become his only quest.

If his father was a tyrant, he may secretly be afraid that he will be as destructive toward women as his father was. If he fails to understand the emotional motivations of his partner or allows her to walk all over him because of his fears, he may snap, becoming abusive just as he may have feared. He may idealize women, but he may also disdain them for what he sees as their weakness and dishonesty. This can cause him to be distrustful and at times abusive. If he acts in an abusive manner he may blame himself and torture himself with guilt and regret or may blame his partner for "driving him to this", ending up with a view that all women are inferior and essentially flawed in some crucial manner.

Second-stage Arians of either sex are inclined to project the image of the ideal self which they lost contact with at the end of first stage onto another individual when falling in love. Since they believe that they will never be able to actualize or resurrect this beautiful self, they are seldom able to believe that this person whom they have idealized will ever truly want them. They may sabotage the relationship through being overly servile and fearful, or they may open themselves up to being used or abused by another individual. They may choose someone who is incapable of or not the least bit interested in loving them.

Resolving relationship problems means understanding the family patterns which led to them, as well as resolving the riddles of first- and second-stage Aries. Aries experiences fulfillment in his or her intimate relationships when these relationships express personal equality and shared inspiration. Through self-knowledge and self-understanding these goals can be achieved.

Famous Arians

First Stage: Hugh Hefner, Fred Flintstone, Charlie Chaplin, Bette Davis, Diana Ross, Casanova.

First/Second Stage: Joan Crawford, Elton John (the gentler version—may be approaching first/third stage), Vincent Van Gogh.

Second Stage: Billie Holiday, Hans Christian Anderson. (It is difficult to find famous examples of this stage of Aries.)

Second/Third Stage: Eric Clapton, Doris Day, Gloria Steinem.

Third Stage: Harry Houdini, Dane Rudhyar (famous astrologer), Jane Goodall, Wilhelm Reich, Ravi Shankar.

First/Third Stage: Anita Bryant.

TAURUS
unconditional love

The older traditions of astrology list the planet Venus as the ruler of Taurus. A more modern tradition lists the planet Earth as its ruler. To my mind both are equally appropriate. Venus of course, corresponds to the Goddess of love. Her romantic exploits are legendary. Taurus is one of the signs concerned directly with assisting the soul to come to a deeper understanding of all forms of love — romantic love in particular.

In the ancient world the Earth was believed to be a living being. Modern discoveries are beginning to lead scientists to reconsider this old idea, and to new theories, such as those presented in James Lovelock's book "Gaia", which seem to indicate some overriding intelligence associated with the Earth itself. It seems to me that if the Earth does indeed have a soul, that soul must possess a tremendous amount of unconditional love to have put up with us for as long as it has. This makes the Earth a very appropriate ruler for Taurus, as the purpose of this sign is to allow the individual to learn to become an embodiment of truly unconditional love.

Many ancient cultures speak of spirits of nature, usually invisible to Man. These Faeries, Elves or Elementals are in their own way responsible for maintaining the balance of nature. Poets, mystics and philosophers who claim to have encountered them commonly speak of them as joyful and loving. While elementals inhabiting storms and dark or desolate locations are inclined to be rather malevolent and brooding, there is also a hidden kingdom of nature which fully expresses the unconditional love of the Earth itself. I sometimes feel that before entering first stage, many Taureans may have spent a certain amount of time in this realm, preparing themselves for the lessons which lay ahead.

Because Taurus is ruled by the element of earth, it is traditionally considered to be a feminine sign. This does not mean that this sign is lacking in masculine qualities, though it does indicate that the early development of these individuals tends to be strongly influenced by the mother.

Because Taurus is a feminine sign, I have used the words "she", "her" and "hers" as neutral terms in this chapter, intended to refer to individuals of either gender.

First Stage

The first-stage Taurus is a simple, loving and optimistic soul. She is filled with joy and gratitude towards the Earth itself and toward all the life which surrounds her, as it supports the pleasure of her own existence. The first-stage Taurean is an innocent sensualist. Like Ferdinand the Bull, she soaks up the sunshine which falls each day upon the fields. At the commencement of the first stage, this individual still feels bathed in the unconditional love of life itself. Therefore there is little need for her to concern herself with much else. Her tie with the Earth may cause her to immerse herself in the joy of simple but honest labor, or to express herself as an artist and lover of beauty. Whatever causes she serves, she serves with unquestioned loyalty.

Above all she seeks to love. She feels a powerful need for an individual or individuals upon whom to bestow her deep capacity for affection. She moves from an isolated reverie, in which she shares in the secret joys of nature, towards a search for those whom she may love unconditionally, to prove her loyalty and express her most fundamental purpose. Unconsciously she feels that the best way to develop her capacity for love is to choose to dedicate herself to those who may be incapable of returning her ardent affections. To love unconditionally is to ask for nothing in return. Without realizing what she is doing, she decides to try and live this ideal in every area of her life, not quite understanding that there are some ways in which she also needs the love of others in order to survive.

She is inclined to gravitate towards those who take without realizing that it is also necessary to give. Family, friends and lovers are inclined to use this individual, and often fail to even acknowledge the value of the gifts which she brings. Many Taureans are born when their parents are really too busy or too self-involved to give them very much of their time. The first-stage Taurean is so loyal and hard working that it is easy to hand her any responsibilities and to rely upon her for her ready assistance and support. She may quickly and unconsciously fall into a servile role within her family. Or she may be neglected and abused.

To the first-stage Taurean these forms of mistreatment really do not matter. The important thing is that she give to those she loves. Her loved ones may agree with her, and can quickly fall into the mind-set that she owes them support, while they owe her nothing. After all, this is her role and chosen lot in life. Or they may be unconsciously envious of her placid and hopeful spirit, as well as the innate purity of her nature, and become actively hostile and abusive in response. In being so accepting, she easily attracts the worst in others, who may feel that in her they have found an easy mark on which to vent their frustrations.

Of course, not all first-stage Taureans attract neglect and abuse from their families. They may instead be born to those who share their own basic approach to life, and so enter their adult lives with their hearts even more openly displayed upon their sleeves. As parents they may, however, attract souls who do not understand the value of the unconditional love which is being offered. The first-stage Taurean may be gravely tested by her offspring. Can they still love a child who responds to their attentions with disdain or outright abuse? It is certain that they can, but they will bear deep wounds in attempting to do so.

To be born to parents or to give birth to children who are incapable of loving her in return is often, though not always, the destiny of a Taurean. Whatever her childhood origins and ultimate family experience, Taurus will always meet her greatest challenges in the arena of her romantic relationships. It is here that she, without fail, will choose those who cannot or will not return her love. Perhaps she is born into a culture where arranged marriages are the rule, and chooses to love a mate who decides not to return love. Perhaps she marries for love, while her partner marries for convenience, money or the ardent service and support which Taurus is always so ready to supply. It is also possible that external circumstances may prevent the fulfillment of love between two individuals who would otherwise be perfect mates for one another. Or, Taurus may choose as a partner someone who, while technically "in love", is not truly capable of sharing or giving their love, perhaps due to the selfishness of their nature or the emotional wounds they carry.

Taurus always feels pain when confronted with this sort of situation, and yet in her heart believes that she can love no other. Unconsciously she is drawn again and again into situations where she must learn to love without thought of reward. While she always attempts to love in as pure a manner as possible, she never gives up hope of one day being loved in return. In reality she is attempting to take a giant leap which she is really not yet ready for. This form of intimate relationship is the most difficult form of relationship through which to express unconditional love. And, in fact, although we are ultimately meant to develop the ability to love all beings in this manner, we are not truly meant to receive nothing in return from our mates. The highest form of partnership always expresses itself through a loving interchange.

While Taurus may undoubtedly experience much pain, she is at first undaunted. Deep within her being, she feels that everything will be fine in the end. She knows that love is the greatest power in the Universe, and unconsciously trusts the promptings of her soul in choosing this form of dedication. It is certainly true that love will eventually win out, but it will not do so in the manner in which she is hoping, nor reach its highest fulfillment for her until many lifetimes have passed. Not understanding these facts, the Taurean goes ahead in blissful ignorance. But with the passing of time, it is inevitable that she will one day be gravely disillusioned, and so lose her innocence. As she progresses, she gradually begins her fall from Grace. As time passes, her ability to trust life and to feel in blissful communion with the life which surrounds her gradually erodes away into nothing. Her inner sources of salvation, strength and contentment disappear, leaving insecurity and confusion in their wake.

First/Second-Stage Transition

Innocence begins to decline, and with it departs the inner security which comes of an underlying sense of being a beloved child of the Earth, whose only need is to express true love and loyalty. Taurus cannot understand why the door to romantic fulfillment continues time after time to slam shut in her face. In first stage, even though others seldom expressed their love towards her, she did not doubt that it somehow still existed beneath the surface, nor did she doubt her own innate worthiness of being loved.

Now she finds her simple happiness interrupted by momentary waves of panic, during which she desperately seeks reassurance from the outside world. At times she remains the blissful, innocent babe that she has always been; at other times she feels like a terrified and abandoned child. Others may placate her fears at the time that they are expressed, but once her panic subsides, they continue to neglect or abuse her as before. At other times they prompt her to suppress her fears, by hinting that if she does not continue to play the role they expect of her, they will abandon her completely.

She tries to avoid the fears which she is feeling, and continue with the activities which fulfill her, and the loyalties she is attempting to perfect.

"If I only love them well enough, then they will one day love me in return", she says to herself, and keeps on going. But secretly she is becoming more and more panicked, less hopeful and less trusting, and may perhaps become subject to blind rages, as her deeper self finally rebels against the status quo. He is repressing her inner voice, as it screams its lack of satisfaction, and the more she does so the more driven she becomes.

She is desperately searching for someone to tell her that he loves her, but subconsciously she cannot allow such a situation to exist. Avoiding her inner voice, she becomes cut off from her last remaining source of inner security. Eventually she can avoid the truth no longer, and must come to the crushing realization that she is truly unloved and unwanted. With this revelation her sense of optimism, as well as faith in herself and in life, dissolve completely. Filled with fear and insecurity, she passes into the second stage.

Second Stage

The second-stage individual suffers from the results of symbolically having walked for miles and miles on only one leg. To love unconditionally without concern or consideration for the self requires a level of mastery of which she is not yet capable. She now no longer remembers her original goal of learning how to love unconditionally. She has loved others as unconditionally as she possibly can, but has forgotten to love herself. Now she suffers from the results of this imbalance and is only aware of feeling deeply, deeply unloved. She seems to be a bottomless pit of emotional emptiness. In second stage, she attempts to come to terms with her loneliness as best she can, using whatever techniques she can to escape or to resolve her personal difficulties. Because the root of the problem is subconscious, her every effort is doomed to failure, until she learns to look within. This necessary examination of the roots of her own experience will only happen as she passes through the transition into third stage.

She may seek love by becoming something of a tragic, romantic idealist. She seeks the great love, the magical love, the perfect image of beauty and salvation. She builds an image of brilliance around herself, seeing herself as an irresistible yet tragic artist. She may build a fantasy around another individual and pursue him hopelessly, for unconsciously she still inevitably chooses someone who cannot or will not return her love. She may return to love again the same individual she has loved before in many different lifetimes, who is still incapable of intimacy or unwilling to return her advances.

She may even choose another second-stage Taurean, unconsciously hoping against hope that here at last is someone else who can truly understand her. But with both carrying similar unconscious programming, their relationship is doomed to failure, either through their own defensive maneuvers, or through the ill-winds of external fate. Romeo and Juliet were almost certainly second-stage Taureans. Most likely these lovers will sabotage the relationship themselves, for the second-stage Taurean lover is always passionate, but seldom stable in her responses. She is too fearful to express herself in a steady manner.

The depth of her need to be loved, combined with her fears and fantasies may cause her to fool herself about the nature of those to whom she is attracted, and she is likely to choose a completely inappropriate individual upon whom to shower affection. He tends to chase love away because of her neediness and insecurity, and may repel the love she seeks through becoming too demanding or being incapable of revealing her true self and true feelings because of an overwhelming fear of rejection. She may be too manipulative and strategic in her approach to romance, ultimately acting in a very self-centered manner, unable to perceive the views and feelings of another because she is trapped in her own personal world of agony. This is extremely ironic, because under the surface she has the best of intentions, and still remains capable of deep and lasting love and affection. The catch is that she must receive love and reassurance before she will be able to relax and allow love to take its course, and her anxiety usually prevents her from doing so.

Until she learns to reprogram her unconscious responses, she will achieve no lasting satisfaction. Because she can receive little sense of fulfillment and security from others, she may turn to other forms of escape such as physical pleasures or addictions. The second-stage Taurean may become addicted to drugs or alcohol as a way of dealing with her inner pain and as a means of providing herself with a substitute for the intimacy she so desperately needs.

She may become addicted to food as her way of feeding and nurturing herself on a physical level, since she seems unable to do so on an emotional level. Hypersexuality may be another form of escape from the emptiness which haunts her. He may tell herself that she does not want love, all she wants is sex. Or she may become compulsively promiscuous, always secretly hoping that one night she will find herself in the arms of her true love.

She may become overly attached to material things, believing her bank account to be more reliable than the human world which surrounds her. Diamonds are a girl's (or boy's) best friend. The strain of her constant lack of romantic fulfillment may prove too much, and she may long to be removed from the fray. She deeply needs love, and so may surrender to one who professes to love her deeply, even if the Taurean herself does not feel the same depth of passion. The relationship offers or seems to offer security, if not depth. For a time she has refuge, although she cannot remain in this false refuge forever. (Even a lifetime is not forever). Her courage is for a time lost, and she seems to lie to herself, if not also to the other person involved.

She may choose a lifetime, or a period within a lifetime in which she decides to make the world pay for the suffering she has endured. She becomes compulsively self-centered, perhaps compulsively self-destructive as well, for her frustration is great and she secretly hates herself for betraying her primary ideal of love. She seeks unconditional love from others, for she feels it to be her due, but returns their devotion with stony silence or disdainful abuse. She may succeed in attracting an opportunity to receive unconditional love, and yet her fear and cynicism will prevent her from opening to receive it. This response is of course another blind alley, and if not recognized as such will inevitably lead to a self-destructive course during the lifetime in which it is chosen.

As second stage draws to a close, this individual finds herself completely bereft of all the resources necessary to deal with the situation she finds herself in. Nothing remains but to surrender to the great unknown, realizing that despair leads to emptiness, and that only emptiness can be filled with wisdom.

Second/Third-Stage Transition

The second/third-stage transition begins as this individual decides to seek some form of objective understanding concerning her life situation. As long as she is coping blindly with the feelings and situations in which she finds herself, she will remain in second stage. As she becomes drawn toward the quest for self-knowledge, she begins a process which will eventually reveal undreamed of resources that lie hidden deep within her.

She must learn to take conscious responsibility for her own life. If she finds herself constantly being rejected by others, she must learn not to blame coincidence or a cruel and mindless fate. Nor is it the fault of the opposite sex, or even of her own parents, although patterns experienced within the family of origin can provide important keys to assist in unraveling her own personal riddle.

To move to third stage we must learn to uncover our own unconscious motivations for the things we do and the experiences we tend to attract. Starting with the assumption that we are the authors of our own destiny, we then begin to unravel the mess which we seem to have created for ourselves. When we get to the end, we find that it was not a mess at all, but rather a gift disguised as a challenge to be overcome.

Let us examine the various common forms of response to second stage, to see how they can be traced to their basic origin and then reprogrammed. Some individuals enter the second/third-stage transition because they decide that they can no longer survive any more heartbreak. They have experienced so many lifetimes of unrequited love that they are in a complete panic by this stage.

An important part of the process of this transition involves achieving a realistic picture of one's own identity. This individual must overcome her tendency to be too subjective and to become excessively involved with the dramas of her own life. She must develop an ability to take an objective look at her own basic qualities and capabilities. The development of personal skills and talents becomes highly important at this stage. She must learn to become inwardly-directed instead of looking outside of herself for fulfillment or distraction. Self-respect and self-appreciation must become the cornerstone upon which she is to build, and this can often be achieved through activities which make use of her innate abilities.

Although her approach to life is often simple and at times rustic during first stage, the trials of the second stage lend her much sophistication. By the time she has reached the second/third-stage transition, she has often acquired much in the way of intellectual skill, and may approach life in the spirit of a social scientist. The development of her mental skills may also be of great value to her as she goes about the process of resurrecting her original strengths. Whatever she does must be done for her own satisfaction alone, and not to achieve acclaim or appreciation from others. Exploring her inner world for its own sake is extremely important.

The inner quest is also of value in order to find a way to end her emotional suffering, and to learn how to be loved, but as long as Taurus quests only with this goal in mind, she will unfortunately be inclined to miss the boat. Only as she finds herself interesting enough to want to know more about will she begin to be able to build the foundation which will allow her to experience the love of another. The more she develops herself and her own relationship with herself, the more she will acquire a sense of personal honor. Initially, of course, she finds herself drawn away from this process again and again in the pursuit of some tantalizing but ill-fated romantic experience. Yet each time she returns to her rightful path, she finds it more and more interesting and fulfilling.

It is important that her quest be the discovery of self for the sake of self, and that it not degenerate into a desire to make something of herself in the eyes of the world; for this is yet another form of compensation—seeking unconditional love from society to fill the inner void. This does not mean that outer success should be avoided, only that it should not be sought as a substitute for self-esteem.

As the second/third-stage Taurean begins to pay attention to her talents once again (they first made their presence known in early first stage), she finds that she is beginning to build an alternative version of herself. At this stage she still experiences deep personal insecurity. And yet, she is building an alter-ego which she knows to be of great value. The more she acts from and defines herself in terms of this personal integrity, the more she will be inclined to develop a sense of inner peace and security.

She may have had a vengeful streak. Others may have mistreated her, eventually causing her to feel justified in returning their negative treatment with thoughtless anger, abuse or dishonesty. Sometimes the wrong people have gotten blamed for her suffering. She may also have forgotten to honor herself in her impulsive quest to achieve fulfillment and an end to personal suffering. Choosing to treat herself and others with integrity gives her an opportunity to begin breaking out of these vicious circles.

Like a starving man she has been storming the strongholds where the food is hidden, trying again and again to breach walls which have never yielded to her in the past, and cannot possibly do so in the future. So many seasons have passed, that in her haste she has failed to notice the rich fertile fields which have grown up all about her, simply waiting to be harvested. Unconsciously this individual is hoping that by choosing those who will likely reject her, she can somehow fix the pattern. She desperately hopes that the challenging individual she attempts to love can be magically induced to return her love. If she can achieve the unattainable, she will prove at last that she is truly desirable. When this pattern operates it shows that the individual does not understand what the challenge actually is!

Usually by the time late-second stage has been reached the individual in question has forgotten the exact nature of her original purpose. Her quest was to become the embodiment of unconditional love. He subtly misinterpreted this to mean that she should learn to love others unconditionally. To embody unconditional love means more than simply being able to prove that one is capable of its expression. Once the original goal is achieved, the expression of love occurs naturally and spontaneously, without a hint of fear or insecurity. However, if one does not embody love, one cannot love oneself unconditionally. And if one does not love oneself unconditionally, then a deep insecurity is bound to assert itself whenever one attempts to love someone else, even if we tell ourselves that we are not asking for anything in return.

Because the Taurean lacked the necessary sense of unconditional self-love, she has subjected herself to a series of lifetimes which, by the end of second stage, have created so great an imbalance that this individual often becomes almost incapable of loving others in a truly genuine manner. When this occurs, it is difficult for this individual to face such a truth honestly, or without self-recrimination, for her highest ideal is to love and be loving. How did she come to fall so far shy of the goal which she originally set for herself?

Unconsciously she assumed that others would determine and measure her success for her. In her initial dim recognition of her ultimate purpose, she felt that all she needed to do was love and to please others to the point where they would love and acknowledge her in return;

then she would have achieved the goal. And yet life does not work like this. Unconditional love is its own reward. In addition, some people are incapable of appreciating the efforts which others make on their behalf, because they have not yet reached the point in their own evolution where such an understanding is possible. By the end of second stage, the Taurean may be angry that no one has returned their love, and yet it is not the responsibility of anyone else to do so.

To pass into third stage, Taurus needs to define for herself what unconditional love truly is. It is not necessary to describe this quality as unconditional love, for all true love is unconditional. In fact love is omnipresent, and is ultimately the substance out of which all things are formed. We do not have to work to express or generate love, we simply need to get out its way. Love is not something to give or to receive, but rather something we must learn to allow.

By the end of second-stage Taurus, most natives of this sign have become rather self-centered and neurotic (as have most natives of every sign). Consciously or unconsciously these tendencies cause this individual to feel like a failure who could not possibly be much further away from her highest ideals than she now is. If she can reach an understanding of what love really is, then she will be able to allow this pure source of life to heal her. If only she had known centuries ago that the first step to embodying unconditional love is to allow it deliberate access to one's own self.

One of the keys to the transition from the second to the third stage of Taurus involves learning how to step aside from one's own emotional reactions to achieve a state of inner quiet where the voice of the inner self can be heard. This practice enables an individual to fall naturally into alignment with Universal Truth, so that she can claim the love which has been waiting all around her.

I have these words for second/third-stage Taurus: Let your true self be shown to you. Love is all around you. It is a pure love, a Divine Love, and it has been waiting all this time for you to become aware of its presence. When you make this love your foundation, then you cannot lose. You will learn how to share love with others, rather than approaching them in need. All the time you spent bewailing the fact that you could not find love and that you could not find the answer, and all the while love had answered long ago and was waiting for you to notice!

This is the kind of peak experience which must inevitably take place in second/third-stage Taurus. And while you are waiting for it to happen to you, or for you to happen to it, there are a few practical, less esoteric steps which can be taken in order to prepare for its arrival. They are simply this: In every way that you can possibly imagine, practice being loving with yourself, with no conditions whatsoever. For all signs, an important key to second/third stage involves watching yourself; watching yourself day to day. When are you self-condemning? When do you not give to yourself? When are you self-critical? And most importantly, when are you tempted to become involved in a relationship—and I'm not just speaking of romantic relationships here, although these are the most important —which may be in any manner self-destructive, or threatening to the new sense of self which you are in the process of building?

Because it has been so many lifetimes since this individual has been intimately loved, each opportunity for a relationship that comes along can seem like the last. In this situation, it is easy to panic and to deny reason or intuition, and to dive once again into the fray; or, to act defensively and destructively, pushing away the very love you seek, before it has a chance to really hurt you. At this stage the need for intimate love is so deep that it is almost certainly guaranteed to push everyone else away. You are left with only one recourse, and that is to provide it for yourself. Only you can give yourself as much as you now need. Then, and only then, shall it all be added unto you.

Taurus sets this riddle up for herself to gain direct access to a very pure and powerful form of Divine Love. On a soul level, she wishes to know it for what it truly is, and to become one with it, unite with it, ultimately to become it. And so she certainly shall. Such is her inevitable destiny.

In first-stage Taurus the individual always selects lovers or mates who do not love them in return, and so the results of this pattern are always faced in the second/third-stage transition. Another common pattern is that of also choosing as members of one's family those who are unable or unwilling to grant the individual the love or nurturing which she may seek—especially in childhood. This tendency will also inevitably follow the individual into the transition, usually in the form of a powerful tie to one or both parents which involves a painful feeling of unfulfilled love.

This parental figure or figures symbolize the ultimate authority which Taurus subconsciously believes will grant her heart worthiness. "If only she would love me, then I would finally be assured that all my fears have been an illusion." She is like a child who longs to awaken from a nightmare to feel the safety and security of a parent's embrace. However, in this situation it is often the relationship with the parent(s) which is the nightmare, nor is this necessarily only the fault of the parent. For most of us, our early childhood experience is designed to help us to pick up where we have left off in our prior incarnations. If the soul has been used to choosing to seek the love of those unable or unwilling to give love, she will be inclined to continue to repeat this pattern until something has been done consciously to correct the problem. A Taurean who experiences difficulty with one or both of her parents has simply chosen these individuals in the same manner in which she would go about choosing a lover. Therefore, it is essential that Taurus learn to let this individual go.

Our parents and our children (for this pattern can also be played out with a child) are free and independent individuals in their own right. They have their own karmic patterns and life lessons to deal with, and must be allowed to attend to such things in their own manner. As long as we continue to project a negative image upon a parent or a grown child we will to a certain extent limit the freedom of that individual. In wishing that someone would change, and learn to love you more, or treat you better, you are paradoxically reinforcing the old pattern within your own mind.

For Taurus, a negative parent represents an unjust authority whose love she aches for. A child in the same position is just a replacement for a parent, once all hope has been given up. "If I can't be loved by an authority, I will try to be loved in an authoritative position. I'll give you everything I missed. Then you can't help but love me." Although Taureans will usually select an actor who is somewhat compatible with the role, the shock is that it is really her unconscious fantasy which is being played out upon the other person. This is also true in the case of her romantic entanglements, and until the outer authority is placed within where it really belongs, both individuals will be inclined to remain somewhat trapped.

If Taurus can snap out of this illusion, and move on to create her own life in a more constructive spirit, this will allow the other individual(s) involved the freedom to do likewise — in their own way and in their own time. Trying to change others rarely works. Changing ourselves can then create an unintentional domino effect, bringing surprising changes in others which we may never have considered. But we must first let go of all outer expectations and concentrate only on our primary responsibility ---- ourselves.

By late second stage, there are certain Taureans who will have given up all hope of ever truly being loved. To them relationships represent nothing but the possibility of pain. They barricade themselves inside their own little world, escaping into solitude and fantasy. Or they act out their frustrations upon the outer world. They may play a game called "Before I let you in you must prove that you can love me unconditionally, even though that is completely impossible." They may keep a lover on a string, never fully committing, but always holding out that tiny bit of hope, while they test and test, forever seeking evidence of the impossible. Many individuals with this tendency are truly good-hearted. Their behavior is as compulsive as that of those who constantly storm the gates of love, and is in fact a reaction against their own previous tendency to do just that. They may be contemptuous of the dedicated lovers which they manage to attract, because these individuals remind them too much of themselves.

While the second-stage Taurean who hides away in solitude, or immerses herself in a search for wealth or power may appear less vulnerable than her apparently more romantic sister or brother, in fact she may have an even greater element of hidden sensitivity. Remember that it is not the possession of worldly goods or the acceptance of great responsibility that present a problem. It is only when such things are sought as a form of compensation for feelings of emotional lack that difficulties are eventually bound to manifest.

The second-stage Taurean who hides the truth from herself may seem to have a hard task laid out for her. However, her greatest difficulty lies in actually becoming aware of what she is doing. Once she realizes that she has been hiding, her moment of liberation is not far away. This individual must acknowledge her deep fears of intimacy. Once she awakens, she may find that her sensitivity threatens to overwhelm her. He must learn to see in it her own potential to experience the best that life has to offer. Then, as in all situations, she must work to develop the ability to be loving and supportive of herself and begin to prepare for the experience of receiving Divine Love.

Unconditional love is not only possible, it is in fact inevitable. Others cannot fail to respond to you in the manner which you expect. They will treat you as you treat them, and even more importantly, as you treat yourself. These are simple concepts to speak of, or to understand on an intellectual level. The true mystery of life is how to live them, and it is the Taurean who has the greatest ultimate potential of solving this riddle. When her response to life is healed, the Taurean will inevitably experience deep personal satisfaction in all of her relationships.

Once true unconditional love for the self has been achieved, the individual finds that she is now able to have unconditional trust in the life force and her own life pattern, whatever it may be. Because she trusts life, she knows that she is worthy and will be loved. She no longer needs to escape. She no longer requires any form of addictive behavior, nor needs to escape into the arms of one for whom she does not truly experience personal love. Instead she now possesses a great impersonal love for all beings and has achieved or will soon achieve a fulfilling form of mutual union with a truly compatible, loving mate. Having become the embodiment of unconditional love, she passes into the third stage of her development.

Third Stage

The Third-stage Taurean may be placid and serene, yet, like a steaming locomotive, potent and unstoppable as she heads in the direction of her chosen destination. The tenacity of first stage and the stubbornness of second stage have given way to the certain determination of third stage. Inspired by a love of life, Taurus uses this great power to fulfill whatever may be her life purpose -- for love can fulfill itself in almost any form. Third-stage Taureans can be found in almost any walk of life. More than any other sign of the zodiac, their future is an open book. The rest of the astrological chart will tend to indicate the chosen life direction of the individual.

Love seeks to express itself, and universal love seeks the higher good of all beings. To fulfill this divine imperative, the third-stage Taurean will choose perhaps to be a protector, healer or agent of transformation for some aspect of the world at large. The artistic temperament is common among natives of this sign, and third stage bestows complete artistic freedom. Because she has spent so many lifetimes giving unconditionally to the world, this individual will find that in third stage she always receives assistance from others as she pursues her chosen calling. She may express her unconditional love for herself and all beings through works of beauty designed to evoke new levels of awareness.

The third-stage Taurean possesses a strong social conscience and may therefore be strongly committed to some form of social action designed to better the lot of the world and its inhabitants. He or she may be found in the world of politics, joined with those who attempt to transform the status quo in some unconventional manner, or utilizing her artistic or literary talents to affect mass consciousness in some manner.

As a healer this individual excels, especially in any position requiring that loving attention be given out to others. Optimistic, loving acceptance can do wonders, and this individual's trust in life is highly contagious. While the presence of this individual is extremely reassuring to anyone experiencing physical difficulties, certain individuals in the third stage of Taurus are also potent spiritual and emotional healers. Because they have spent so much time during the second/third stage exploring and realigning their own inner world, they are often able to contact the deeper reaches of the collective mind and inspire and assist others to do likewise. They are guides, allowing full exploration of the inner world, giving those whom they serve the love and inspiration which makes it possible for them to conquer their inner darkness and re-emerge into full daylight.

It is also possible for the third-stage Taurean to have no special role in the external world. Instead, this individual takes quiet pride in her possession of the greatest gift in all the world, bestowing it upon all whom she may encounter. Love, pure and simple, is her gift and her inheritance. In fame or in obscurity, great spiritual leader or simple-hearted lover, this individual finds fulfillment through living from the law of her own inner being.

Taurus at the Crossroads
First/Third-Stage Transition

At the end of first stage, Taurus has two choices. She can continue to trust life, despite the perplexity she feels over the treatment she has received from others, or she can choose instead to doubt herself, wondering if she is indeed worthy to draw from the well which never runs dry. As her heart crumbles she may seek solace in the natural world which has always befriended her. But will she be able to forget her grief long enough to listen to the spirit which speaks from within?

To achieve the transition between the first and third stage of Taurus, this individual must learn to be objective about her own life situation before it is too late. If she reacts, she will be lost. If she decides to actively analyze her situation, she may be able to understand that she has been sending others a subtle message, which has offered them an opportunity to use and abuse her. If she becomes lost in self-pity, she will almost certainly follow the path of least resistance into second stage. If she can instead decide to break away from all who threaten to oppress her emotionally, she may have a chance to avoid many future problems.

She must learn to see the value of her own heart. She must remember that she is indeed a good soul, and must vow not to lose her special and rare capacity to love. Instead of casting pearls before swine, she would be better served by choosing to stand for simple justice within the world, starting with a decision to practice equality in all her relationships, regardless of how much she may be tempted to give without restraint. Her loving nature gives her great potential as a positive social force. If she can transfer her ideals to a larger sphere of influence and strive to achieve and apply her objective understanding of the world around her, she will avoid the suffering of the second stage. Inspired by a greater ideal, she will be freed of her need for others, and may be able to comprehend another of the secrets which will allow her to enter the third stage — the secret of true self-love and self recognition.

Childhood Conditions and Relationship Patterns

While the relationship patterns of Taurus have obviously been discussed above, there are a few things which remain to be said concerning her relationships with her parents. In traditional astrology Taurus is considered to be an Earth sign. One of the four elements of the Ancients, Earth is associated with the physical, material world and with our needs for sustenance, pleasure and physical affection. Because of this emphasis upon primal needs, the Taurean tends to experience the mother's influence as being generally more powerful than that of the father. Mother represents primal, physical fulfillment as well as female beauty (or ugliness) personified.

In early first stage the bond with the mother is likely to be serene and fulfilling. From the mother, the Taurean learns to love and to appreciate beauty and pleasure. She feels gratitude towards her mother for all she has given, and wishes to give to her in return. Yet, no matter how much she does for her, once she is old enough to contribute in some manner to the welfare of the family, she may feel that it is not good enough. After a while, especially as first stage progresses, her mother may be inclined to agree with her. She may come into her next lifetime expecting the impossible from herself, as far as what she feels she must give to her family. And they therefore become increasingly demanding of her as well.

The Taurean male has a powerful tie to his mother, for good or for ill. There is often an almost emotionally incestuous relationship between the two of them. If there is great love expressed in the relationship, the danger, in first or second stage at least, is that the relationship will threaten to devour them both. Unconsciously he may not be able to allow his romantic relationships to succeed, because this would betray his union with his mother. If their relationship is outwardly negative and filled with conflict, this may lead him to feel a lack of trust towards the opposite sex. He may be filled with anger and resentment and may be inclined to be quite manipulative in his relationships, as a result of the fears engendered by this primary relationship. It is also possible for a single mother/son relationship to express both of these patterns. Because our mother is our primary love relationship, regardless of our sex, a daughter with these patterns expressed in her relationship with her mother may be affected similarly.

Another pattern can also emerge in the mother/daughter relationship. Mother and daughter may find themselves engaged in a vicious competition for the love of the father. Even if this is not actually the case, it is easy for the insecure Taurus female to feel that her mother outdoes her in terms of feminine beauty. If there does exist an actual competition between the mother and the daughter, whether for the attention of the father or just to prove who is the most attractive, this can be destructive in many ways. The daughter can be left with lifelong insecurities. Because she wants to love her mother, she may feel guilty for feeling in competition with her and resentful of her. This is damaging to her self-esteem. She may feel that she must always scramble to achieve any kind of romantic fulfillment or attention from the opposite sex. She may also be inclined to be attracted to triangles, falling in love with a married man for example, as she tries once again, unconsciously, to steal her father's love away from her mother.

Father may be absent, or mother may dominate to the point where she prevents the father and the child from building a complete relationship. If the father is not hidden in the background, she may be difficult and demanding as well. This is often crushing to her son's self-esteem, interfering with the child's ability to form balanced relationships in her adult years. For a daughter this may be just as difficult, for she will tend to seek relationships with men which are just as destructive as her relationship with her father once was. Taurus in first and second stage may play out their pattern of unrequited love with either a distant and demanding father or an overpowering and exacting mother. If they can learn to seek the infinite source of love within themselves, then they will be set free.

Taureans born into third stage generally receive tremendous emotional support from both of their parents. Although their relationship with their mother tends to remain close, by third stage they also tend to experience a positive and fulfilling relationship with their father, who represents symbolically their new understanding of Divine Love. For Taurus the mother represents personal love and the father represents divine love. The third-stage Taurus understands that they are in fact both equally important.

Famous Taureans

First Stage: Cinderella — without the Prince; Pepe LePew. (It is almost impossible to find famous examples of first-stage Taureans. I have known individuals in this stage in my life, but there is little reason why they should be in the public eye.)
Second Stage: Romeo and Juliet, Hero and Leander, Lee Majors, Melissa Gilbert, James Brown, Billy Joel, Beatrice Arthur (close to the transition), Adolph Hitler.
Second/Third Stage: Bianca Jagger, Carol Burnett, Sigmund Freud, Dr. Benjamin Spock, Stevie Wonder, Salvador Dali, Malcolm X, William Shakespeare, Leonardo Da Vinci.

Third Stage: Audrey Hepburn, Shirley MacLaine (both of the previous examples passed through the second/third stage in their lifetimes), Gautama Buddha.

First/Third Stage: Cinderella — with the Prince.

GEMINI
youthful genius

According to traditional astrological lore, Gemini is considered an air sign. The element of air is associated with the mind, and is one of the two masculine elements. Because Gemini is therefore considered one of the six masculine signs, I have used the words "he", "him" and "his" as neutral terms to refer to either gender. Even though Gemini is termed a masculine sign, this does not necessarily mean that individuals born under this sign will be lacking in feminine qualities. It simply indicates that they will tend to require more support and encouragement from their fathers, than those individuals born under the feminine signs of the zodiac.

Gemini, more than anyone else, is at home in the mental world. If Taurus spends time in the world of the faeries before being reborn, Gemini at that time inhabits a world filled with the joys of knowledge and wonders of life as they present themselves to the objective observer. Whether he studies the natural world or dwells himself in the kingdom of the faeries, he does so as a scientist or an artist who seeks to express some vital truth.

He is fascinated with humanity, yet feels like an outsider. Gifted artist, scientist or eternal student, his goal is to develop the skills, talents or essential knowledge which will take humanity ahead. He brings the world to its next step, whatever that may be.

First Stage

For Gemini, the first goal is to develop the skills and knowledge necessary to the fulfillment of his purpose. His initial lifetimes generally bring him into contact with an environment which affords him ample opportunity to develop these skills or experiment with and collect whatever knowledge may be necessary. Early in his lifetime he discovers that he possesses a natural talent and affinity for some specific science, art or field of human endeavor. It is also quite possible for this individual to be multi-talented, for the concrete purpose of each Gemini is unique and may

75

require that he master several different disciplines. Whatever path of development he may pursue, he is inclined to be extremely dedicated in his pursuit of skill or knowledge.

His one-track mind tends to isolate him, although in truth he bears a great deal of love for humanity. He secretly longs to be a part of society, yet at this stage his pursuits seem to demand most of his resources of time and energy. In addition, he feels more comfortable in the world of ideas than he does in the sphere of emotions and relationships. Between lifetimes he has spent so much time on what the mystics might call the mental plane, that his emotional nature is not well developed. Emotions to him are confusing. They do not fit the program. They are not logical, and he really does not understand where they fit in.

He is usually quite shy in the presence of others, and even when he does attempt to reach out to them, finds that they do not easily relate to or understand his ideas. And so he tends to spend most of his first-stage lifetimes living a hermit-like existence. He feels that if he can make a lasting contribution to the welfare of humanity, then he will become a truly valued member of society. And so he dreams of the day when his discoveries can be given to the people, and he can be loved and appreciated by all. Despite his capacity for mental achievement, he is touchingly naive on an emotional level.

As first stage progresses, he tends to sacrifice opportunities for human companionship in favor of pursuing his work and studies, feeling that once he has completed his research, made the big discovery or achieved artistic excellence, then he will be judged worthy to receive the love which he desires. Because he chooses to continue to develop the parts of his personality which are already highly developed, while ignoring those areas of life which will allow him to become a complete human being, he gradually becomes more and more lopsided. He may excel in the sciences or the mystical or creative arts, but while his mental skills develop far ahead of most other individuals, his emotional nature remains child-like and unformed, lagging behind the development of those who surround him.

As first stage reaches its completion, the skills and knowledge which he possesses have been developed to the point where they are finally ready to be shared with the rest of humanity. While he understands that the pursuit of knowledge is an endless quest, he has at last reached the point where he can begin to present what he possesses. Like a gleeful child he begins to share his gifts with the people, never imagining the difficulties which may lie ahead for him.

In some cases he may find that the people receive his gifts gladly, and this pleases him, for at last he is receiving the acclaim and attention which he has always wanted. Yet he has always required intimate acceptance as well as universal acclaim, and when the people see what he is capable of, they are inclined to worship him from afar. He is placed upon a pedestal and seen as someone to be honored and admired, but inwardly he finds that this does not bring him the fulfillment he longed for. He also needs to be accepted as one of them, an equal, and the position they place him in creates a subtle distance. The people may admire him, but it seems that they almost fear him, or wish to worship his image, rather than to share unconditionally and informally in his joy of discovery.

He also finds all this acclaim subtly unsettling, for he knows that he is not just a big hero. Secretly he is aware that he also has a very vulnerable side, which no one, it seems, ever wants to see. They want him to fulfill the role of a leader, and ironically he has set up the very circumstances which have encouraged others to view him in this manner. His shyness causes him to withhold his emotional nature from others. Because people only wish to relate to him as a guide or leader, he begins to feel that perhaps his underdeveloped emotional self may be unacceptable and unlovable. He may come to wonder how secure his position in society actually is.

Because this latter part of the first stage of Gemini tends to last for several lifetimes, he may find himself presenting his talents in many different places and at many different times. In less fortunate situations than the one represented above, he will meet with an unwelcome surprise. Even if he is mentally prepared for it, he can never be emotionally prepared.

As much as the people need the gifts he has to offer, they may also not yet be ready for them. They may not want to see what he has to give, for it asks them to change their way of life and perhaps also their most basic thoughts or beliefs. Human nature tends to be conservative and finds change unsettling, especially on the mental plane. Many people wish to maintain their old philosophies, as they give them a degree of mental security which they may feel to be necessary to their survival. Because Geminis in first stage have little understanding of human emotion, this individual is unlikely to comprehend this tendency in human nature.

Gemini individuals have the capacity to open the doorway to a whole new world. In the world at large, there exist those who would rather see the way barred. Not everyone shares his love for truth and knowledge for their own sake. Gemini's ideas may clash with existing political or religious ideologies, which may not wish to relinquish their powerful hold upon the minds of the public. And so he may meet with rejection or even persecution for what he has to say. For this individual such an experience is quite traumatic and surprising. In his innocence he had hoped to earn the love of the people through the presentation of his gifts. This experience tends to create a lasting fear of rejection and a sense of personal alienation which will follow him through many lifetimes. In time it leads to the subtle disintegration of personality which is the beginning of the transition into the second stage.

First/Second-Stage Transition

The first/second stage transition Gemini lives life under constant pressure. Whatever his public role may be, he is extremely involved with it. If he is passing through a phase of public acceptance he will feel greatly burdened by the people's need to perceive him as a more than human icon of perfection. He is a tower of strength who may secretly doubt the soundness of his own foundations. Even if he is not burdened by self-doubt, he will certainly feel swamped by his responsibilities, and often unappreciated and in need of support.

If he is less fortunate, he will be experiencing rejection or persecution at the hands of those he seeks to serve. He will attempt to hold his ground at any cost, but the stress, pressure and ultimately the trauma of doing so is one day destined to shatter him to the core. He may also find within the course of one lifetime that he moves from a position of popularity to one of oppression and infamy, as the fickle winds of public opinion shift against him.

At the same time, while he attempts to hold to his ideas and principles, and continues to expound them in a rational manner, his emotional needs are becoming stronger and do not wish to be denied. His mental perspective still dominates, but tension is increasing, and each new rejection wounds his Achilles' heel — his hidden, child-like emotional nature — more and more. At last he finds that something is building up within him which he cannot control. Until the very last, he will use every effort of his will to maintain his hold upon his principles and preserve his self-control, but eventually his emotions will spill over and wrest control away from him.

He has been rejected, or admired, but he has seldom been loved. He is not a purely rational being, and much as he may attempt to live only in this world, ultimately he will succumb to the needs and drives of his emotional nature. At the end of the first/second-stage transition he collapses in defeat. He was unable to give the people what they wanted. Even when he was able to give them what they needed, he seemed only to have been accepted for a short time. The dream of his glorious admission into the brotherhood of man has been delivered stillborn. He doesn't really trust himself anymore. With his trust in himself and his own decisions visibly weakened, he consciously or unconsciously gives the control of his own personality over to the wounded child within himself, and as he does so, he passes into second stage.

Second Stage

Although he may be unaware of this fact, the second-stage Gemini is almost completely dominated by his emotional self and his often irrational beliefs and impulses. Emotionally he is undeveloped and the child within him now dominates, doing everything in its power to cope with the rejection which it fears to be inevitable. Subconsciously this individual believes personal acceptance to be impossible, and so struggles to avoid any form of personal rejection, or failing that to compensate in whatever manner may be possible. He is convinced that sharing himself with the world will inevitably lead to rejection, and that it is not possible for him to ever be loved for who he truly is.

When others acclaim him for his qualities of genius, their adulation does not seem real. They seem to only love him for being superior to them. To maintain their adulation he feels he must hide his emotional self, and hide it he does whenever and wherever possible. Of course if he is hiding his emotions, he cannot share them, and so is doomed to remain in lonely isolation. He is also acutely aware that others might easily reject him even for his best qualities and if that is so, it seems as though life will never really be secure. It is no wonder that he finds it so difficult to trust others. He doesn't really understand what went wrong, and may feel that he must have failed the people in some way, and therefore also tends to doubt and distrust himself.

He copes in whatever way he can while using the child-like logic of his now dominant emotional nature. Hiding his sensitivity from others, he uses his mental-self as a shield between himself and the world, and so that he may not seem to be dominated by his emotions. Yet that is exactly what he is. The non-rational part of himself now dominates, influencing all of his decisions. He is constantly on the defensive, always expecting to be betrayed or rejected once again.

Unconsciously he must invent some explanation for the traumas which he has experienced in the past. He will decide that it was either his fault or the people's fault that his message was not well received. If he decides that it is his fault, he wonders constantly what he did that was so wrong. How was it that he failed so profoundly in his quest to please his audience? He may innocently assume more positive intentions in others than can actually be there. Like a child trying to please the adults, he tries to be constantly "good". He does not know what he did wrong, and easily assumes that others may know better than he does, the truth about society and what constitutes an acceptable form of service.

This form of second-stage Gemini is easily led into doing whatever others want, even if this means selling himself short or allowing himself to be used by others. He may suffer from an excess of humility, habitually downplaying his talents, abilities and actual worth as an individual. He may hide his true talents, accepting whatever treatment or mistreatment he may receive from those in authority — subconsciously, almost everyone — allowing them to dictate what his own actions and personal limitations should be.

Like a faithful dog he tries very hard to please, hoping that one day he will produce or perform that one special, magical action, that service which will win him true acceptance. Meanwhile, his talents, his sense of self and his true feelings are stifled, as he is continually passed over and taken for granted. He is likely to put tremendous pressure on himself to perform, setting high or impossible standards of achievement in his chosen area of work or service.

He may still be involved in some endeavor which corresponds to his true soul-purpose, yet inevitably finds himself restricted or unappreciated. He may hold back, secretly holding dreams which are unrealized, or which remain hidden even from himself, refusing to pursue his true purpose, because he fears being too controversial. If this is the case, he will still attempt to please the people in some manner, perhaps in a more menial form of occupation, or through the patterns of relationship which he expresses in his personal life. He may serve those whose love he seeks, yet be unable to experience true intimacy in his relationships, for he unconsciously holds back much of himself, expecting rejection to follow upon the revelation of his true self.

Being locked in a corner is difficult for any child, and this is exactly what he is experiencing. Inevitably panic and frustration build up. Although he tries to be constantly on his best behavior, eventually his feelings must erupt, and they usually do so in a highly chaotic manner. He may be consciously or unconsciously self-destructive, lashing out with bouts of uncontrolled rage within the confines of his intimate environment. His rage may have the effect of destroying or damaging his health, or may take the form of crippling depressions stemming from low self-esteem, or could be expressed directly towards his family and others with whom he lives.

He may blame those closest to him for his failures, for he feels trapped into taking actions which will please others, and often tends to feel personally enslaved by those around him. His uncontrollable eruption of emotion is also a cry for help. He is asking others to release him, or to help him to release himself from the impossible burdens which he carries. Although he wants help, once his emotional crisis has passed, he may refuse any form of assistance. He feels that he must constantly carry whatever responsibilities seem to have been entrusted to him, even if they amount to nothing less than slavery, for otherwise he feels he will not have a right to belong to society, and may not even be able to survive as an individual. He may live in isolation, or drive away his nearest and dearest, in which case he must throw his tantrums to an audience of one.

Another type of second-stage Gemini individual will tend to blame others for the rejection which he has experienced, and decide that rather than attempting to be a good child, he will instead become a bad child. He will usually attempt, consciously or unconsciously, to find a way to make the world pay for having wronged him. In either case, the child hides behind his genius and uses the genius to mediate with the outside world. The emotional self pulls the strings, using mental talents to buy him acceptance in the first case, or to turn the tables on the world in the second case.

The "bad-child Gemini" is an artful dodger and a master of deviance, who may go so far as to become a psychopathic liar. At the very least he is a teller of tall tales. He tries to manipulate those around him into loving him or looking up to him, feeling falsely that he can somehow win himself a place in the world that way. As innocent as his more honest fellow he might hope that by spinning the right tale the whole world and the life which it allows him to live will be magically transformed. He may not trust others easily and expects high standards of behavior and honesty from them, while unconsciously living out a double standard as he fools himself into believing his own lies.

He still remembers when he held high standards of thought and behavior, and may believe that he is still the same person he was before the transition into second stage began. In a sense he is right, for his true self does have the nobility which he remembers. He may be constantly on the lookout for the betrayal which he expects to re-occur, and when he sees evidence of it, either in reality or in his own imagination, he is quick to take vengeance, perhaps secretly. This is a very difficult pattern, for it may operate consciously, unconsciously, or in a combination of both.

The bad child may not just be seeking vengeance, he may believe that dishonesty is truly the only way to gain acceptance, or even in some cases to ensure his own survival; for it must be remembered that his true gifts have been often and perhaps even violently rejected in the past. He desperately needs love and may also be, like a child, constantly testing for and seeking unconditional love, then challenging its existence by misbehaving. He may be seeking attention as a way of asking for help and external discipline, for he certainly cannot handle his own life once his patterns have reached this stage of complexity. This form of Gemini may experience constant or periodic waves of remorse, feeling that he truly must be bad or inferior and wishing that there were some other alternative. Once he learns to stop blaming others for his misery, and begins the sincere search for self-transformation, the transition into third stage will begin.

A third alternative to the second stage of Gemini also exists. This pattern could be described more as an "adolescent" form of response rather than a child-like or childish way of handling a crisis. In this version the ideals remain intact, and the individual continues to operate from a highly ethical standard of behavior. Nor does he make the mistake of blaming himself for having been rejected by society. He or she does not choose to "sell out" in the hopes that he will thereby be fully accepted by others.

Instead this individual becomes mentally attached to a seemingly hopeless battle with the corrupt forms of social expression which he envisions to run counter to the expression of his or her life purpose. This individual becomes locked into a pattern of noble rebellion which is eternally destined to fail, due to the fact that he tends to see "the powers that be" as far more powerful and effective than he himself could ever be alone. This pattern can also be difficult to surmount, for the individual may initially be unable to perceive that his or her troubles actually stem from an inner attitude or belief, rather than a set of outer circumstances over which one cannot gain control.

Identifying oneself as the noble and oppressed rebel continually attracts just that very situation into this individual's life. Seldom does he understand that he actually possesses far more power than he realizes. He is inclined to choose the difficult cause and the difficult way of going about a cause, when he could be far more effective utilizing a different set of tactics and different manner of approach to an easier problem, should he choose to tackle it.

Healthy responses to second stage include the "good child" who chooses to lead a simple life within the dictates of society as it is, and the playfully "bad" and rebellious child, who instead of acting destructively towards himself or others, employs his sense of humor and capacity to play the harmless trickster to gain attention from and enlighten others about the limitations of their beliefs and attitudes. To have a healthy response to the second stage of Gemini, the individual must cultivate patience and contentment, and avoid feelings of frustration, martyrdom or blame. Even the healthy "good child" is inclined to become overly humble, while often learning to live contentedly in the moment. The latter response, however, will serve him well during the transition into third stage. On the other hand, a more rebellious response to second stage can easily get out of hand or be misunderstood by others, even though the playful, mischievous aspect of second-stage Gemini can be a side-effect enjoyed by others during this transition.

Second/Third-Stage Transition

This transition commences when the individual begins to admit to himself that he is in pain, or at the very least that his life has become too limited, and that nothing he himself can do with his known personal resources will resolve the inner difficulties he is facing. To accept and admit this form of inner helplessness and frustration takes a great deal of courage, and the beginning of this transition is often extremely difficult, as it is for all signs. Initially this individual may swing between frantic seeking and deep feelings of inner despair and hopelessness.

He may fall back into blaming others and rebelling against them, if he has previously been a "bad child". He may fall back into selling himself out to lowest bidder, if he has been the "good child". But whatever choice he makes, he will be unable to stay with it for long once the truth begins to dawn, for he will understand that the old ways are the path of his undoing, and that he must somehow find a way to save himself from them.

Anyone who sincerely seeks answers eventually finds them, and for Gemini the answer lies in the part of himself which he has been hiding for so long. His emotional self has become his Achilles' heel, mainly because he has always believed that it would be. Many lifetimes ago he made the decision that it was unsafe for him to be vulnerable towards others. He may have decided that people could never be trusted. In isolating his emotional self from the outside world, he also removed himself from the only source of true support and sustenance which he had — himself! His vulnerability became a weakness to be denied — inwardly as well as outwardly.

All of his true emotional innocence, never acknowledged for its beauty or its basic right to exist, has been hidden like a dirty secret, as he struggled on, attempting to survive without ever nourishing or giving any attention to it. Now he must learn to give unconditional support to this childlike part of himself. This is not at first an easy thing to do, for it is human nature not to want to dwell on one's own weaknesses. We tend to believe that the weaker parts of ourselves prove that we are somehow inferior and unworthy; yet there is nothing wrong with starting at the beginning. We all do this in many ways each day. Gemini's "weaker"' emotional nature is not a failing, just an underdeveloped part in need of support. To pass through this transition, this individual needs to learn how to take an entirely new attitude towards himself.

He must learn unconditional self-acceptance. This does not mean indulging the self and letting it get away with anything. Nor does it mean setting 'reasonable' standards by which the self can be 'judged'. What it does mean is learning to live with a responsible attitude of care and consideration for oneself, exactly as if one was attempting to become one's own loving parent.

We all suffer insecurities which seem child-like. This less developed part of ourselves needs to look to the more mature aspects of the self for guidance and reassurance. When we live from the inner child, it is this inner child which struggles to make the decisions about how to guide and nurture itself. The child within always requires parental guidance, and until we learn differently we will tend to emulate our own parents, not only in the way in which we treat our own children, but also as we go about attempting to parent that childlike part of us which is within us.

This means that as adults we internalize our mother and father, and begin to parent ourselves as we were by them. The second-stage Gemini experiences either rigid discipline, which tends to produce the "good child," or neglect, which will usually result in a "bad child" response.

Some Geminis born into the transition are gifted with a parent or set of parents who are truly adept at helping him to learn to honor and take genuine responsibility for himself. If they are truly wise, they will intuitively comprehend that this individual is somehow innately less comfortable with his or her emotional responses then most people. They will make an extra effort to create a safe, firm and loving environment in which this individual can discover that what seems to be an inner weakness is really a strength waiting to be developed. The mother is particularly important to the second/third-stage Gemini, for she provides a direct line to her child's deeper emotional nature.

Whatever the early childhood situation, as Gemini matures, he must learn how to properly parent himself. If the early home experience was mainly positive, the process will be easier, but nonetheless it must be undergone in order for the individual to achieve true independence. Daily habits of thought and internal action must be monitored. In the second/third-stage transition of every sign, the daily habits of internal thought and action take on great and usually underestimated importance. It is so important to treat oneself lovingly in one's thoughts. Condemnation is not loving, nor is self-indulgence.

As Gemini learns to be more nurturing of and responsible for his inner self and outer choices, he gradually learns to be more vulnerable to his feeling nature. The initial process of discovery of emotions which lie beneath the surface can be very painful. He may have a hard time finding others to assist him with this process, because he usually finds it so difficult to trust others. He soon learns that secretly he also finds it difficult to trust himself. And yet he must go forward and work to be emotionally self-supporting, for at this point any other choice may lead to his complete undoing. Eventually the dam breaks and he begins to develop the ability to trust inner feelings.

The more he trusts himself and the more he supports himself, the more he finds his attitude towards the outside world transforming. He learns not to seek external approval. He ceases to feel so angry at the world, for he begins to comprehend that it is not their fault. He may decide to suspend his beliefs concerning society and the world at large, choosing instead to concern himself exclusively with his inner world for a certain period of time. He does not separate himself, nor is he excessively self-centered. Instead, this individual is learning how to trust life and may begin to experience contact with something larger than himself, the Divine Mind, of which we are all a part.

Gradually he begins to understand that he is constantly being nurtured by this Primal Source of Being. As he begins to accept his emotional nature, his mental world also begins to transform, and he becomes able to perceive life from an archetypal level of consciousness. He begins to see and understand the tides of evolution. He is like a prophet who will always be ahead of his time, but now that he knows how time works and what the needs of the people truly are, he understands that he need never suffer again as a result.

While it is certain that few will ever be capable of truly understanding him, he now has unflagging inner support. And because he no longer views his emotional self as a weakness, he begins to be able to attract those few who are capable of understanding and honoring him for who he is as an individual. True friendship and intimate love become his inheritance. Once this individual has become his or her own best friend, and surrounded himself with the love and friendship which reflect this state of being, then he will be able to enter the third stage of his development.

Third Stage

The child genius becomes the wise eternal youth. Playfulness is an aspect of universal being. It is therefore also an aspect of all third-stage individuals, yet none more so than Gemini. For many lifetimes, he has felt himself to be but a child. He was the shy child waiting at the fringes of life, hoping to find the thing which would entrance his fellows enough to gain him admittance. Or he was the alienated child, misbehaving in his certainty that he would never receive their welcome. Now he has learned that the key is to include himself, merely to play. Being his own best friend, he need no longer fear or expect rejection and so can now be free to accept himself as the child he is, capable of enjoying the sunshine long after others have grown too old and serious to do so.

In second stage, he was often completely at the mercy of his own unconscious forces. Now he has accepted and befriended the irrational aspects of his being, and allows himself to be guided by his own powerful bond with the natural rhythms of life. He is always in the right place at the right time, as he effortlessly follows the life path which is in harmony with the inner law of his being. His self-expression is natural and unaffected, and he is completely at home with the often considerable talent which he often possesses.

He seems playful, innocent and perhaps simple, but he is also a deep thinker. Never would he impose upon anyone any form of knowledge or understanding which they were unprepared for. By now he may be an insightful observer of human culture and evolution, and may veil some of his teachings in allegory. Certainly the lightness with which he approaches the truth gives it a sense of completeness. His enthusiasm draws us into the future with him, entering into entirely new worlds of being. He playfully leads the people past their limitations, and sometimes, making positive use of his old faculty for sleight-of-hand, leads them to believe that they have made these new discoveries all by themselves.

Because he has conquered his fears, his trust in life is now so great that it proves to be a constant source of inspiration to all who surround him. Each day is new to him, as trust and enthusiasm provide him with a simple, but profound key to the mysteries of life. Loving and loyal, with a deep appreciation for all forms of relationship and a true capacity for transformative intimacy, he is like a little child on a sunny day who has gone ahead to explore the unknown path, and now lies gleefully in wait for his companions to catch him up.

First/Third-Stage Transition

As the first stage of Gemini draws to a close, the individual finds himself in a perilous situation. Having spent so many years in isolation, he or she must now share his great discoveries and vulnerable persona with an unpredictable public. If he is to avoid becoming permanently scarred by this experience, it is important for him to discover that he is never truly alone. The crossroads therefore opens to Gemini in the form of a profound opportunity for mystical experience. He is offered an opportunity to understand that all which he stands for, he is standing for on behalf of the greater whole. The message which he carries is not his own exclusive property. He must learn not to identify his knowledge with himself.

The crossroads may also come in the form of a warning which Gemini may be inclined to ignore. He may be warned that he is very far ahead of his time, and that he should prepare himself for the stresses which must result from this situation. If he can acquire the proper attitude before it is too late, or even after he has gone through a certain amount of trauma in his dealings with the public, then he will not be flung helplessly into the second stage.

There is of course a great temptation inherent in late first-stage Gemini, to lay claim to the ownership of one's knowledge, to say, "This is my discovery, and therefore I am of value as an individual!" This is due to the fact that the individual has come to believe, consciously or unconsciously, that his or her knowledge and wisdom will bring personal validation from the people, giving him a sense of belonging and a way of being one of them. And yet it is this very temptation which ultimately gives others the power to hurt or control him. He must learn to perceive his own value on an essential level, without ever needing to prove it to anyone. He must also learn to understand the ultimate and enduring value of his contribution, no matter how it may or may not prove to be accepted, and if possible he must understand this before his contribution is made public. He must come to understand that his value and integrity as an individual stem directly from his willingness to risk all which he must risk in order to make the contribution which his soul urges him to make. His personal integrity may be all that he has to hold on to.

While he should support his own interests in whatever practical or legal manner may be necessary, emotionally he must learn detachment. Only in this manner does he learn to support himself as he faces the challenges which lie before him on the path. Though he goes forward in service to the knowledge or wisdom which he carries, his ability to be not personally identified with his message allows him to perceive and accept the divine support which surrounds him at all times.

If he is able to do this, his attitude towards himself will reach a state of near perfect balance; and if he allows himself to feel support on a subtle inner level, he will also attract it on a personal level. The more he masters the challenges of the first/third-stage transition of Gemini, the more fulfilling and supportive his personal life will become. He learns to view life with a sense of humor. He gains the courage to be himself at all times and in all situations. Becoming a profound student of human nature and human evolution, he learns also how to be in the right place at the right time. As all temptation to hide himself or to seek the approval of the public fades, he finds that he has passed some of the most difficult tests and challenges which life has to offer. Receiving emotional support internally as well as externally, he is now able to be wise at the same time as he may be controversial. Seemingly without effort, he passes into the third stage of his development.

Childhood Conditions and Relationship Patterns

In first and second stage this individual generally tends to be born into a family whose members are uncomfortable with the expression of emotion. The early childhood environment may place great stress upon intellectual values, the family is inclined to communicate verbally rather than on a more intimate level. Little use is made of non-verbal means of communication and there is often very little physical affection expressed to this child. This sort of childhood environment often makes Geminis feel lonely and alienated even within their own homes. This makes it very difficult for them to constructively bridge the gap between themselves and the greater world once they have become adults.

In first stage and in early second stage of the "good child" phase of Gemini there are often some bright spots in all of this. While members of the family may be reserved with one another, beneath the surface they experience genuine love and feelings of affection for each other. The family often expresses great loyalty toward all of its members, helping Gemini to build his strong sense of personal integrity and basic love of humanity.

Father is fascinating. He may not be present a great deal, but when he is, the family revolves around him. Subconsciously he represents Gemini's tendency to emphasize the value of his mental capabilities. In early childhood, Gemini will be inclined to place his father upon a pedestal. He greatly admires his father's skills and abilities and wishes to emulate them. He wants his father to teach him all about life and the fascinating things which lie waiting to be discovered. To the Gemini child Daddy seems to know everything and to be constantly involved in fascinating and important projects.

However, somewhere in the process of passing through the second stage, the bond with the father begins to be disrupted. In second stage it is common for the child to experience a sudden interruption in his or her paternal relationship. Gemini children often lose their fathers, whether it be through divorce, death or physical or emotional abandonment. As Gemini children mature, a distance often develops between the father and the child, often because the father is not comfortable with his own emotional nature.

As the transition between the second and third stage approaches, the relationship between father and child may degenerate into open conflict. The difficulties with the father subconsciously reflect Gemini's over-emphasis upon the intellectual aspect of his nature. As time goes by he learns that this part of himself, which he once valued so highly, is beginning to let him down. Once he has made peace with his own emotions and created a balance within himself, he will find that he once again has a close and fulfilling relationship with his father. By third stage, this becomes possible, as he is finally able to see his own father and both of his parents clearly.

To Gemini the mother subconsciously reflects his or her emotional tendencies. In first stage she may be emotionally cold, distant or uninvolved. In second stage she may be volatile and irrational. In either stage he is rarely able to understand her feelings or appreciate the motives behind her actions. A child who is born into the second/third-stage transition or into the third stage will have a mother who is highly nurturing as well as playful and inspiring. If he is at the beginning of the second/third-stage transition he may at first fail to understand her emotional nature and the gifts which she offers.

Gemini's relationship with his mother reflects his relationship to his own emotions. This is why she is often of such crucial importance during the transition into third stage. In most stages he finds his mother rather elusive. She may unwittingly or purposefully avoid contact, and in his later stages he may find her difficult to understand because her wisdom stems from a highly developed emotional source. To achieve emotional union with his mother is to achieve union with his own emotional nature and to understand the strength of his own vulnerability.

Childhood experiences, except in third stage, often teach Gemini not to trust others. His early bonds with others tend to be disruptive and unpredictable. This may or may not be the fault of his parents, as it is important to remember that he has his own destiny which must be allowed to express itself, even if it must sometimes do so through certain difficult early experiences.

Geminis are usually not very confident with the opposite sex. The female Gemini does not trust men. Her father may have let her down in some essential way which she has never been able to understand. The male Gemini, on the other hand, may not be able to understand women. He does not usually know why his mother acted the way that she did, be her behavior positive or negative. He may place too much emphasis upon his partner's outward appearance and behavior, because he feels the need to present an attractive and acceptable image to the outside world. Subconsciously, the approval of the outside world corresponds to the approval of his father, which is often still highly important to this individual. In certain stages of his development, he may not have felt equal to his father or to the standards which his father set for him. This may create another feeling of insecurity in his intimate relationships, as he compares himself to other men and secretly wonders if he may fail to measure up.

Third-stage Geminis of either sex achieve fulfillment in their personal relationships because of their understanding of the feminine principle of life. The female Gemini thrives in the understanding of her own feminine powers, which gives her confidence in her own power to love. It is important for her to come to terms with her own relationship with her father and the masculine principle, and to have achieved a harmony between the masculine and feminine aspects of her personality before external fulfillment can be achieved. Male Geminis in third stage have great appreciation for the feminine aspect of nature too, and are able to find a partner who is a constant source of inspiration and support. Again, a positive relationship with the mother is of great value to these individuals, allowing them to easily recreate similar experiences of harmony in their adult relationships with women.

Famous Geminis

First Stage: Jacques Cousteau, Arlo Gucci, Prince, Bob Dylan, Frank Lloyd Wright.
First/Second Stage: John F. Kennedy.

Second Stage: John Wayne, Marilyn Monroe, Joan Collins, Judy Garland, the Artful Dodger.
Second/Third Stage: John Bradshaw.
Third Stage: Paul McCartney, Norman Vincent Peale, Walt Whitman, Isadora Duncan.

CANCER
divine protection

Astrologically speaking, each sign of the zodiac is considered to be under the rulership of one of the four elements of the ancients. These four elements are fire, earth, air and Cancer's element of water. Water is the element of deep, subjective feeling. In Cancer it takes the form of a deep well of caring, which has as its highest goal the welfare of all beings, or at the very least the welfare of those whose destiny has been entrusted to the individual.

Cancer is the sign of the Great Mother, and is traditionally considered to be one of the six feminine signs. Because of this I have used the words 'she,' 'her' and 'hers' as neutral terms in the following description, which is intended to refer to either gender. Although Cancerians are strongly influenced by their mothers, and are capable of strong emotional responses to life, the description of cancer as a feminine sign does not indicate that these individuals are in any way lacking in masculine qualities.

Cancerian loves physical existence for its own sake, and not just for what it offers her as an individual. He or she instinctively understands the balance of nature and the sanctity of all life, and enters life seeking to enhance, nurture and maintain this balance in some manner. Their purpose: to nurture what is most precious in life.

First Stage

The soul's first task is to develop the ability to nurture and protect some aspect of life, and in first stage this is usually done through individual family relationships. Through knowing what it means to truly nurture another individual or individuals, the capacity to nourish life in all of its forms is developed. The family is like a training ground for all of the qualities which are necessary to this soul's greater purpose. Of course, this does not devalue the experience or make it just a "preparation for something greater". And first-stage Cancerians are usually unaware

95

of any purpose beyond that which exists in their own small personal arena.

No one is as dedicated a family member and parent as the first-stage Cancerian. This individual is usually born into comfortable and natural surroundings. They often choose to live in an environment or society of individuals living in harmony with nature and with one another. Their family experience is constructive and nurturing. There may be individuals in their environment who are concerned with larger social or spiritual issues, but the Cancerian remains largely unaffected by these topics. Their life revolves around their home and the simple enjoyment of the natural world which surrounds them.

They will grow up to marry "the boy or girl next door" and proceed to put all of their efforts into raising a family of their own. If you are the child of a first-stage Cancerian, you are fortunate indeed, for these individuals will spare no effort to properly provide for their offspring in every way.

In their early lifetimes, they may have little experience of what it means to be a parent, but their lack of experience presents no danger, as what they lack in knowledge, they make up for in sincerity, and they usually receive a great deal of external support. In addition, the children which they attract into their family are at first quite easy to handle, usually being well-balanced first or third-stage individuals themselves. As the years roll by, this individual develops a deep understanding of the most precious experiences of love and life which can exist within this physical world.

In time their parental skills increase, as does their emotional depth. They are capable of feeling very deeply for those they love, and their capacity to be patient with others and to suffer through the normal trials and tribulations of family life grows with each passing year. They often develop a keen insight into human nature, and as they have a tendency to rear a large brood, they also learn how to manage others through proper discipline and to use all of their natural talents and abilities to move or influence those who may surround them. These skills, along with the objective foresight which they often develop in the process of guiding others, will come to serve the Cancerian well once she reaches the third stage of her development and to unfold her larger purpose.

However, as first stage progresses, other character traits begin to make themselves felt, as a result of the imbalanced perspective which an excessively nurturing role is bound over time to create. It is only a matter of time before these imbalances build one upon another as the transition between first and second stage approaches.

First/Second-Stage Transition

As Cancerians progress through first stage, a darker side to their emotional dedication may gradually appear. The individual may develop a tendency to live too much through the lives of others. Individual development is often shelved for the sake of family needs, and when children reach maturity and attempt a fully independent life of their own the Cancerian may find it very difficult to let go and face the emptiness which exists within themselves. Her keen insight into human emotion can make her a master manipulator, constantly attempting to control those around her, often cultivating a false form of dependence in those around her in order to stave off the loneliness which she feels within.

Should she begin to create such false responsibilities for herself, she will obviously suffer their consequences, and may begin to feel stifled and overwhelmed by her family experience. As she nears second stage, she may run from the responsibility of knowing herself. Or she may feel irrationally chained to her family, yearning for the outside experience which will bring her self-knowledge, yet somehow feeling that to seek fulfillment only for herself would be disloyal.

Instead of immersing herself in a family situation, while experiencing a great, smoldering ambivalence, she may attempt to avoid commitment. As a youth this can take the form of an inability to commit to any form of serious relationship, despite a strong desire to do so. Certain first/second-stage Cancerians will run many times from the altar, despite flirting constantly with permanence. This individual will most likely feel immense guilt and self-loathing at being unable to live up to her own and her family's expectations, yet every time she comes close to a permanent relationship, she feels an irrational sense of panic, as though she were about to be swallowed up. She has spent too many lifetimes living only for the sake of others.

In first/second-stage transition the soul can no longer continue this form of self-immolation without paying a price, and so she consciously or unconsciously rebels. If she continues to immerse herself in family, she may feel enormously restless and unfulfilled; if she suppresses these feelings she may attempt to live her life through others, which can never be a healthy pattern for herself or the rest of the family. If she feels driven instinctively to search for herself, she will never be able to do so in clear conscience, for she still identifies fulfillment and security with the home, and will not be able to allow herself to feel like a worthwhile human being without shouldering a certain amount of family responsibility. Whoever said that you cannot have your cake and eat it too must have been a frustrated first/second-stage Cancerian.

An older soul with much capacity for dedication, as well as a great unconscious fund of self-knowledge developed during previous lifetimes spent in other signs, may feel no sense of ambivalence at this point. And yet for this individual, the danger still exists that she may fail to develop herself as an independent individual. And so life must move forward and become more complex. For this individual the transition will begin with some form of family upheaval. She may have become too wrapped up in her children and neglected her mate, and so finds that the family dissolves through separation and divorce. Or, her increasing capacity to nurture may attract severely troubled souls who incarnate as her children, but prove incapable of receiving the nourishment which she provides.

The family will no longer be her peaceful refuge and deep source of personal satisfaction. Whatever her situation, she is usually not inclined to look too deeply at her own life, but if she were, it would seem to her that she could never win. Profoundly unsettled within herself, whether she acknowledges it or not, the Cancerian passes into the second stage.

Second Stage

Here the family is subject to constant upheaval in one form or another. Most Cancerians, after experiencing the first stirrings of ambivalence during the first/second-stage transition are inclined to suppress these feelings whenever possible. They dedicate themselves to the only thing which really seems to have meaning, relevance or sanctity in their lives: the welfare of their family. Yet they often find themselves wishing they could be freed from this burdensome responsibility.

The soul has a powerful need for growth and transformation, which when suppressed or unacknowledged tends to express itself in the external circumstances of the individual. For the Cancerian this inner urge causes the family to be constantly torn apart by the currents of change. We are never alone in our experiences, nor does any event which may occur have meaning and relevance for only one of the individuals involved. If her family suffers in any way during the second stage of her development, this experience is a necessary part of the soul growth of all the individuals involved. Consciously, this individual is seldom able to understand that there may be a purpose to the suffering which surrounds her, and so she suffers more than anyone, as she watches her loved ones cope with the powerful challenges which they must inevitably face. Because we are usually surrounded in life by individuals close to our own level of development, most of the members of her family will also be experiencing their own version of the tumultuous second-stage development.

The upheaval which the family tends to experience at this stage may be of internal or external origin. External upheaval may come out of nowhere. This individual may be living a life of quiet desperation, apparently at peace with her family and its attendant responsibilities, while secretly wishing she could be freed from such burdensome demands, when suddenly the family will be subjected to some powerfully destructive external force or circumstance. The family may suffer through war, social or political upheaval and persecution, or natural disaster of one form or another.

To experience the loss or separation from all or several

members of her family is deeply traumatic to this individual. She may remember having secretly wished to be freed from her responsibilities, and may now feel an overwhelming sense of guilt. Given the subjective nature of one's emotions in a circumstance such as this, it is hard for her not to feel somehow responsible for the suffering of her family. After several lifetimes in this pattern, she may suffer a great deal of inner frustration and impotence, feeling that whatever is precious to her may have no hope of ultimate survival. She can never forget the great vulnerability of all she cares about, and this awareness creates a constant, gnawing pain, which she must often suppress rather than acknowledge.

Family disruption can also occur from within. The individual may choose an inappropriate partner. This possibility is somewhat likely at this stage, for the individual may tend to put less emphasis upon the quality of her relationship with her mate, unconsciously viewing her as more of a means to the end of creating a family. Having a tendency to suppress many of her emotions and inner life reactions may allow her to easily fool herself about the basic nature of another individual. The family disharmony and dysfunction resulting from such an insecure foundation may tend to create an atmosphere of constant conflict and insecurity, often leaving those entrusted to her care with long-term negative effects. Such a situation may sometimes lead to permanent estrangement between the Cancerian and one or more of her children.

Yet another possibility involves the birth of a highly disruptive individual into an otherwise peaceful and harmonious family setting. In second stage the Cancerian may attract deeply troubled souls as children, who seek her wisdom, understanding and innate nurturing capability, but for one reason or another may be unable to receive, honor or appreciate the gifts which their Cancerian parent has to offer. Natural law sees to it that there is no waste of effort, yet for many years, or perhaps an entire lifetime, the Cancerian may wonder where she has gone wrong and may experience a tremendous sense of futility and frustration when her troubled child fails to respond to her ministrations.

Difficult children born to this stage Cancerian are often involved in a deeply entangled version of mid to late second-stage development within their own sign, where no one else can take responsibility for their growth and development. And there they shall remain, lost until they themselves determine to find a way out of the tangled web which all must weave at some time or other, in the path of a soul's evolution. When they finally choose to do so, the love which their parent or guardian provided them will be recalled and appreciated, as it provides much needed reassurance. The support of a loving parent will then assist them to maintain the will required to complete their own personal process of transformation. Even if this transformation does not take place until a later lifetime, the gifts of their Cancerian parent will remain with them on a subliminal level. No effort is ever lost. In the meantime, the personal loss which this process often causes the Cancerian to undergo helps to prompt her to seek larger answers and to release what by now has often become a masochistic attachment to family and the responsibilities or assumed responsibilities attendant to it.

In a simpler scenario, it is also possible for the Cancerian parent to build her life around an (understandably) self-centered child, for example a first-stage Aries, only to find that her offspring grows up completely unappreciative and abandons the nest along with its over-attentive guardian. This experience can also prompt a similar form of re-evaluation.

The form which the disruption takes is largely dependent upon the needs of the individual in question. For example, the individual who builds her world around her relationships with her children may experience abuse or abandonment from her self-centered offspring. The second-stage Cancerian who is more selflessly bound up in the welfare of her offspring may attract the (apparently) hopelessly troubled child; an experience designed to cause her to consider the larger causes found in the overall context of life, and to begin to consider herself as well as others.

In general, upheaval caused by external, natural or political forces is more common in the first part of second stage. That which stems from personal causes occurs more towards the middle of second stage. Second stage may end after a series of disruptions cause the individual to question more deeply, or it may continue through yet another phase where the family is no longer subject to those disruptions over which the individual has little or no control.

Instead she now closes off emotionally and goes into a highly defensive mode of operation. He experiences a great deal of personal insecurity which may take the form of paranoia and a series of irrational fears, often having no apparent conscious cause. There is often a reluctance to experience some aspect of the deeper emotional content of life, for the hidden inner pain which this individual carries may be considerable. She may build a protective shell about herself, in her environment and the private confines of her own psyche, being unable or unwilling to admit any outside force or individual. Suspicious and often cynical, she unconsciously remembers a time when hostile external forces destroyed all which she held dear. Now she does everything in her power to protect herself and her environment from anything which may appear at all threatening.

This individual may experience difficulty in relating deeply to her family, and the ambivalence which has been a part of her being for many lifetimes now creates a powerful form of inner tension which cannot be denied. Whether she wants to or not, this individual is often involved in a love/hate relationship with those she is closest to. Resentful of the power that her emotions and her family have over her, she may begin to feel that her only route in life is to become compulsively self-centered, for in this manner she may feel that she can control her life and her experiences.

She may become a control freak, feeling that denial of emotion constitutes personal strength, perhaps choosing to lord it over others as a way of compensating for the deep sense of powerlessness which she fears she could re-experience at any moment. Paradoxically, it is she herself who may now become the source of family disruption, as she may neglect others while attempting to protect or bolster her own inner stronghold. She may even become abusive as she struggles with little ultimate satisfaction to contain the forces which rage within her.

She may become obsessed with power, attempting to become the strongest person alive. He may obsessively attempt to develop unlimited physical, economic, social, or political power, unconsciously believing that if she is strong enough she will be able to defend what she cares about. And yet her efforts are futile, for she truly feels herself to be arrayed against the entire world, and no matter how powerful she may become as an individual, she will never be able to ensure perfect outer security for herself and those she loves.

Of course, not every second-stage Cancerian will express all of these possible reactions to the circumstances in which she finds herself. However, by the end of second stage, this individual may find herself quite literally trapped in a hell of her own making. In order to discover just how she has created her own suffering, and how she can right things once again, she will need to enter the second/third-stage transition.

Second/Third-Stage

For some Cancerians this transition may be entered with relative ease. Others will find themselves dragged kicking and screaming into the realization of their need to re-evaluate their approach to life. Those who find entry into the transition easiest are the ones willing to admit their deep dissatisfaction with life, and who ardently seek an alternative, realizing that personal independence is an important key which must be developed. This kind of second/third-stage Cancerian hears a call to self-discovery which cannot be denied. He or she wishes to develop personal strength and to explore her own individual talents. She seeks to discover what she cares about most, and to move beyond merely meeting the needs of the people around her.

At some point in second/third stage, it may be important for this individual to live at least part of a lifetime dedicated to self-development alone, without the need to assume family responsibilities. To do this she may need to move completely away from her family of origin, and may also choose to remain single or to avoid creating a family of her own upon maturity.

At first she will struggle with guilt and obligation, as a

war rages between her individual needs and her apparent responsibilities. Her family may be in turmoil and may seem to require constant attention. And yet if she examines her life objectively, this individual can often find a way to meet her true responsibilities to others (if indeed there actually are any) and still be able to fulfill the quest for self which must now be her primary objective.

Emotional manipulation is often very much a part of her life at this stage. She must learn to transcend a pattern of dysfunctional family life which has often been her inheritance for the last several lifetimes. The family into which she is born or into which she marries does not value the rights or development of the individual. Instead each person lives through the other, and a pattern of manipulation emerges as each person struggles to force the others to meet her own needs.

Almost every second/third-stage transition individual sooner or later faces the need to pull herself out of an environment which operates according to the second-stage principles of "what you don't see won't hurt you", "let sleeping dogs lie" and "it must be someone else's fault." Certain second and second/third-stage Cancerians are easy prey for those who wish them to take the responsibility implied in the last statement, and must learn to realize that as long as they themselves are not whole, they cannot truly aid others. Also, until those around them are truly willing to wake up the dogs and take a good look at them, no one, no matter how enlightened they may be, can offer lasting aid or assistance.

In many ways, this is a struggle everyone faces. For the Cancerian, the key to its resolution lies in recognizing that one truly does wish to give to those around oneself, and that to do so requires a commitment to develop the discrimination to be able to recognize that giving someone what they want is not always the same thing as giving them what they need. The second/third-stage transition Cancerian is attracted to the larger world, and if she sets herself free to learn of this larger world and of her true relationship to it, she will ultimately be a far more effective agent for the lasting change of many other individuals. Only then will she actually be able to also aid her family, should they be ready and willing, by having developed the skills which will enable her to do so.

This individual must learn that to truly love another involves allowing them the right to pursue their own development at their own pace and in their own way. This means sometimes making the difficult decision of letting someone else go in a direction which is ultimately going to cause them some pain. To attempt to change them will not work, and to prevent or delay their rendezvous with destiny only robs them of the opportunity to learn from life as we all must. To understand this concept properly will allow this individual the freedom to pursue her own true needs in life, rather than giving in to the manipulative demands of various family members. For in giving in to their apparent need to cling to her, she is not only denying herself something she truly needs, she is also delaying their opportunity to learn of a new way of being, even if they should be consciously unwilling to accept such an experience.

This understanding applies equally to the family one is born to and to the family which one may choose to raise. A parent has certain responsibilities, beyond which the child is accountable for her own destiny. Any individual in the process of the second/third-stage transition naturally tends to come from a highly dysfunctional background. As she becomes more honest with herself, she may discover that her family seems to have suffered at her hands. This can be a crushing realization for most Cancerians, one which they may attempt to ignore, with the attendant risk of anaesthetizing much of their own inner being, or one which may cause them to become overwhelmed with deep feelings of guilt.

It is important for this individual to realize that although parents most certainly do have their responsibilities, from the vantage point of the soul, the child is also responsible for choosing a difficult parent. Rather than condemning herself as having been totally responsible for their suffering, she must realize that on a soul level "we are all in this together". Somewhere she must find the strength to forgive herself, so that she will be free to move forward and build a better future. If the Cancerian individual is the first to awaken in the family, she may begin by hopelessly asking herself, "What have I done?" But she will end by realizing her overwhelming influence as the catalyst which has freed them all.

Beyond the obvious concerns of caring for the helpless, and being loving towards those around her (without becoming entangled), her only true responsibility is to seek the full development of the self. Everything else follows out of this line. "Seek ye first the kingdom of God..." the Bible says. Although she has always known this to be true on some level, for so many lifetimes her sense of obligation would not allow her to answer the call. If she did, she may have attempted to do so in such an impulsive, unconscious and overly self-centered manner that she ultimately ended up missing the boat. When she understands that the development of her true self will eventually benefit all who surround her, she experiences a tremendous feeling of liberation and a profound sense of having been redeemed.

In second/third stage, it is also necessary for this individual to come to terms with the spiritual reality of which she is a part. In second stage she has tended to feel, whether she wishes to acknowledge this fact or not, that she is really the helpless victim of random fate. She has suffered under an inability to properly care for those she loves. To resurrect her purpose, she must understand the true source of all enduring power, and learn to become a vehicle for the force which seeks to nurture all which is most precious upon this Earth.

She is at first frightened and reluctant to become involved with life's spiritual realities. She feels that she must maintain control, even if her hold upon life is by no means complete. The mystical aspect of her being seems at first to be a great unknown, which could easily become uncontrollable and dangerous. Danger is not what she wants, for she has had enough of that already. Her first contacts with spiritual truth and the presence of the Divine may feel too overwhelming. Because this form of experience can tend to sweep over an individual, and often by its very nature seems to demand some form of ultimate surrender, the Cancerian native is inclined to be innately suspicious of it.

On a deeply instinctive level, she may feel she is being invaded, and all past invasions have been negative and destructive to all which she holds dear. Why should she trust this alien, external force, when all other external forces have proved themselves to act to her detriment? She may also struggle with a presence which seems bent on dismantling her ego, which at this stage she may be attempting to fortify and enhance, as a means of defense against any hostile possibilities.

Because she begins her encounters with spiritual reality in a suspicious manner, her outer world may reflect this expectation, causing her to encounter frightening manifestations of the occult, or gurus or teachers who are domineering and invasive. Many individuals encounter such experiences as they begin to explore the spiritual life. In time, they pass beyond them. The Cancerian however, can have her progress slowed considerably by situations such as these, for due to her inner psychological dynamics, this individual may find these experiences highly traumatic.

The solution to this dilemma lies, in part, in the Cancerian individual's need to draw upon the truths which lie within herself. Her journey must be a personal one, and she must be clearly aware that the wisdom and knowledge which she receives comes from within, and is an intimate and personal aspect of herself, which she need not fear will get out of control. Many people must prepare themselves mentally to accept their first concrete spiritual experiences. The Cancerian must prepare herself emotionally for hers. It is through the emotional, devotional aspect of her being that the truth will come. Even those who have come to refuse emotion in the quest for personal strength will, in the quietness which they create for themselves alone, be able to touch their own form of ultimate truth.

The Cancerian makes her encounter with the Divine through symbolism and imagery, creativity and nature. She may return to nature for solace, achieving a sense of oneness which communicates the secret keys to the kingdom. She may learn to draw upon her own emotional nature and creativity, allowing those visions which correspond to her deepest values to surface from the silence within. In surrendering to those truths within herself, she finds that a deeper power has always been there ready and waiting to serve her. She discovers that she may always turn to her own creative forces, and in the process discover an archetypical reality which leads her home to the larger world which is to be found within.

Some Cancerians may find their road home through a conventional form of religious practice or through an established and enduring spiritual framework involving imagery and symbolism, employing ritual as the means of touching and transforming the individual. The spiritual tradition with which she becomes involved, may or may not be widely known or accepted in our culture at the present time. For this individual the sense of history which she experiences along her path is immensely comforting and represents a genuine call back to the roots of her highest ideals. Within this framework however, she must still walk an often solitary and intensely personal path towards her ultimate realizations.

As the inner source of the greater life begins to speak to her and then through her, she discovers the key to eternal peace and security. Long has she sought this road. She sees clearly the omnipresence of the greater life. Understanding that spiritually speaking there is no death, she begins to conquer her fear of loss. She comes to understand the process of evolution, and to know that she has never been solely responsible for the suffering of others. She learns once again to trust the ways of nature and to abandon her old fears. While she can never become personally powerful enough to protect those she loves from the destructive forces surrounding them, she comes to discover that there is a greater power, which can act through her, and which is capable of preserving and protecting all that holds enduring value in life. It can only act when she allows it to do so, and it is her great privilege to discover that her true purpose is to allow it to do just that.

She sees that what she had always felt to be true was in fact a reality. Life is inherently sacred. And although there is a purpose for suffering, and an eventual need for an end to all things, there are also sacred vehicles for life which must be enabled to live and to flourish now in this world which surrounds us all. The more she surrenders to the life force, the more wisdom she will gain, as she allows herself to be used as a vehicle for the defense and nurturance of those specific sacred forms which she has come to the world to promote and care for. She allows this spiritual power to speak and act through her, and so attains completion, and passes fully into the third stage of development.

Third Stage

Deep inner peace, and an enduring sense of personal security characterize an individual at this stage of development. Sheltered by the infinite world which she knows to be the home of all, this individual is gracefully detached yet warm, nurturing and compassionate. The older soul in this stage is in constant contact with the life force which surrounds her. A younger soul in third stage may not be consciously aware of her contact with the whole of life. A hidden power which lies unquestioned within this individual provides her with the inspiration and confidence in life which allows her to fulfill her larger purpose.

She lives from the inner voice, and possesses an unshakable faith in the way of all things and, yet, the native of third-stage Cancer also possesses a deep sense of loyalty to her community and to some aspect of the larger world of which she is a part. While she is inclined to step back and allow things to take their course when the situation requires that she do so, she is also capable of stepping in to make a difference whenever there is truly a need for her to take action.

Always acting on her inner promptings, this individual never makes the mistake of attempting to act from the power of her own limited personality alone. Consciously or unconsciously she realizes that all things are possible when action is taken in accordance with spiritual reality. Therefore she allows herself to be utilized as a powerful vehicle to preserve and enhance some aspect of life which is essential to the development of mankind or to the natural kingdom which surrounds her.

She may be involved in politics or social welfare. She may be an ecologist or an iconoclast, an artist or a mystic. Whatever path she chooses, or more accurately, whatever path chooses her, she will walk it in perfect faith, having full confidence in the truth which speaks to her from within. She is in many ways a loner, although she is at peace with her surroundings and lives in balance with her family and all of her worldly responsibilities. She has found the Self, and needs much time to commune with it. Nor is she concerned with social opinion. She is finally freed to be her own person, and knows now that she need not deny any aspect of her true self.

While all third-stage individuals have achieved a certain level of mastery over their own intuitive capabilities, it could be said that the Cancerian is the most intuitive of them all. Even living in the heart of the city, she is truly at-one with nature, and so comes to grasp the essential truths of life more with the heart than with the mind. She understands that as we think, so we are, and so she chooses to cultivate her inner silence so that she may hear the voice of the greater whole as it speaks within her. She may or may not be able to instruct others concerning this aspect of her personal philosophy, but whether or not she comprehends these truths intellectually, she lives them naturally and unquestioningly, making Cancer truly the sign which expresses the greatest inner peace and understanding.

She may be so surrendered to the greater whole, that it would seem that she is in danger of actually melting away. And while many denizens of this sign may in actuality be taken by the faeries, this individual will never lose herself in a purely mystical world for, above all else, she is a worshipper of life. And so she serves, at times with very notable impact, at other times imperceptibly, yet always nurturing whatever is most truly precious in life, both within and beyond her personal self.

Cancer at the Crossroads
First/Third-Stage Transition

As the first-stage draws to a close, this individual begins to feel a profound sense of conflict between herself and the needs of her family and those around her. She struggles to find within herself some means of reconciling these opposing needs and desires. In most cases she will fail and, so attempting to deny some aspect of herself, will pass into the troubled waters of the second stage.

All Cancerians, as they reach the end of first-stage, will be offered an opportunity to avoid the stormy journey which lies in wait for them. As they reach the crossroads, they find that two paths now lie before them. One path leads steeply upwards towards a land of sunshine, while the path of least resistance slopes gently down into the wake of a hurricane.

It is important to realize that the suffering which may be experienced in second stage is never necessary. I have not written this book in order to scare those who are presently living a peaceful family existence. Please do not begin to fear for the future welfare of your loved ones. In fact, if this chapter has made you afraid that some tragedy may befall those you care about, it is more likely that you have already experienced this kind of situation in a previous lifetime. Cancerians who are clingy and fearful with family members may have experienced difficult events related to the family, somewhere in their past soul history. The purpose of writing about the second stage of Cancer is to provide some sense of meaning to those who have already experienced the disruptions which were described above. If these difficulties lie ahead it is usually possible to diffuse them by coming to terms with the inner conflicts represented by the second stage of Cancer. Doing this will allow the individual concerned to bypass second stage or to begin the second/third-stage transition, if the difficulties of second stage have already begun.

To overcome her personal conflicts, the first/second-stage Cancerian must learn to seek her answers through an understanding of the larger social, spiritual and evolutionary forces which surround her. This is very difficult for Cancerians to do, for they are accustomed to taking responsibility only for their own lives and the lives of those closest to them. They have learned to be highly self-contained.

Every first/second or first/third-stage Cancerian is haunted by a nagging sense of guilt, fueled by the belief that they are constantly being tempted to deny the values which they hold most dear. Despite their confusion, it is very difficult for them to admit to themselves that they are in fact experiencing such a profound sense of ambivalence. Those who are willing to admit that this may be the case, often do so with such underlying self-hatred that they make it impossible for themselves to reach a deeper understanding of the purpose of their situation. They cannot reach a higher level of understanding with such a heavy heart.

Somehow this individual must be willing to admit to her inner demons in a spirit of true humility. True humility requires the ability to accept oneself despite the limits of one's own personal knowledge and wisdom. As this transition approaches, the Cancerian will always be surrounded by higher forces which attempt to prompt her to achieve some form of unconditional self-acceptance.

At this stage Cancerians need to understand that whatever they may be feeling has no bearing upon their value as individuals. Nor need they lose themselves in the process of expressing loyalty to their personal values. The Cancerian must come to understand that her purpose expresses itself at first quietly within her own being, not necessarily in immediate external action or responsibility. Therefore it is of extreme importance that she allow herself the time and energy to develop herself so that her purpose can shine through. The desire to know herself and develop her talents and personal independence is never a selfish urge to be denied. If she allows herself to invest the time in herself, she may find that the truth begins to speak to her through some ancestral spiritual heritage which she has received. If she can allow herself to surrender to the spiritual forces which surround her in the endeavor to guide her, this will enable her to come to a new definition of her most essential purpose.

She must not limit herself to believing that her purpose can only be expressed within the confines of her own earthly family. She must learn to see all of nature, or at the very least all of mankind as her true family. Inner truth beckons her to begin to take her role of leadership within this larger family. If she answers this call of the spirit, she will come to realize that those urges which she feared were too self-centered—were in fact the promptings of her larger self. To embrace her role within the world she must become more truly who she is. Feeding her spirit in an independent manner is essential to this process.

Truly and fully accepting her need for self-exploration and self-development will allow her to release any desires or behavior patterns she may possess which do have destructive potential towards all which she may hold dear. Self-destructive habits will fall away, as will patterns of abuse or manipulation which may have been expressed towards those around her. Inappropriate commitments will no longer tempt her, nor will personal disinterest or infidelity plague those bonds she chooses to maintain.

The first/third-stage Cancerian allows herself to be guided into a new world and a larger relationship with life. This new world is one of immense personal freedom, yet also one of deep, loving reverence for all life. She learns to allow the higher aspects of the life force itself to determine the role she is to play within the world, rather than relying upon an outmoded collection of personal "shields" and emotionally based guilt complexes or attachments to run her life and imprison her spirit. Light of heart, she effortlessly ascends the path towards the Sun.

Childhood Conditions and Relationship Patterns

Cancer is a water sign. On a psychological level, the element of water corresponds to one's emotional nature. Because the emotional nature of the Cancerian is the dominant force within her psyche, the mother, who archetypically represents the emotional and material aspects of life, generally tends to be the dominant force within the family.

In early first-stage her emotions are strong and nurturing. She inspires her child with the love which she feels for her family. Male or female, this child usually chooses to emulate her in many ways. The boundless love which the Cancerian receives from her mother helps to build within her a strong feeling for the value of the family. The relationship with the father is also positive, although he is usually more of a background figure. He may be active in certain community projects or have strong spiritual or philosophical ideals, which his child acknowledges to be important, but which are seldom of interest to the youthful Cancerian.

As the soul progresses and begins to head towards the second stage of its development, her mother begins to reflect back to her the emotional conflicts and tendencies which she is developing. The mother may be over-emotional, controlling or manipulative. She may dominate excessively and attempt to gain all of her emotional sustenance from her children, building powerful guilt complexes in them as she does so. Many mothers of first and second-stage Cancerians combine the positive maternal traits described above with the negative traits just mentioned. This makes life very confusing for the offspring. Feelings of love, gratitude and loyalty combine with tremendous guilt and a desire to escape from her all-powerful grasp. These same feelings are later projected out onto the family which the Cancerian chooses to create for herself, or may cause the individual to avoid the commitments of family and marriage.

As second stage progresses, the relationship with the father grows more distant. He is weaker than the mother, and although he may have strong spiritual, philosophical or political ideals, the Cancerian child may grow to disdain him for his weakness. The father of the Cancerian is quietly embodying—often in an underdeveloped or impractical form —many of the qualities which the Cancerian needs to express in order to complete herself. As long as she clings exclusively to the positive or negative relationship which she has with her mother, she will be unable to experience a truly balanced life. She may have to struggle with the feeling that she cannot trust her father, before she will be able to assimilate the gifts which this individual may have to offer her. This situation becomes even more difficult if the Cancerian has an absent or abandoning father, which is relatively common towards the end of second stage.

Another common second-stage situation occurs when the Cancerian soul who has developed a powerful ability to nurture others finds herself attracted to parents whose understanding of how to be a parent is minimal or largely undeveloped. The child wishes to share what she knows with these individuals. In some ways she is often able to instruct them as she grows: "Here, let me show you how to raise me". But this situation is a complex and difficult one because, of course, she is still the child and they are still the parents. The neglect or abuse which she experiences at their hands may give her a strong desire to grow up and show that she can do better, but she may find that as an adult she is still haunted by their legacy and may end up making some serious mistakes of her own.

As an adult she may find that her parents become very dependent upon her, as she suffers with the conflict between ministering to their needs and having a life of her own. Still she may feel that she has never truly reached them with the most important parts of her personal message. The frustrations she experiences in attempting to communicate with her family may inspire her to take on a teaching role. This sort of vocation may be a stepping stone, allowing her to acquire certain necessary traits as she begins the transition between the second and third stage of her development.

An individual born into the second/third-stage transition may have childhood experiences which are very similar to those of second stage, as previously described. In addition, she may find that should she develop any mystical inclinations, her family may attempt to hold her back, discouraging the pursuit of these interests. In this and other areas she may have to struggle to gain her freedom from their overwhelming tendency to want to control her life - long after she should have achieved complete independence.

A child born into third stage will finally reap the results of all the years which she has spent giving to her family and offspring during many previous lifetimes. She comes once again into a highly nurturing environment. She is born into a family with a conscience, for while its members are close and loving, they are also involved in the larger community in a way which makes a difference. While her mother is still often the dominant individual in the family, her powerful emotions are once again used in a constructive manner. Nor does she concern herself with her family to the exclusion of her own personal needs or larger responsibilities. She may be strongly involved in her own spiritual pursuits, passing much of her powerful ability to live according to her faith on to her children. Her spirituality allows her to love her children in a truly unconditional manner.

As third stage progresses the father begins to develop his own strengths, and the Cancerian child is finally able to enjoy a close and satisfying relationship with this individual. At last she understands her father's social and spiritual ideals. A strong intellectual rapport may exist between father and child. Both of her parents support her unconditionally, allowing her to experience total freedom, as she moves into adulthood, to choose her own path of destiny.

Childhood relationships may affect adult intimate relationships in the following manner. The first-stage Cancerian female is inclined to seek a protective father figure who can help her to create the family which she desires. In early first stage she will be likely to attract the sort of individual she seeks, but as first stage progresses her tendency to focus on her children to the exclusion of all else may create problems in the relationship. She may not have been very close to her father, and so may not really notice the distance which is being created in her own marriage.

Later in first stage, or as she progresses into second stage, it may become more difficult for her to attract a positive mate. She has not experienced a strong relationship with her father and may find it difficult to understand men or to see them clearly. She may attract a weak individual, who prompts her to take all of the family responsibilities upon herself, or she may attract a domineering tyrant who seems at first to have the strong, nurturing qualities which her father lacked. Marital relationships are inclined to break down as the individual enters second stage, and this of course leads to an upheaval and the subsequent disintegration of the family.

The male Cancerian in first stage experiences an extremely powerful bond with his mother. At first this is positive. He will seek a partner who is very similar to his mother and who can be brought into the fold as one of the family. His mate and his mother will in all likelihood become close friends. As lifetimes progress this bond may become unbalanced. He places his mother on a pedestal, unconsciously believing that no other woman can equal her. She may be possessive of their relationship, and this tendency may ultimately sabotage any marriage or permanent relationship which he may attempt to create. Or he may feel such a powerful need to break free of her influence that he is unable to commit to any other intimate relationships, for fear of being imprisoned once again. These two patterns can co-exist, as the Cancerian man chooses to marry a woman who reminds him subconsciously of his mother, despite the fact that she herself may disapprove of the union. He later abandons the relationship and his family in a desperate bid for personal freedom. While he may justify his behavior in the present, he will carry a tremendous amount of suppressed guilt into future lifetimes, which will need to be unraveled as he acquires the ability to have compassion for himself and his past actions.

It is also possible for a male Cancerian in second stage to idealize his mother to such an extent that he begins to believe that women can do no wrong. In first stage this tendency will cause him to attract a truly constructive and loving mate. By second stage, however, it often means that he is suppressing his awareness of his mother's less desirable traits. This tendency may leave him open to destructive forms of domination and emotional manipulation from the women in his life.

The second-stage female may have difficulty finding a partner. She tends to create a protective wall around herself and may not realize that this makes her difficult to approach. Her distant and difficult relationship with her father may cause her to desperately seek a mate who can fulfill the role of the father figure which she lacked during her childhood. Or she may develop a cynical and rejecting stance in her relationships with men. She may disdain what she views as their inherent weakness, while being fearful of any strengths which they may possess, because she does not wish to be dominated or overwhelmed in any way which she may perceive as being invasive. Until she resolves the life patterns set by her relationship with both parents, and learns to trust life and her own inner nature once again, she may move from one unsatisfying relationship to another. She will lose respect for any gentle man whom she can dominate, while she finds she must escape again and again from men who seek to dominate and abuse her, as she always feared that they would.

In second/third stage, Cancerians begin to develop the father function of the psyche. For women this may prompt a strong attraction to a mate or lover who fulfills the role of a fatherly spiritual mentor. While this may be positive for a time, it can also leave them open to subtly destructive forms of emotional manipulation. It is important for the second/third-stage female to develop her own spiritual ideals through deeper contact with the inner self. Spiritual development and emotional support must come from within, before they can be shared and experienced without. The second/third-stage transition is often such an overwhelming experience, that it may prompt the individual to become excessively clinging and overly emotional in her intimate relationships. Cancerians can be very good at manipulating others in an emotional manner, and this tendency may flare up under stress. An individual of either sex must learn to be emotionally independent at this stage, without becoming personally defensive. Only then will true sharing be possible.

It is more common for males at the end of second stage to realize the importance of developing personal independence. However, they may go too far, and attempt to achieve this ideal in a rather compulsive manner. In late-second stage it is likely that the male Cancerian has experienced deep hurt in his relationship with his mother. He may be tied to her through bonds of resentment which eat away at his capacity to have faith in life. He may believe that women can never be trusted and may fear and resent his need for them. If this is the case, he will choose to remain alone or to become involved with women whom he can dominate. He will find these kind of relationships highly unfulfilling, because there can be no intimacy without equality. For Cancerians of either sex to fully mature, intimate relationships which take the form of equal partnerships are extremely important. For lifetimes this individual has related to others only from a superior or inferior level, as he attempted to develop the nurturing faculty.

The compulsively independent second-stage male must learn to take an objective look at his emotional responses to women. If he can realize that we are all individuals—first and foremost—and that it is individuality which he seeks, this may allow him to learn to trust other individuals, who may also happen to be women. Eventually this may allow him to find a partner who can join with him in a mutual quest for self knowledge and self expression.

The third-stage Cancerian will gravitate towards another individual who shares her high level of emotional maturity. Their partnership will be based, not only on equality and true intimacy, but on a dedication to expressing certain ideals in the world at large. They may choose once again to create a family of their own, but whether or not this is the case, they will certainly experience fulfillment in their relationship to their larger family and the greater community as a whole.

Famous Cancerians

First Stage: The old woman who lived in a shoe. (Sorry, first-stage Cancerians usually don't become famous—they're too busy with other things.)

Second Stage: Princess Diana, Ernest Hemingway, Mike Tyson, Rod Stewart, Robin Williams (close to the transition).

Second/Third Stage: George Sand, Arlo Guthrie, The Duke of Windsor (formerly King Edward VIII), Donald Sutherland, Herman Hesse.

Third Stage: Abigail Van Buren, Woody Guthrie, Nelson Mandela, Mary Baker Eddy, Elizabeth Kubler Ross, the Dalai Lama.

First/Third Stage: Harrison Ford, Kim Mitchell.

LEO
joyful leader

The third masculine sign of the zodiac is Leo, considered to be a fixed fire sign. Fixed means enduring, and fire power is life power. Individuals born under this sign have enduring life power which they can apply almost inexhaustibly. Because Leo is a masculine sign, in describing Leo's qualities I have used the words "he", "him" and "his" as neutral terms which can apply to either gender. This does not indicate that individuals born under this sign are necessarily lacking in feminine qualities.

Leo is ruled by the Sun, the center of our solar system, and the source of all life energy. It could be said, symbolically speaking, that before experiencing rebirth, Leo spends much time in this solar realm, a place of almost infinite abundance of energy and enthusiasm.

He is born to inspire the world with his enthusiasm for life. His soul is determined to transform reality, as fire transforms matter from one state to another. His confidence is boundless, but his great power is not infinite. When he learns to draw from a higher source, his triumph will be assured.

First Stage

The first-stage Leo is the Divine Child of the Royal Sun. Destined for great things, this individual will be born into harmonious surroundings which provide him with great advantages. It is as if an eternal summer reigns in his first kingdom. He comes from a world where he is supplied with the best of everything. Under the warm Sun, Leo grows bright, strong and talented. He grows up to become more powerful and more enthusiastic than those who surround him. His father is strong and powerful, providing a positive framework and foundation for the high ideals which this individual will be inclined to uphold and embody. His mother tends to be quietly and unconditionally supportive of whatever his soul's direction may be, even when she herself does not fully comprehend it.

120

For at least the initial segment of the first stage, the individual's innocent enthusiasm creates boundless self-confidence, and his innate reserves of boundless energy spawn an almost insatiable curiosity. Soon the soul has mastered his or her social environment and begins to be able to see and understand things which others are unable to see. This individual possesses a great love of his or her people and an enormous sense of gratitude for benefits he has received; he therefore desires to aid his people with the understanding he has gained.

As time — perhaps lifetimes pass — he may begin to see the inequities which surround him. Perhaps the culture into which he has been born begins to deteriorate, as though there were a hint of autumn air in the late August afternoon. He is still inspired to see how ideal life can be, and with tremendously innocent strength, courage and enthusiasm for life, leads the people out of what is now becoming a crisis situation and into a better world. He leads the people out of negative or limiting circumstances and into a more positive external environment, condition or world view. He may effect lasting social change in some area, or may prove, through the life which he leads, that great things are possible. He is certainly a public hero, whether in a small or a large arena. As lifetimes unfold, he is seen to gather force. He gains more courage, confidence and charisma as time passes.

In the beginning his triumph is spontaneous and easy. However, with time, his increasing sense of self-consciousness and natural desire to continue to move forward at all costs begins to cause trouble. He attempts in each lifetime to surpass the achievements of the previous incarnation. In the first stage of all signs, the basic framework for a new form of ego response is being developed. Unless the soul is highly evolved, it tends to lose contact with the Divine Source as time passes. Therefore, in Leo's case this indicates that the personality, strong but finite as it must be, continues to be pressured to perform the almost impossible.

Leo has many motives for being a high-achiever. In addition to his need for constantly increasing horizons, he also seeks to give to the people, in response to his innate feelings of loyalty and out of his long lasting sense of gratitude for benefits previously received. Leos tend to measure their self-worth on the basis of service given. However, this individual does not just stand around waiting for others to make a request of him. Instead he tends to define the area of need in an independent manner, before taking action. Although the tendency to be self-motivated is undoubtedly quite admirable, it does make his role more stressful. This is due to the fact that he feels that others must acknowledge the importance of his self-chosen contribution, for the people must receive his gift in order for Leo to achieve personal satisfaction.

This may require him to spend a certain amount of each lifetime misunderstood and isolated, while in the process of perfecting his contribution and waiting for the world to catch up to his vision. As first stage progresses, he gradually begins to feel more and more unloved during these phases of his life. Eventually his or her charisma and ingenuity lead to the public acceptance of his goals. He triumphs in leadership and begins to feel loved once again. But with each successful lifetime, the demands placed upon the self grow larger. As this occurs the individual's chances for success gradually grow slimmer. Although he is stronger than most other individuals, he is still a human being and as time passes, moves closer and closer to the outer limitations of his personality.

As first stage progresses, his father tends to become more dictatorial, and his mother more victimized, in reflection of Leo's inner demands upon self and the damaging results of this upon the level of his personality or Lower Self. Eventually he comes to value himself more for what he has been able to achieve than for his innocent joy and love of life. He is acquiring too much social sensitivity, along with a tendency to allow his ideals to become a crushing weight, larger than himself. When this occurs, the transition to second stage is imminent.

First/Second Stage Transition

As the transition between first and second stage begins, the individual's ideals begin to assume almost fanatical importance. He feels that he must achieve the extremely difficult goals which he has set for himself, or see his life fall into utter ruin. He has forgotten the value of who he is, and can only identify with the value of what he must do. His self-confidence is beginning to crumble, as he secretly wonders whether or not he is capable of fulfilling the standards he has set for himself. As he gravitates towards what must become greater and greater positions of challenge and leadership, he will begin to demand more and more of himself. Soon he is requiring himself to become almost superhuman.

He walks a tightrope between conformity and non-conformity, for if he is too different no one will follow him, and if he conforms completely he will lose sight of his unique and independent vision. The pressure mounts, as he feels an increasing need to achieve the goals he has set for himself, and receive the recognition which he now associates with his own personal value as an individual.

Although he desperately requires the success which will provide him with the acclaim he seeks, his goals have by now become unreasonably high. They really stand almost no chance of being achieved by just one small human being working alone. Although he tries to deny the fact that he is finally attempting the impossible, subliminal awareness of this fact may cause him to be in an almost constant state of inner tension. He pushes himself to the limit, never allowing himself a moment's pause as he pursues his obsession. He may become abusive and dictatorial with those around him, demanding no less than perfection from his associates, as well as himself.

He has never failed before, and now the possibility terrifies him. To him it will be final proof that he is less than worthless, totally unlovable. Consciously he would believe such a statement foolish. Beneath the surface, however, this is exactly how he feels. Becoming gradually more frantic, he begins to make mistakes. His feeling of panic escalates until it creates the very thing which he has always feared.

He has never failed before, and when he does his ego is completely crushed. We are speaking here of the complete failure of a lifetime goal. First/second-stage Leos do not fail in an average manner. They do so in a colossal and dramatic fashion. Not only has he shamed himself, but he may also feel deep regret for having let others down. Many people may have been depending upon him, and he has failed them. He may awake to realize how he has abused those who sought to assist him, and now finds it extremely difficult to live with himself.

With his self-worth in ruins, he enters second stage. There this individual will constantly attempt to compensate for the pain and the feelings of inner inferiority which plague him.

Second Stage

Many different coping mechanisms may be chosen here, usually throughout the course of several lifetimes. If one does not work, Leo tries another the next time around. Each soul is an individual, having its own order and its own style, and may not express all of the following alternatives.

As the soul enters second stage, he may at first continue to try to achieve idealistic goals. He is inclined to choose hopeless causes, time and time again, perhaps failing more spectacularly with each effort. He will simply try to climb a bigger mountain next time. He feels that, in conquering it, he will make up for all past failures. Of course this tendency is a prescription for burn-out and self-destruction. No matter what he does, Leo still secretly feels like a failure. He cannot erase the pain of the past, or the beliefs about himself which were developed there, and which must ultimately continue to fulfill themselves until transformed from within. No individual in second stage wants to look too deeply within, for there is too much pain there. Instead he anesthetizes himself and pushes relentlessly forward.

Leo has a creative side, and a humanitarian side. If at this stage, the humanitarian side dominates, he will spare no effort in the loving service of his fellows. However, he can easily be manipulated into giving more than is good for him, because he constantly feels guilty, as though he has not done enough. His self-worth is too low and his ideals are too high. It is hard for him to achieve satisfaction, because regardless of how loving he is, he cannot admit love or intimacy from the outside world. He does not feel that he deserves it, and is afraid that anyone who is close to him will surely see that he is somehow not quite all that he should be.

Alternatively, he may believe that it was his idealism which caused all the trouble. To compensate for his pain he tells himself that others will not accept his idealism, but that he still deserves acclaim. For after all, he must do what he needs to do in order to survive. Inner survival seems dependent upon outer acknowledgment. He attempts to seek some form of acclaim or social success which has no relation to inner ideals. Unable to duplicate the inner stature which he achieved in the first stage, he seeks instead to achieve the image of greatness. He stokes his own ego and hides his personal insecurity in his unconscious. He may manifest a subtle form of resentment towards society, as he tells himself that his goals are being sought only for himself, and that he is answerable to no one else.

Having reached the limits of his personal strength in a previous lifetime, he may now seek followers instead of attempting to develop himself any further, catering to the lowest common denominator in order to retain the illusion of himself as a strong, confident leader. As aggressive, active and apparently self-confident as he may be, in reality he is stagnating, and may be plagued by waves of despair as he momentarily recognizes the futility of all he is doing.

Leo's conflict between conformity and non-conformity may reach a peak at this point. He finds the tension of living on the fence to be too much, and must eventually succumb to the pull which he may feel is exerted upon him from one side or the other. If he conforms, he will lose his vision. If he rebels, he will lose his place in society and the opportunity to become a respected leader. Eventually one side or the other must win. Perhaps each will have its opportunity for expression, sometimes within the course of one lifetime, if not during the several lifetimes spent in second stage.

Falling to one side of the fence, he will likely become angry at society, attempting to convince himself that it was "their" fault that he was unable to achieve something great. He retains his idealism, yet spurns ambition and accomplishment in favor of a life spent on the fringes, which seems the only way to hold to his ideals and to some semblance of self-worth. He becomes the noble non-conformist. This type of Leo often becomes extremely cynical as an individual, but as a friend of mine, who has passed through this stage says, a cynic is an idealist! It is impossible to be cynical concerning life unless you also hold high hopes and sacred dreams. This individual may seem angry or cynical towards the world, but secretly he is just as angry at himself, if not more so: he would have loved to conquer the evils which he impotently denounces. At this stage he may become an armchair philosopher or a masochistic martyr for a cause. Or he may become an iconoclast, succeeding in shocking society or overthrowing some of its most sacred cows, achieving enduring infamy in the process. Or he may fail to achieve even that, and end simply as a common criminal.

Leo chooses to conform to society's expectations when he allows his self-worth to become too dependent upon the opinions of others. To hold to sometimes unpopular ideals, which run the risk of isolating him for years, may seem to be too great a risk to run if he secretly fears that he may be unequal to the task which these ideals have set for him. He may renounce his dreams, or hold to them secretly, but outwardly he may begin to act, almost compulsively, as he feels he is expected to. He may attach himself to a leader or to an organization, which subconsciously form a sort of father substitute for him, as he attempts to shine constantly in the eyes of those who possess authority above him. He may become a social climber, seen in all the right places with all the right people.

Alternatively he may give up hope, and become nothing more than a cog in a great wheel, afraid to move in any other direction for fear that his survival may be threatened. He may recall when acclaim for his actions admitted him to the world at large, and may remember suffering in loneliness and poverty prior to having made good upon his dreams and ambitions. Now that he no longer feels strong enough to answer to his true ambitions, he may become terrified of stepping out of line and being without nourishment or support in any form.

The final alternative is to play the role of the lazy lion. He attempts to simulate in his lifestyle the bountiful oneness he experienced before his responsibilities began in first stage. He plays in the Sun, haphazardly allowing life to support him in ways cultivated or stumbled upon with a minimum of effort. He knows this alternative isn't really bringing him any lasting satisfaction, and that he still feels ultimately worthless, but part of him hopes that if he just keeps playing, it will all somehow go away and stop bothering him.

Second-stage Leo seems to be a study in contrasts and extremes. It seems as though the individual unconsciously chooses to play upon all of the polarities inherent in his basic nature. While he continues to place enormous conscious or unconscious pressure upon himself, he becomes unable to hold up under the strain of maintaining a working balance between opposites, and the resulting release of pressure inevitably pushes the pendulum to one extreme or another.

Ambition is another quality dealt with in a pendulum-like manner in second stage. Almost no one is as ambition-less as a certain type of Leo, enmeshed in the false vision-of-self which is brought on by the pressures of this phase. His unconscious sense of hopelessness can completely immobilize him. His dreams are often still-born, for he feels that any form of meaningful achievement is impossible. He may torture himself with resentment and feelings of inferiority, or he may instead choose to anaesthetize himself in some manner, creating his own little world in which to retreat and lick his wounds, real or imagined.

His environment may mirror his inner self in a strange manner, for he will likely find that should he retain his dreams while refusing to act upon them, he will be sadly ignored by all about. But should he attempt to lay his dreams to rest, he may find himself subject to a great deal of external pressure from his nearest and dearest. He may have a parent who has unrealistic expectations, or may marry or choose a close friendship with an individual who is constantly demanding greater performance than he may be willing or able to produce.

The other side of the coin, and not so radically different as it may at first seem, is the second-stage Leo who is obsessed with his own personal ambitions. It would seem that this individual will stop at nothing in order to accomplish the things which he or she has set for himself. True idealism is not really allowed to enter the picture, for this would add an extra burden which the lion secretly feels unable to carry. Above all he seeks to shine in order to compensate for a sense of internal inferiority which drives him mercilessly. He wants to do something big, which everyone will notice. Politics may attract him, (but in this stage only to promote the interests of self), or he may be drawn towards the arts.

The arts for Leo can be a kind of double-edged sword. In second stage, he is too performance oriented. Only if he can accomplish something which seems large or notable to himself or to others does he believe himself worthy of regard. The quest for fame can consume him, and cause him to lose touch with his deeper values. If he does not achieve outward success, he may feel that his life is not worth living. In time, being so other-directed may tend to interfere with his true capacity for artistic genius. And yet the creative experience is a valid doorway to achieving inner contact with the true self. For Leo, this form of expression can be an important pathway into the third stage of development. When he learns to create for the sheer joy of the experience alone, playing only to an audience of one, heedless of the presence or absence of others, he will have discovered a potent key to his own inner being, which will ultimately have the power to set him free.

Until he reaches the second/third-stage transition, this kind of experience is impossible for him. He may vaguely intuit its possibility, and this may be part of the siren song which draws him toward creative endeavor, but so long as he is a slave to his own ego and the inner task-master which it has become, he will never be able to rest, nor know any true, lasting satisfaction.

Second/Third-Stage Transition

As is the case with any sign, the transition into third stage usually begins when the individual's life becomes too painful to cope with, and he or she begins a quest to understand himself and his life from a new level. Or it may begin more peacefully, as the individual becomes drawn to the great within, and gradually begins to shed his emphasis, conscious or unconscious as it may be, upon the outside world and his accomplishments or lack thereof.

Truly there is a greatness within all of us, but for Leo understanding and making contact with that greatness within as it is, and not so much in an attempt to prove or actualize it, is extremely important and forms the entire key to the transition into third stage. Unconditional self-recognition is the central theme at this level.

This is a very simple concept, but achieving it in reality is quite an art, especially for the individual first entering this transition, for Leo always ends the second stage of his or her development in a deep state of personal insecurity. He is drawn again and again to the possibility of self-knowledge, yet it seems tremendously overwhelming, and so he must draw back. He is afraid that he will lose control, and lose all sense of security, for the inner world does not operate according to any of the laws with which he is familiar. If he loses control, he has no sense of mastery, and feels an acute sense of inner weakness which he is constantly trying to overcome or avoid; he cannot abide an experience which seems to weaken him. He senses that the inner voyage will eventually strengthen him, but it seems at first only to terrify him.

The inner quest must inevitably uncover all of his fears and doubts about himself, often producing overwhelming feelings of helplessness. To find the pure solar core within himself, he must first pass through the raging torrents of the river Styx, where he encounters the results of several lifetimes worth of buried emotion. He will alternate between periods when he faces the possibility of drowning and periods when he returns to whatever behavior he has used to cope with the dilemmas of second stage. Finding his life increasingly unfulfilling, he returns again and again to the edge of the river.

One day he realizes that each of his encounters with the river has left him stronger and more refined and purified as an individual. Instead of feeling that he is forced to look within, he begins to enjoy this voyage through his own inner landscape. As his panic subsides, he begins to look around and see some beautiful landmarks. He must still come up for air from time to time, but now his basic perspective begins to shift, and with the shift comes a lasting sense of self-worth which increases steadily as he progresses more deeply.

His leonine courage re-asserts itself, and he begins to take pride in his willingness to see the truth about himself and his life. He is gradually learning to let himself unfold at a smooth and natural pace. He is no longer afraid to see the doorway to the greater Universe which lies within himself, for he no longer feels that he must be all-powerful in order to be worthy of love. He knows that there is a greatness beyond him—and paradoxically also within him—which he could never hope to manage or control; and so he learns to let it be, and let its majesty flow around and within him.

He sees his inner beauty and his inner resources, and delights in the exploration and expression of inner riches which he now knows he possesses. He may again be an artist, or he may exist in any walk of life, but whatever he does, he plays. This individual may play to an audience of thousands, or to an audience of one (himself); to him it makes no difference, for he discovers as he plays, and therein lies the joy. He is now third stage.

To reach this point Leo must ruthlessly extinguish any vestiges of conditional self-love which he might hold.

"I will be beautiful and wonderful when I accomplish this."

"What will people think?"

"If I cannot carry the world, I am unworthy."

"I am nobody."

"I am better than everybody (or most other people)."

"I will show them—then they'll see, they never should have rejected me."

On and on goes the inner dialogue inherited from second-stage Leo.

His experiences during first and second stage have seduced him into believing that he must practice a highly conditional form of self-love. Spiritually speaking, he has over-emphasized the father force, while neglecting the mother force. On an archetypical level the mother's function is that of providing unconditional love to her offspring. It is she who looks at her child and loves him or her solely for what he or she is in essence. Under natural circumstances a child need do nothing to earn its mother's love. She is the safe place to which her child may return no matter what. In her arms he can perceive his own limitless perfection, with no need to actualize it, unless he should desire to do so.

While the mother force and our relationship to it is experienced at an external level during our childhood, the true home of this force is within. Likewise, the father force is also carried within us. It is this force which impels us to realize our potentials — to challenge ourselves, and to bring what we stand for into concrete manifestation in the greater world in which we all must live. The father's function, archetypally speaking, is to encourage us to do. The father draws the child away from the safety of his mother's arms, and out into the greater world to play his role as an individual. He encourages his offspring as they make their first tentative steps out into the world, and guides them step-by step into the adult world which they must eventually inherit. The mother loves her child as he or she is. The father loves his child as he or she will become.

Of course these are only archetypal, and in some ways symbolic, functions. In reality both parents often play both roles. However, on a subliminal level mother and father still stand as powerful symbols of these archetypal realities. Many childhood situations are of course less than ideal. When the function of either parent goes astray during an individual's childhood experience, it is usually an indication that a corresponding imbalance is to be found within the psyche of the individual involved.

When the father force becomes unbalanced, it expresses itself as conditional love. The child is judged upon his or her performance. When there is no safe place to return to (because on a soul level the individual has lost contact with the mother aspect of his or her own inner nature) the pressure to perform becomes unnaturally acute. Anxiety is intense, and expresses itself either in ruthless ambition, or a subconscious program dooming the individual to failure.

Both the mother aspect and the father aspect exist as inner qualities within us all. For Leo the voice of the inner father often shouts so loudly that he drowns out all other voices. And yet this voice is not Leo's true self. Leo must learn to isolate this aspect of his being and understand it to be the source of his motivations and the foundation of his most basic relationship to self. Then he can begin to set it aside, as he learns to listen to the still, small voice within, which in this case is the feminine aspect of his being.

LEO

Childhood patterns in the present life can give clues as to how his or her own inner structure has been built. Commonly Leo experiences a demanding and domineering father figure, while his mother is more likely to be passive and perhaps victimized. Until the second/third-stage transition has been completed, Leo often spends his entire life trying to please his father, or failing due to a belief that to do so would be impossible. He may also choose to rebel in anger against the power which he resents his father for possessing. His mother represents his own personality as it experiences subjugation due to the demands which he places upon himself.

For some Leos the pattern is less obvious. They may be born into a fatherless household, or lose their father at an early age, or find that he abandons them psychologically and emotionally. Every sign will respond differently to this kind of experience. In second stage, Leo may feel abandoned and unloved, and may unconsciously decide that he did something to displease his father, and to cause himself to be abandoned. With no external father figure to assist him in forming a realistic relationship with this aspect of the life force, his own inner archetype tends to take on super-human proportions. Again he is tyrannized from within.

Leo can also experience an excessively demanding mother. In this case, it is almost as if the father force has taken over the physical mother, at least in terms of his own inner unconscious dynamics. This can be one of the most difficult patterns, for it causes the appearance of a lack of a safe place to retreat to — nowhere where he can be accepted for who he truly is — as an individual.

For each sign, the importance of monitoring one's inner habits of thought and emotion upon a daily basis, during the transition into third stage, cannot be sufficiently underscored. The individual is born with an extremely tenacious, unconscious set of habits which must be transformed in order to reach personal liberation. First the patterns must be clearly identified, so that Leo can observe their effect upon his or her daily life. New thoughts, images and perspectives must be substituted so that eventually the inertia of the subconscious or unconscious mind begins to work in his favor. Sometimes it seems that no progress is being made, but new forms of being, once established on a subconscious level, ultimately create enduring transformation.

The more an individual is able to cultivate an attitude of openness to the discovery of his true self, the more successful he will be in overcoming old patterns of intensely destructive ambition, excessive responsibility, self-criticism or sheer despair. He must learn to act as though his inner self contained some miraculously hidden mystery just waiting to be discovered. When the individual actively begins to pursue the magic of life, it can safely be assumed that the mid-point of this transition has most likely been achieved. For some, the quest for the mystery of life occurs because of an outer event which provides a mystical transformation of his or her life perspective. For no matter how long we have been pursuing the magic of life, it is a sure bet that it has been pursuing us for even longer. Such an experience challenges one's rigid definition of life, often opening up a whole new world to be explored. But for Leo it may hold a greater importance even than this, for it is certain indication that *something* seeks this individual because it knows and realizes his or her true worth. Something already knows intimately the character of Leo's True Being.

This experience also teaches Leo yet another important lesson — he does not have to do it all himself. The onus is not on him. There is nothing he need do to make himself worthy, except to recognize that he already is. The Spirit of Life truly makes no demands, yet there are certain responsibilities, such as a willingness to be constantly aware, and to overcome the tendency to lie to oneself. Ultimately this new path leads again to the achievement of greatness, but the greatness is far less important than the experience of the moment.

Third Stage

No one is more selflessly involved with himself than a third-stage Leo. He finds himself endlessly fascinating, yet is totally without any form of offensive egotism. Easily lost in the moment, he is just as fascinated with life. He is enthusiastic and curious. Whatever he does, he does for the sheer joy of the experience. He exists in a state of reverence for life, completely absorbed in childlike concentration upon all that interests him. He does not care what impression he may leave, as he is constantly caught in a spontaneous act of self-recollection.

Because he has freed himself from all outward pressure to perform, his talents and strengths re-emerge in all their glory. He responds to this experience with awe and humility. The greatness which he discovers in himself fascinates him in the same way in which the natural world itself does. He knows that he is no more the owner and author of his own capabilities than he is of the beauty which surrounds him. No longer need he carry the burdens of the world, for he understands that it is subject to a greater purpose than he can ever hope to fathom. He serves not by attempting to stretch his own limits as a human being, but by being open to the greater force which seeks to act through him. He will not take the burdens of others upon himself, but will stand ready to assist and inspire those who seek the benefit of his wisdom.

He appreciates the humor of life, embracing its mysteries with an ease which astounds those closest to him. Paradoxically, as he plays his way through life, he may once again accomplish great things. As the power of the infinite acts through him, he will most likely surpass even the greatest achievements of his own past. To him the greatness of life now lies in the experience of the moment. His accomplishments, although affording a fulfillment all their own, are not the final goal. He allows the dream to move through him with no attachment to its outcome. In perfect trust, he is a totally surrendered, joyous virtuoso. He walks through life leaving no footprints, yet he is never forgotten. He returns to the leadership role which his soul has chosen, but the role falls lightly upon him now, for he secretly knows that he is just another follower of the Divine Impulse.

Leo at the Crossroads
First/Third-Stage Transition

How can Leo at the end of second stage —where his pride is being challenged to its utmost, as he experiences almost constant pressure, with no time to think for himself —ever manage to escape from his illusions long enough to discover the secrets of his own inner world? Answer: Through drawing upon the power of his own most basic sense of personal integrity.

At the end of second stage he may be under pressure to prove that he possesses integrity, or at least to appear as if he might. But does placing himself under constant pressure, and subjecting those who surround him to the same rigorous scheduling or serious danger really represent an act of integrity? Could his time be better served by choosing a less hopeless quest?

Patience and forethought are part of our responsibility to life as a whole. If Leo at this stage can have the courage to admit that he does not know everything, then perhaps he can pause to reconsider the fundamental basis of his assumptions. He must achieve a complete shift in his perspective before it is too late. The inner voice whispers this truth to him, as those closest to him may attempt to warn him that he is approaching the ultimate failure. They urge him to stay his course in order to avoid disaster. But it is hard to admit that he might be wrong. Where will he be if he abandons his quest? He fears that he will have no value in his own eyes, or in the eyes of the world. Yet he needs to ask himself how he might be seen in the eyes of God.

To do this, he must listen within, for the Divine Spirit of life may not be asking him to fulfill what he now believes must be his duty. It calls him to a higher goal. Perhaps if Moses had continued to listen to the voice of God after he had left the mountain, he would not have needed to lose his temper. Perhaps what he stands for is more important than what he actually accomplishes. Perhaps he can learn to respond to his purpose creatively rather than obsessively, embracing the unknown with enthusiasm rather than responding to it with a compulsive need to control. When he realizes that nothing which he does can be done under his own power alone, he will be set free. These are the things which this individual shall come to understand. This is what he shall know, if he at last allows himself to retreat, to take time away from the goals which have come to possess him, to go to the mountain, and speak to the Divine Within.

Ironically, once the transformation has begun, this individual may return to the same goals and activities which he pursued before his departure. Outwardly nothing has changed. Yet inwardly he lives in a completely different world. His attitude has changed, and so has his destiny. Whether he should succeed or fail in the eyes of the world, he knows that he is fulfilling his true purpose. Paradoxically he now has a much greater chance of success than he ever had before. And he can enjoy the process far more now that he has let go of his attachment to it.

But what if he or she has been unable to listen to the inner voice? Then failure is inevitable, necessary and, in the final analysis, kind. With his life in ruins, he may finally be able to turn to the Source of Life in a new spirit of humility. Failure is not a disaster. Instead it is an integral part of the creative process of life. If it leads him to the mountain, so much the better- it has more than fulfilled its purpose. And if he does not have the self-respect and humility to seek out this higher purpose, he will pass inevitably into the second stage. Ultimately it is of no consequence whether this individual reaches the mountain sooner or later. With lifetimes to fulfill the special destiny which is set for him, surely time is on his side.

Childhood Conditions and Relationship Patterns

Leo is a fire sign and, as we have discussed in the chapter relating to Aries, fire represents the spiritual principle of life and the personal ideals of the individual. Subconsciously the element of fire is associated with the father principle. To the Leonine child, the father subconsciously represents his or her spiritual drives and conscious mental perspective towards life. Since these drives are dominant within his or her psyche, generally speaking, the child will also experience the father as being the dominant member of the household.

In first stage, he may hold an important role within his community. He is physically strong and on the move. Leo looks up to him and wants to be just like him. The mother of a first-stage Leo is inclined to be emotional and rather dreamy. She has a caring and compassionate nature, and

136

may offer solace and support to those whom others might be inclined to overlook. Leo emulates the strength of his father and the altruism of his mother.

In second stage the father is still dominant. He is psychologically strong, and often highly opinionated. The mother remains sensitive and emotionally oriented. She may appear to be somewhat victimized by her role within the family. The dominance of the father may be less constructive than it was during first stage. He is inclined to be demanding and critical of his wife and children. Part of the reason that Leo chooses a strong father is so that he or she can be shown the ropes, given instruction concerning the way in which the world functions. Leo wants to learn about society, so that he can play his role within it and transform it. He is seeking guidelines and may already be overly sensitive to these guidelines. If his parents impress him with too many "shoulds" it will only add to the pressure he is already under.

If Leo sees his mother victimized by her role, it may cause him to feel that he must be especially protective of his own emotions and altruistic drives. It may cause him to adopt the subconscious belief that perhaps his ideals don't stand much of a chance when confronted with the forces of the world. As second stage progresses, the power of the father or of the father image increases, while the influence of the mother diminishes. Mother may be caring but weak, she may be emotionally disturbed, or she may be absent altogether. It is his mother who has the ability to provide him with unconditional love—to care for who he is in essence, rather than demanding that he perform according to a standard. The more demanding he becomes of himself as an individual, the more he will be inclined to lose contact with the mother force, internally as well as externally.

Leo's father is a figure of authority, and how the individual deals with his father's influence will determine the role which he will choose to play in his adult life. It is impossible for the Leo individual to have neutral feelings towards his or her father. As a youth he will be inclined to idealize his father and to place him on a pedestal, or to reject him and plot rebellion. If he idealizes his father, he will seek to emulate him, and become prone to developing an over-inflated personal ego. If his father is inclined to be rejecting and demanding of this individual, upon maturity he will likely adopt an overly conformist attitude towards life. Subconsciously he identifies "the powers that be" with the father that he is still trying to please.

The Leo who chooses to consciously reject his father's influence will be inclined to mature into a cynical idealist or spirited rebel. In this case his father still represents "the powers that be" whom Leo believes to be opposed to his or her innate ideals as an individual. In his youth his opinions may be in deep conflict with those of his father.

A Leo who completely abandons his or her ambitions may do so as a result of excessive pressure from both parents. As the inner and outer pressure mounts, he collapses under its strain, truly believing that he is incapable of achieving anything. In later second-stage Leo it is also possible for the individual to be so dependent upon the support of his father, that he or she will completely collapse, should the father withdraw in any manner. As second stage progresses, it is possible for Leo to be born into a family where the father, instead of being all-powerful, is actually rather ineffectual. This is a sign that this individual is beginning to lose all personal drive and confidence in his or her ideals.

This kind of early home environment can also create a "lazy lion", with little or no ambition, but it can also spur Leo on into the second/third-stage transition. With father's influence weakened, he may be able to draw closer to his mother, who may be able to re-inspire his innate idealism, as she teaches him to accept himself for who he is, rather than what he does. Another kind of late second-stage scenario occurs when Leo's father becomes excessively tyrannical, literally driving his offspring over the brink, where life must be reconsidered.

In third stage, Leo's father is once again strong and opinionated. But his opinions, instead of being hard, are flexible, uplifting and inspiring. He has a humorous and playful attitude towards life. He often has strong intuitive abilities, and is able to look into his children and immediately recognize their purpose and potential, which he unconditionally supports them in fulfilling. He is patient and spontaneous in his encouragement. The child feels that in his father he has an ally and lifelong playmate, who will always respect him. While he still remains very strongly influenced by his father, their relationship is now one of greater equality than was ever possible during the earlier stages of his development.

In third-stage Leo, the mother's innate sensitivity is once again a strength. She is intuitive and empathic, and very much aware of her own strengths as an individual. While she is mature and independent, she may also possess a streak of childlike wonder, and in her company Leo learns never to tire of his exploration of life or his own individuality. She believes in magic and miracles, and her beliefs often turn into reality. She is the living representation of the fulfilled altruism of Leo.

When the first or second-stage Leo male matures, he may be upset to find that others often view him as something of a male chauvinist. He would certainly be unhappy to think of himself in this light. He may see women as more emotional than men, and therefore possibly weaker. He may be attracted to a woman whom he can save or teach in some way. Through her he may unconsciously hope to make up for the suffering which his mother experienced during his own childhood. He wants to be a hero like his father, or take the place of the tyrant which he may have perceived his father to be. His mother's unhappiness may have subtly unsettled him. He may not realize that in attempting to rescue a woman whom he subconsciously associates with mother, he is really trying to save a part of himself. If his self-worth is low, he may find that eventually she becomes the dominant force in the relationship, controlling and manipulating him through her emotional melodramas.

The first-stage Leo who has experienced a relatively carefree childhood may seek a mate who can serve him or assist him in fulfilling the less important or less interesting aspects of becoming who he is. As he progresses he will begin to seek a Muse—a woman who can become his source of creative or philosophical inspiration in life. He may place her on a pedestal which will not allow her to be human or to express her own desires. Further along in second stage, his adulation may turn to contempt. He may blame her for his failures and insecurities, requiring her to be someone whom he can lord it over.

LEO

Whether male or female, Leo's "shoulds" can also interfere with a smoothly running relationship. Because true relating requires spontaneous sharing between two individuals who can be themselves in each other's presence, intimacy is difficult to achieve for someone who feels that he will only be worthy of love if he becomes something which he is not capable of being. The stress of constantly feeling compelled to put on a good show, coupled with the constant fear that he may be found out to be less than he should be, cause him to be overly demanding and difficult to live with. If the stress continues, he may eventually withdraw.

The Leo female has an image of a strong, fatherly, dominant male. She may try to seek a partner who can live up to the powerful father image which she has cultivated. Since her father is often a rather rare and strong individual, and her image of him is even larger than he is himself, she may have a very difficult time finding someone who can fit the bill. Another difficulty lies in the fact that she may not wish to be under his thumb, as she felt her mother was in the relationship with her father. This means that when she does find a powerful partner, the two may engage in a battle of wills. She wants him to be strong and dominant, yet at the same time, does not wish to be dominated by him.

An alternative response for the first or second-stage Leo female is to identify with her mother. She may feel as weak and sensitive as she observed her mother to be, and hopes for a protective father figure to care for her, so that she can subconsciously play out the role of the beloved little girl. She seeks a positive form of dominance, but may end up experiencing the negative manifestation of the Leonine father image, as her protector gradually turns into a tyrannizing bully.

The Leo female needs to develop confidence in her own strengths. Even the Leo female who subconsciously emulates her father appears more self-assured than she actually is. She has made contact with her own strength, but still fears that some man may come and take it all away from her. The male Leo needs to understand and respect his own emotional nature, rather than projecting it outside of himself, where it will continue to cause havoc until attended to.

The third-stage individual tends to seek a mate who can share his or her ability to see beyond the surface of life. Together they can adventure in a self-determined world, appreciating all that life has to offer. A relationship with a third-stage Leo has a great deal to offer any individual who is ready to enter the world of childlike wisdom, in which the resurrected Lion dwells.

Famous Leos

First Stage: Moses, Neil Armstrong, Jean-Luc Picard, Arnold Schwarzenegger, Alan Leo (an old soul and famous astrologer of the previous century), Earvin "Magic" Johnson, Bill Clinton. (Are the last two examples close to the transition?)
First/Second Stage: Davey Crockett.
Second Stage: Whitney Houston, Madonna (an interesting study, as she also has many traits of first and third stage; perhaps she is making a quick trip through second stage?), Benito Mussolini, Sean Penn, Roman Polanski, Mick Jagger (probably close to the transition).
Second/Third Stage: Percy Byshe Shelley, Kate Bush, Carl Jung.
Third Stage: George Bernard Shaw, Alfred Tennyson, Rupert Brooke, Tony Bennett.

VIRGO
world healer

Virgo is the third feminine sign of the zodiac, ruled by the element of earth. Because Virgo is traditionally considered a feminine sign, I have used the words "she", "her" and "hers" throughout this chapter. These terms are meant to refer to either gender and do not in any way indicate that individuals born under the sign of Virgo are in any way lacking in masculinity.

An old myth associated with the constellation of Virgo states that this constellation was once a Divine Virgin Goddess who dwelt upon the Earth but, because of the corruption of humanity, withdrew into the heavens where She now watches and waits for the inhabitants of the Earth to return to the ways of truth and to nature. Symbolically She represents natural harmony and the true rhythm of the Universe. Because humanity has temporarily abandoned the principles which She represents, they seem to exist only in a very distant and abstract manner. Most of the human race has moved so far away from its beginnings of natural harmony that they are unable to recognize this eternal truth, because their perceptions have become too distorted. The dream of inner and outer harmony and an ordered and reasonable universe seems very, very far away.

Prior to being reborn, Virgo dwells in a state of perfect, natural harmony. Here she comes to understand the natural order and true pattern of earthly experience. Armed with this knowledge, and the inspiration and natural skill it provides in her, she is reborn, an emissary of the Celestial Virgin. She understands and embodies the state of natural harmony to which humanity needs to return.

This individual contains within herself a pure and innocent form of understanding regarding some aspect of the natural state of being. It is interesting to note that souls experiencing their first series of lifetimes as a human being are most likely to be born under the sign of Virgo or the sign of Pisces. This does not mean that all Virgos are young souls, although many are. What it does mean is that all Virgos possess a certain innocence, a sense of having been untried. They seem to take longer to adapt to

Earth life than do individuals of most other signs. Virgo will spend her first series of incarnations learning how to be a healer. Although her vision is initially quite powerful in its simplicity, she will not find the process of saving the world to be quite as easy as she might imagine.

This individual has the capacity to heal some aspect of the world or its people. In order to be capable of fulfilling this ideal, she must at first lose contact with the natural truth which is found within her. He must take on the mantle of blindness (on a spiritual or psychological level) in order to know what it is like to be in darkness. Discovering the keys which will allow her to emerge from the imbalances which she acquires enables her to guide and assist others.

First Stage

Many souls with the Sun in Virgo are experiencing their first series of lifetimes upon this Earth. Those who are not are returning here from a very highly refined state of consciousness, and will usually encounter certain difficulties in re-acclimatizing themselves to life within the human world. Because such a high degree of sensitivity exists in all cases, the individual requires special circumstances in order to develop the skills and knowledge necessary to prepare her for her mission.

At the beginning of the first stage this individual will be born into a very protected environment. On a spiritual level, and sometimes also on a conscious level, those who comes to are aware of her true identity, and have made an agreement to do everything in their power to assist her in fulfilling and fostering her potentials. Her parents and others who have chosen to assist her throughout her life, have a deep understanding of her innate gifts and purpose. As she matures, she will receive further assistance from others who also recognize her potential and are committed to assisting her in adapting to her earthly existence.

She is protected from most external negative influences, and often leads a highly privileged life. Given the best of everything, she receives every opportunity to develop her often considerable talents, responding very much like a child prodigy. With all her special talents and abilities, she often remains quite child-like for most of her life, always dependent upon those in her surrounding environment who are charged with the function of supporting, assisting, and protecting her.

The material and spiritual forces of life are all on her side, as step by step she is guided towards the expression of her ultimate purpose. The soul has training wheels; her stunning successes often do not seem fully earned, for they are seldom achieved by her effort alone. And yet it is important that these early experiences take place, for they are building an absolutely essential foundation for the truly individualized accomplishments which will occur once the soul has independently reached its full potential.

The first stage Virgo is often shy and retiring, and may feel alienated from society as a whole and from anyone who exists in the world outside of her own personal sphere. She may have entered the world during a time and culture essentially foreign to her basic nature. She senses that she is different from most other people and tends to retreat within, unsure of her ultimate potential for acceptance. Were it not for the support she receives, she would be incredibly lonely. As it is she nonetheless often lacks for the companionship of others.

All of her life she may feel like the new kid at school, very much ahead of all of the other children, yet socially backward, and perhaps doomed to be excluded because of her undeniable differences. She possesses all of the hallmarks of an overprotected child, and while this pattern will eventually create serious difficulties for this individual, it is the only path which she is capable of taking at this stage of her development.

In early first stage her innocent trust in life and in those who care for her tends to ease her path through life; she remains content in her secure, if limited environment. However, as first stage progresses and her complexity increases, she may begin to question her circumstances more deeply as she gradually becomes less trusting and more frustrated in her isolation. Others seldom understand her suffering, although there are usually those who may envy her opportunities. They sense her differences and may be repelled by them, and their resentment of the positions which seem to come so easily to her may unwittingly cause her to make more enemies than she does friends.

Some first-stage Virgos allow their easy success and privileged position to go to their heads, causing their egos to become enflamed. They may abuse their opportunities, acting destructively or carelessly towards those who are beneath them. This only builds karma for the individual concerned, who is literally living in a fantasy world and a true fool's paradise. Secretly she knows that she has never really proven herself, and that she is therefore heading for a fall. As she enters the first/second-stage transition, her self-worth may plummet lower than it would have had she retained some semblance of her original humility. As it is, her behavior ultimately serves to isolate her more and more as she becomes bored and lonely, and may eventually grow frightened of trying anything new for fear she might fail, destroying the image which she has created of herself.

Humble or proud as she may be, eventually her loneliness becomes too much to bear. Her walled garden begins to feel like a prison, and deep within her being she longs for her freedom and a chance to stretch her wings. When this occurs, the transition into second stage begins.

Transition to Second Stage

At this point the soul requires a taste of true independence. She has formed a personality out of the simple clay which life has offered her. Now she needs to fire this clay through the tests and trials of unguarded experience. This need may show itself consciously as a desire to leave the fold, but more often it operates solely on an unconscious level as the individual begins to feel her old life disintegrate as the protective defenses which shelter her begin to fall away.

She has had ample opportunity to develop her skills and talents, and to achieve a basic sense of individual identity. Now it is time to take the training wheels off. She must now learn to go it alone, and so all external assistance is gradually withdrawn. Her experience of love up until now has usually only been that which she has experienced through the attentions of her "caretakers". She has rarely had much opportunity to experience true love and intimacy, as it is shared among equals, and therefore the departure of those souls who have offered her initial assistance feels like a crushing form of abandonment.

Although she may attempt to hide her feelings from herself, in her quietest moments she experiences an overwhelming sense of fear. It is terrifying to try to make it in a strange world all by herself. He may feel like a small child abandoned in a city where she does not speak the language. Symbolically speaking, this is exactly what she is. However, since she may in actual fact be an adult as this transformation takes place, these feelings may be very hard on her self-worth. She is supposed to be a competent adult.

While this transition may occur within the context of an existing lifetime, it is also possible for a soul who has achieved the triumphant completion of first stage in a previous incarnation to begin a more sudden transition which commences at the start of her next lifetime. In this case she may be born into a life of poverty, or experience a tremendous amount of childhood neglect.

This form of experience obviously comes as a great shock to the system, although on a very deep level she has longed for a taste of some of the worst that life has to offer. Despite the fact that the road to second stage is immensely difficult, it could be said that there is no better way to learn about real living, and no better way to develop the true strengths of one's individuality. On a conscious level, however, this experience tends to be quite a blow to self-esteem, for she may have become used to seeing herself as something of an aristocrat, and may still expect to be fussed over and cared for.

Whether she is born into the transition or experiences it at some point in the course of her adult lifetime, she finds one day that all of the safeguards which had once protected her from life's harsh realities have now been removed, and there is nothing to stop her enemies from closing in. Many of the individuals who sensed her differences and were threatened by them, who became jealous of her "instant" success in first stage, as well as those who may have been wounded by the innocent arrogance of her previous actions, may now close in for the kill.

The next step in her journey takes her through the darkness of the earthly experience. She is often placed in an extremely vulnerable position, with very little to protect her from the worst which life has to offer. She may feel as though she is running down a dark tunnel which grows gradually more narrow, as wolves snap constantly at her heels. She may struggle, she may panic and she may again and again seek assistance which is just no longer there; until at last, having received the first true wounds of her soul's history, she realizes that she is truly alone. She has nowhere to turn.

Initially her psyche simply cannot cope with the stresses to which it is subjected, and so she has no other choice but to block out her awareness of many of her life experiences. She cannot run away. Life always finds her. There is no one truly there to help her, and so her only recourse is to anaesthetize herself in some manner. In order to cope with her life situation, she begins to close the door upon her inner self and her capacity to perceive and assimilate experience, and so passes into the second stage of her development.

Second Stage

In all ways truly abandoned, she now races down the tunnel, outwardly and inwardly attempting to escape from all that seems opposed to her or likely to bring her any form of pain whatsoever. She has come to believe in her own weaknesses rather than her own strengths. She truly believes that she is not strong enough to protect herself from all that seems to assail her from without, and so finds her only true refuge within. Ultimately this realization will serve her well, but for now she misinterprets it and consciously and unconsciously does all she can to preserve a feeling of inner security by choosing to remove her consciousness from those parts of herself which experience pain. She soon masters the art of subtle retreat, quietly avoiding any real contact with the outside world, or with any feeling or situation which she believes might cause her to lose the control which she believes she must at all costs maintain.

Because she longs always for the security which she has left behind, she may still seek someone to depend upon. However, since it is no longer in her best interests to do so, she does not attract those who are capable of having her best interests in mind. Those to whom she turns for assistance usually turn out to be wolves in sheep's clothing, always hoping to take advantage of her in return for providing her falsely with the sense of security she seeks. She is easy to fool, because she expends so much effort trying to deny her true feelings to herself. Eager to accept the fruits of her own self-deception, she is often equally eager to accept the lies of others.

She works very hard to become unaware of what she is actually doing to herself, for the reality of it all is very hard on her pride. She does not like to think of herself as weak and desperate. However, truth can be denied, but it can never be destroyed. Anyone who could offer her real assistance will do so by encouraging independence, which she will usually decline to accept at this stage of her development, since to do so means acquiring full contact with her true self. She is loath to do so, as her survival seems to depend upon distancing herself from her inner pain, and from those aspects of herself which have the power to make her feel truly vulnerable. She does not realize that the same parts of her which make her feel vulnerable also hold the keys to the infinite and invincible power of her true individuality.

She has a great deal of difficulty with intimacy, and usually avoids it like the plague, for to be intimate with another not only creates an incredible feeling of personal vulnerability, it also means that one must be intimate with oneself which, at this stage, is ultimately her greatest fear. She has many reasons to avoid intimacy. Consciously or unconsciously she still remembers having been traumatically abandoned in the past and fears this experience may re-occur. She knows from first-hand experience that there are those who actively seek to harm and to take advantage of her when she is down. She senses that she is somehow different from others and that she may therefore be unlikely to meet with full acceptance from them. In addition, her self-worth has been damaged enormously by her past experiences and her own chosen responses to the situations in which she found herself. He feels secretly unworthy of sharing herself with another. As if all of this is not enough, she may also fear the loss of control which true surrender to the love of another may entail.

In her more quiet moments she realizes that she is lying to herself and that she has failed to develop a spine and is therefore spinning her wheels. She knows that she is not accomplishing her chosen purpose. She is stuck in the mud due to her own unwillingness to see. She simply does not know what else to do and feels incredibly helpless. Despite her constant use of all her personal defense mechanisms, she still tends to suffer from an almost constant sensory overload. Because she is still so new, the experience of life is often simply too much for her.

The more pain and difficulty she experiences, the more she shuts down, until she reaches the point where she literally ceases to assimilate any of her experience. Like a broken record, she replays the patterns which seem to promise protection and security. She becomes completely alienated from her true feelings, both emotionally and physically. After several lifetimes this tendency produces, in some individuals, chronic or congenital physical afflictions or handicaps. Common areas of difficulty are the nervous system or the spine and legs — the latter representing an inability to stand it here, to stand up to one's full potential height or to stand alone in life. Sometimes a health breakdown can be a way of calling for help, seeking the dependency of first-stage Virgo which by now, must always come at a very high price.

Some individuals experiencing the second stage of their journey through the constellation of Virgo are deeply aware of their need to go it alone. They may decide from the beginning, or after a series of experiences of being let down by those whom they seek to depend upon, that they must learn to stand alone in the world no matter what the cost. Through the power of personal will they attempt to develop their skills and powers in order to make a successful go at self-sufficiency.

Because of an unconscious fear of being incapable of mastering their skills or demonstrating a lack of true personal competence and independence, these individuals are inclined to be somewhat perfectionistic and overly control-oriented. They possess high standards for themselves, and usually over-emphasize a mental approach to all aspects of life. The rational mind allows them to limit and control their lives so that they will have a greater sense of control over their experiences and activities. They do not wish to be betrayed by their own emotions which is not to say that they do not possess a strong emotional nature, merely that they feel it necessary to contain their responses in order to survive in an often hostile world.

This type of second-stage Virgo is very much like the third little pig who built a house of stone with which to shut the wolf out. As second stage progresses this individual usually manages to have her life controlled to the point where she is no longer pursued by the wolves which haunt the steps of an early second-stage individual. However, she may eventually find that along with the wolves, she has managed to shut out much of the positive experiences which life has to offer.

Not all Virgos possess the critical tendencies for which the coffee-table astrology books have made them famous. When a critical streak emerges it is often due to insecurity and doubt about one's ability to master her life situation. (Remember that Virgo is subconsciously aware that she may not yet be very adept at meeting life's challenges.) By maintaining high standards and feeling that she conforms to those standards, or judging others as either beneath herself or as meeting the grades of excellence which she has set, this individual is able to feel secure in her own worth.

A critical or fastidious tendency can also come about through feeling unconsciously that the world and those within it are essentially hostile to her own well-being. She remembers the wolves and now sees their shadows all around her. Excessive cleanliness may seem to keep her safe in a hostile world. In addition, she unconsciously knows that she still holds knowledge within herself which the world can use to make itself whole. When she feels impotent in expressing these truths, she may become bitter, cynical and unforgiving in her criticism of a thankless world.

This form of response to second-stage Virgo is valuable in that it does provide the individual with a sense of her own personal competence. Eventually the life she leads becomes too dry. Alone and perfectly preserved, she stands somehow outside the world of those who truly live. He may grow tired of living in a perfectly ordered desert wasteland, or perhaps she succumbs to paranoia and obsessive behavior. Eventually she grows tired of being isolated through the excessive judgment she practices towards those who surround her.

Second-stage Virgos can be incredible perfectionists, as in the classical examples given in popular astrology books, or they may swing to the other extreme, becoming disorganized, irresponsible and neglectful. This is usually due to the fact that their true life purpose weighs heavily upon them and they may believe that they will be unable to summon the necessary strength and courage to fulfill their chosen calling.

Whatever may be her response to the second stage, eventually the pain of stagnation becomes too great and produces the humility which allows her to seek a solution other than the ones under which she has previously been operating. "There must be some alternative to the way I feel." When Virgo says this with true sincerity and willingness, she passes into the transition to the final stage of her development.

Second/Third-Stage Transition

To the outside observer it would seem that the second stage of Virgo is really in most ways a colossal waste of time. However there is a purpose to this journey into the darkness. In first stage this individual innocently believed that all she needed to do was land upon the Earth and set up shop, and she would be able to begin healing the world. However, life does not work like this.

In essence Virgo is required to take the burdens of the world upon herself, living through at least some of the diseases of mind and spirit which afflict the people before she will truly have the ability to set others free. She must live out the dictum: "Physician heal thyself." Then she will be able to say to others, "I have been there and back, and I know there is a way out. If I can do it, you can do it." This approach works wonders, enabling others to look into her eyes and know that what she says is true, and be strengthened and inspired by her example.

Therefore, the second stage of Virgo represents a very much simplified, yet greatly intensified, taste of what it means to be in the second stage of any sign. In all signs the basic response to the second stage is to batten down the hatches -- to try and stay safe by not looking too deeply at what is going on in one's life. Self-worth is low, and there is a tendency to be overwhelmed by one's experiences. Virgo digs herself in deeper — perhaps than anyone else. While this might seem to be a waste of time, in the process of extricating herself she becomes an expert in self-transformation.

The transition to third stage may begin when the individual can no longer suppress her feelings of pain. The soul may be in a panic. The individual seeks a solution, any solution, and knows above all that she is helpless when it comes to coping with life and with her day-to-day response to it. The individual may try to fall back upon early second-stage behavior by attempting to depend upon others, but this form of behavior will no longer work. In her heart of hearts she is seeking answers, and so she is unlikely to be taken in by a complete charlatan. Those whom she seeks to depend upon may find her too hot to handle, for her pain and the resulting demands which it causes her to place upon others is just too much. Sooner or later, if she is lucky, she will find a guide who forces her to stand up on her own two feet and begin the necessary process of self-development.

As second stage progresses the general pattern is for the early home environment to become increasingly difficult. Many Virgo's enter the second/third-stage transition as a result of the abuses to which they have been subject, and the resulting traumas which have made it impossible for them to live a normal life. While some may enter this transition in a panic, others approach the change in a state of anesthesia and numbness. Their life is empty and meaningless. There is no pain but, likewise, there is no joy or pleasure. The life within them must move somewhere, and so beneath the surface, passions stir. This individual may wake up one day and, without consciously knowing the reason why, make a decision that a change must now occur.

Perhaps it seems that the change is made for her. A mate, a parent, a child or even an employer may decide that it is time for her to begin a new inner life, and she seems to be dragged into self-analysis and a new level of awareness kicking and screaming. However, no one else can actually cause us to change, and if she is truly ready for the transition, her reluctance will not last, although at first she will suffer serious doubts at various points along the way.

Once the willingness to change has been achieved, the first (and ultimately the only) step is to begin the process of listening within, allowing herself to feel and regain contact with all of the aspects of the self from which she has been alienated. Above all, it is crucial that this individual learn to stop lying to herself in any way.

She has to commit herself to seeking true strength. Is she still seeking to depend upon others while lying to herself about her motives or the real nature of those with whom she is involved? Or does she believe that refusing intimacy and standing physically alone and invulnerable constitutes a true state of power and independence. Real strength consists of the capacity to be openly and responsibly intimate without being needy or dependent. This is a tall order, and it can only be accomplished through the long and arduous process of learning to trust oneself and one's environment.

He needs to get all of her pieces back. Does she have any mental, emotional or physical blind spots? Where is she refusing to feel, where is she refusing to see? She may need help finding all of her pieces and putting them back into order in a balanced manner. Step by step and bit by bit she needs to learn to listen to what her real self is saying to her. She gradually learns how to heal herself and recognizes that, miraculously, all of the tools to do so are there at her disposal in the great within, which once frightened and overwhelmed her.

Once she is in contact again with all of herself — physical, sexual, emotional, mental and spiritual — she can begin the process of balancing her responses in each of these various areas. It is important that no one aspect of self be allowed to drown out the rest of her being. For example, she must learn not to become overly rational, while denying the reality of her emotional or spiritual responses. On the other hand she must not allow her newly found emotional responses to overwhelm her reason and cause her to collapse, a helpless victim to herself.

When all of the aspects of self are balanced, the tremendous power of the inner voice emerges. The inner voice is the greatest key to self healing and self-realization which anyone possesses. Once it has been found, the mid-point of the transition into third stage has been reached. More and more the individual will learn to rely upon this aspect of her being, as it teaches her how to stand alone but never lonely, and to be intimate without endangering or losing the Self.

Now she finds that the inner voice tells her the Truth

about self and about life and about her relationship to the Whole. It reveals to her the truth and the perfect pattern of those around her, whom she now perceives in love and compassion. Having triumphed in the resurrection of self, she now finds herself a natural born healer, and so passes into the third stage.

Third Stage

Now in third stage, this individual can finally get on with her ultimate purpose of healing the Earth and its people in her own chosen manner. She has learned never to judge for, in the process of resurrecting herself she came to realize that love was the only key and the only power which could ever affect a change in her basic circumstances, interpretation, and experience of life. To judge or condemn merely freezes us in our tracks. Because she has learned unconditional self-acceptance in the process of healing herself, she now has the ability to provide unconditional acceptance and understanding to any individual she may encounter. She has come through the long dark tunnel in graceful and perfect form, and though she may be the living embodiment of some higher ideal, because of her past experiences, she still retains her full humanity.

She is relaxed and natural and perfectly at home within the physical world in which she lives. Indeed she also realizes that the physical and spiritual worlds interpenetrate each other and are one. She lives in simplicity within the union of both of these worlds. Possessing a quiet trust in life and a total confidence in her own inner voice, she has a powerful calming affect upon others. Those who wander in the darkness can look into her eyes and see there perfect evidence that there truly is a way out. Certainly they can know that where they are, she has been, and perhaps she has been someplace worse. "If I can do it, so can you," her spirit says in the silence.

The third-stage Virgo has no dependencies, and is confident and competent as she goes about the process of fulfilling her personal life mission. She loses the perfectionist tendency which is often a part of second stage, where great personal insecurity prompted the individual to attempt to legislate all aspects of her life. Needing no one, she is nonetheless capable of deep personal intimacy, now being able to unite with life without fear of being violated or of weakening herself. She does not hide her vulnerabilities from others, and takes total personal responsibility at all times.

Her purpose may involve physical, mental or emotional healing of other individuals, or she may heal upon a collective level, expressing her purpose politically, artistically, scientifically or environmentally. Her natural talents are developed and perfected, yet unless her purpose requires her to be personally expressive, she tends to go about her business in a spirit of quiet humility. She has an enormous capacity for long-term dedication, yet when circumstances warrant, or her inner voice indicates it, she can be off in a moment pursuing whatever course of action may be necessary in order to further her purpose or her process of self-actualization.

One can also heal through the expression of wholeness. This alternative expression of third stage lends itself to many different lifestyles and ways of being. If this form of self-expression is chosen, she need not necessarily be retiring or dedicated completely to some specific form of service. Instead she may possess an endless spirit of adventure, constantly demonstrating her oneness with nature and her own inner being, by seeking out challenging circumstances, perhaps in social or geographical wildernesses, and always emerging on top.

Healer or free spirit, she knows that through the state of oneness which is our divine inheritance, even seeming impossibilities become naturally possible.

Virgo at the Crossroads
First/Third-Stage Transition

The fork in the road occurs for Virgo as she begins to see all external assistance withdrawing from her. Perhaps her wisest advisor, before taking necessary leave, will attempt to inform her that if she can summon up the necessary courage to rely upon and trust her inner self completely, then she will find that she possesses all the power that she needs, deep within her being. "You are ready now for your greatest challenge," she whispers as the wind carries her to distant lands, "remember to trust yourself above all else.

Question deeply, and do not lose your trust in life, even as the storm rages all about you."

Without the will to find true strength, this transition cannot be accomplished. But even with the determination to do so, she will find the process very difficult, and perhaps terrifying at first. She will have been warned that above all else she must not run from her feelings. And yet when she faces her ultimate challenge, in complete isolation—as she must do—this advice seems very much like being told not to close the windows in a hurricane or leave her doors unlocked while ax murderers roam the streets.

As she searches within, all she may at first encounter is her own personal terror, agony and profound feelings of helplessness. She feels so small, when once she may have felt so large, that it is a great blow to her personal ego. Her next hurdle is to overcome the temptation to hide behind her own emotions, to indulge her feelings of helplessness or lose herself in self-pity. It is very difficult to solve the riddle of the self with no clues to go by, but she must remember that somewhere within her there lies the still, small voice.

She must recall her original ideals, and trust the guidance of her teachers. Somewhere seemingly beyond herself and her own personal concerns lies the key to becoming all she is. She must literally or figuratively step into the wilderness and trust that there is a spiritual force which will support her when all external supports have failed. She must surrender to the greater whole and follow its voice within her heart. And this is why she must keep her doors and windows unlocked.

When she gives herself over completely to this higher being, within and without, she will have passed the greatest test which any man or woman can ever face. She must never undervalue the process she is involved in, or the results which it begins to yield. When she succeeds in meeting the storm unarmed, she will have returned to a true state of innocence and completion. Never having fully departed from it, she is truly her own greatest gift to the world.

All third-stage individuals must learn to become agents for the greater whole. Therefore the first/third-stage Virgo must always remember the essential oneness which exists between herself and her enemies. She may be very different from those who confront her, but this does not mean that they do not come from the same ultimate starting point that she does. All around her other human beings exist with the same essential fears, longings and desires. Her "enemies" are merely wounded souls who, believing that they are trapped in their suffering, can see no other recourse but to lash out blindly at others.

If she can remember her purpose, while forgetting herself, she will lose her fear and become instead an open vessel for a greater power which seeks to heal all who suffer. Perhaps this is the real reason why "the wolves close in" at the end of first-stage Virgo. Those who need her healing powers are attracted to her, while at the same time experiencing an unconscious, instinctive need to test her mettle.

At the end of first-stage Virgo, all external guidance is withdrawn from the individual. If she still persists in seeking assistance, she will fall into illusion. Should she become lost in self-pity at her seeming abandonment, she will also fall into illusion. Even if she tries to "tough it out" alone, relying upon the largely undeveloped powers of her own ego, she will still fail to reach what could be her highest potential.

Only if she allows herself to seek the only true guidance that there is — the Divine Guidance which can be found within herself and from no other source — will she triumph. She will learn that her only true essential self is her spiritual self, and that this aspect of her being can be harmed by no one. Invulnerable and invincible, she is now wiser than those who assail her, and will be certain to succeed in every way that matters. Perhaps this transition may seem to be too difficult, especially for one who, if not a young soul, is at the very least a new soul. But we all possess the potential of the highest power within ourselves. In the innocence of the Virgin lies the trust of a child, and through this deep form of trust profound rebirth can occur.

Nor need Virgo fear that in bypassing second stage she will sacrifice the experience necessary to the development of her future abilities as a healer; if she can avoid the great wound which assails us all, she will become an expert in preventive medicine of the most valuable sort. She will emerge with the ability to show others how they can preserve their own individual integrity.

Childhood Conditions and Relationship Patterns

Virgo is an earth sign. As we have discussed previously, every sign is symbolically ruled by one of the four elements of the ancients. The element of earth symbolizes the physical nature. It relates to our capacity to experience physical intimacy with another individual, to our relationship with our own bodies, and to our capacity to deal with the material world with maximum efficiency. Obviously our ability to relate to ourselves and others on a primal physical level, as well as our capacity to deal most immediately with the concrete world which surrounds us, is more related to our mother's influence than to our father's. Because this is the case, the Virgo individual will generally tend to be more influenced by her relationship with her mother rather than her father.

On a subconscious level, Virgo's mother symbolizes her relationship to the natural world, and her own physical and emotional being. Virgo's mother also acts as a good indicator of the basic stability of her personal ego. Because one of the early goals of the individual as she passes through this sign is to adapt to an earthly world which she cannot easily understand, the bond with her mother is of crucial importance.

In early first stage, her mother is her number one fan. She may be her favorite child and will be given her unconditional support and admiration. Because in her eyes she can do no wrong, there may be a danger of the first-stage Virgo developing an ego problem, or having difficulty knowing her natural limits in life. If her mother is wise, she will provide proper limits and balanced discipline, along with the abundant encouragement which she finds it so easy to supply to this individual.

As first stage progresses, their bond will remain strong. The mother and child will often share common values and interests. Their relationship may be more intellectually and philosophically stimulating than emotionally and physically nurturing. The Virgo child may idealize her mother, but in many cases may not realize that the two of them are not actually close physically or emotionally.

As the individual progresses towards second stage it is common for the early mother/child bonding process to be interrupted in some way. This may be due to a childhood illness, an extremely difficult birth or some other form of external interference or sudden emergency. On the other hand, the mother herself may be uncomfortable with her physical, sexual or emotional nature. While she may love her child, she may have difficulty expressing her feelings, and may be afraid of the surrender to her own emotional and physical nature which true motherhood requires. Where the mother/child bond remains strong on all levels, it is still common for the relationship with the mother to be severely disrupted at some point during the childhood.

At the beginning of first stage, the child's relationship with her father is similar to the relationship with the mother. The child looks up to the father, expecting him to show her how to live in the world. Initially Virgo tends to accept her father's ideals, although she may not fully understand them. Whatever her father does seems important to the child and as first stage progresses, it also seems so important to the father that he may have little time left over to spend with his child. This may cause Virgo's mother to experience a great deal of stress, and to feel that all of the responsibility for caring for the household is being left to her. The fear that all of the practical requirements of life may not be fully met is passed on to her child, who may develop fears and worries concerning the fulfillment of life's day-to-day necessities.

As first stage progresses, and the transition into second-stage approaches, the relationship with the father may grow more distant. He may be completely wrapped up in his career, feeling that children should be seen and not heard. On the rare occasions when he does grace the family with his presence, he may seem cold and distant. He may also be domineering and abusive, expecting the impossible from his offspring, while severely damaging their self-esteem and their ability to relate to those whom they may encounter outside of the family sanctuary. Alternatively, he may be irresponsible or largely absent.

Subconsciously Virgo's father represents her relationship with her own source of spiritual guidance and the promptings of her soul as it seeks to fulfill its chosen purpose. The distance between the father and the child symbolizes Virgo's tendency to lose contact with her inner source of spiritual guidance as she heads towards the second stage. The tyrannical tendencies of her father represent Virgo's feeling that her soul is expecting too much from her, by expecting her to face the darker aspects of the human experience.

In second stage, Virgo's relationship with her mother becomes more powerful and more subject to conflict, confusion and upheaval. The mother/child bond experiences greater disruption, sometimes the child herself may end up pushing the mother away, thereby creating greater feelings of personal isolation. The child often develops sexual fears or conflicts as a result of her early experiences.

One or both of her parents often has a strong, perhaps overly rigid moral code. The child is given many "shoulds" and "shouldn'ts", and very little acceptance as an individual. She is taught to fear the world. Nature and other people are not to be trusted. She may be taught to be judgmental of others and made to feel that she is never adequate, because there is always some standard which she is not measuring up to.

Although both parents may be present during second stage, the child often feels emotionally like an orphan. In early second stage, she may actually be one. Many Virgos in early second stage lose one or both parents, or are adopted as children. Regardless of circumstances, the child still feels a great longing to be somehow reunited with the father she may never have been close to. Her relationship with her mother may be close by virtue of an ego-damaging form of symbiosis or even deeply rooted feelings of resentment. A truly balanced and nurturing mother/child bond is extremely rare. The difficulty which Virgo experiences in bonding with her mother is a direct reflection of the soul's difficulty in bonding with the Earth.

Things improve as we move towards third stage. While some second/third-stage Virgos are born into a family situation which still expresses the nightmarish tendencies of second stage, others are more fortunate, and are graced with a truly wise and nurturing mother or mother substitute. This individual may herself be in a process of emotional or physical self-healing. She is learning to move beyond a sometimes fearful and rigid response to life in order to trust herself again, and Virgo learns with her. She will most likely be in second/third-stage or even third stage herself, and may guide her child as she moves forward to fulfill her true destiny. If Virgo's mother does not directly aid her in the transition into third stage, her relationship with her may prove to be so destructive that it goads her toward making the necessary changes in her life responses.

A child born into second/third stage will experience similar patterns in her relationship with the father. The tendencies expressed by the father during second stage may intensify. Or the child may be born to an individual who is just beginning to take an interest in developing her own parenting skills. If this is the case, the child will learn to slowly trust her father, for it has often been many lifetimes since this individual has experienced a positive paternal relationship. Symbolically her reunion with the father corresponds to her increasing ability to listen to the voice within and to trust in her own sources of spiritual strength and knowledge.

In third stage, the bond with the mother once again reaches complete fulfillment. There is a deeply gentle and refined relationship between the mother and the child. This individual chooses a mother who has developed the capacity to recognize and appreciate the inherent Divinity and individuality of others. She is wise in the ways of the world, but her wisdom is fluid rather than dogmatic. Her spirituality comes from within and includes an appreciation for the natural world and her own physical and emotional being.

In this stage the child finally enjoys a much longed for feeling of intimacy with her father. In the earlier stages, the father's involvements took him away from the family. If he was present, he was either irresponsible, or was forced out of the picture by the mother's dominance. In third stage, she is still subtly dominant, mainly because the father holds her in such high regard. At this stage the father takes his share of the responsibility for the care of her child. He is physically and emotionally present in the nurturing process.

Under this care young Virgo thrives. While her parents are nurturing, they are also careful to encourage independence. The child grows up in an atmosphere which has a strong link with nature. Her parents are not just her parents, but also each other's lovers, and her spirit is nourished in the light which results from their union.

As an adult the first-stage Virgo individual may remain close to her parents and to those who protect and assist her in life. She may fail to reach full maturity as an individual, and may therefore choose to remain single. Should she choose to marry or become involved in a long-term relationship, it will usually be with someone who will protect and support her as an individual. A female Virgo will probably choose a strong provider or someone who can give her a great deal of attention and emotional support. She innocently expects to be taken care of and looked after, seldom realizing the one-sidedness of this kind of relationship. As she nears the end of first stage, she may be abandoned by her partner, as she grows tired of doing all of the giving and most of the work.

A male Virgo tends to choose a similar relationship, but in this case he usually expects to receive frequent massages to her ego. He needs to be a star in the family he creates, just as he was a star in the family into which he was born. He expects an easy road in life, and does not wish his wife to surpass him in her career. If she does he may become abusive and demeaning. While Virgos in early first stage can usually find relationships which are reasonably fulfilling and satisfying to all concerned, as they reach the end of first stage, both males and females may be abandoned by mates who grow tired of being their baby-sitters.

Second-stage Virgos have great problems with intimacy. While second-stage Geminis may have a great fear of rejection, second-stage Virgos are more frightened of abandonment. While the two may seem similar, in reality they are not. Gemini's fear of rejection is really a fear that her true self will be seen and found wanting by others. It is a fear of lack of recognition. Virgo's fear is of losing support and nourishment for some unknown reason. This can make some early second-stage Virgos extremely clingy in their relationships. Almost from the start they are saying, "Please don't leave me. I would die if you left me. You can't leave me, because I was abused and abandoned in my childhood, and I deserve to be taken care of now." While this response is understandable, it usually has the result of chasing people away.

And so Virgo becomes bitter and defensive. She may have trouble letting people get close, because she is terrified that they will leave as soon as she becomes attached. This fear is understandable, because this is exactly what has happened so many times before. The individual may instead develop strength and independence, while a part of herself withers away. As second stage progresses, intimacy becomes frightening for another reason. Virgo is afraid to feel. She has too much pain hidden away, and it will cost her too much to open up and let it out.

Because this individual has had difficulty with her mother, the second-stage Virgo may have sexual problems. She may have inhibitions or distortions in her response, or she may be curiously detached from her sexuality, seeing it as just another bodily function, maybe not quite as important as all of the others. Alternatively, she may overemphasize her sexuality as her last contact with herself and as a means of bolstering her ego. Sexuality may become an escapist pastime, but emotionally she may be afraid to surrender to anyone.

Males in second-stage Virgo have a very difficult time, because they do not wish to admit any weakness, and so may be even more closed off from others. Their difficulties with their mother will affect them more deeply, and they may feel an enormous amount of anger towards the opposite sex because of this. Alternatively their confidence may be crippled in some important way.

In second/third stage, the individual is learning to be vulnerable once again. Because of this her fears of abandonment will surface once again. She needs to learn to rely upon the power of her inner voice to give her the strength to stand alone without being aloof, while remaining open to the outpouring of her own emotions. She must develop the courage to relate to others without personal expectations. Because she is developing the ability to heal others, she must be careful not to attract those who seek to depend on her. Her calling in the larger world is to be a healer, but in her personal life she must only share with, not seek to uplift, her partner.

Intimate relationships are a very important part of the fulfillment of the third stage of Virgo. A third-stage Virgo makes an excellent lover, for she is a strong individual who is nonetheless capable of powerful physical and emotional surrender. But she cannot abide dependency. To love this individual you must be able to stand alone, yet dive deeply. Those who are mature enough to be able to handle it will experience a truly wise and unconditional form of union should they choose a third-stage Virgo as their partner.

Famous Virgos

First Stage: Freddie Mercury, Michael Jackson (very close to the transition).

Second Stage: Aristotle Onassis, Greta Garbo, Elvis Costello (close to the transition).

Second/Third Stage: Kristy McNichol, Sophia Loren.

Third Stage: D. H. Lawrence, Leo Tolstoy, Mary Stewart, Mother Theresa.

LIBRA
right relationship

Libra is an air sign. One of the four elements, air is associated with the mental and social realms of experience. In this sign, the focus is on the social or interpersonal aspects of the air element. Some elements are considered feminine by nature, others masculine. Because air is considered a masculine element, I have used the words "he", "him" and "his" in the description that follows. These terms are neutral, and refer to individuals of either gender.

Before experiencing rebirth, we all have the opportunity to set aside the need for a personal ego and to merge with life itself, experiencing our true place in the larger reality. Once we have developed our full potential as individuals, we can return to that state of oneness without running the risk of losing ourselves, having fully achieved the ability to play our part in the greater scheme of things.

Until that point is reached, most of us tend to forget that we are truly all one, as we go about the process of mastering the physical world and actualizing our own potential as individuals. The Libran, however, is initially reluctant to leave this state of oneness, and consciously or unconsciously longs always to return to it. On a deeper level than most, his heart has been touched by this experience of unity. He seeks to serve the ideals which it represents.

As he moves toward the physical plane, he comes to understand how the forces of nature create through union. He perceives union as the highest form of beauty, and harmony as the key to universal justice. He sees the power which is unleashed in the human world when two or more individuals join in the name of love. He also experiences the need to develop his individuality, as we all do. And yet he does not wish to lose the experience of unity in doing so, and so longs to exalt himself through personal love. He seeks also to serve the cause of harmony and justice within the human world, and it is these twin urges which draw him into incarnation.

First Stage

Because he has lingered so long upon a higher plane of unity before being reborn, during first stage he is inclined to find his way into an earthly home which reflects the experience of harmony to which he has grown accustomed. This environment embodies the most basic qualities and higher longings of his or her true inner nature.

Usually he experiences a secure, most often rural existence where harmonious associations prevail both in the home and in the environment at large. The soul experiences a paradisical state of natural harmony both without and within. His greatest longing is to make true contact with another individual, to experience that state of oneness from which he has come, without losing the sense of personal identity which has come from being a separate individual.

Because this individual instinctively gravitates towards those places and individuals which possess a natural harmony with his basic nature, he or she is able to consummate and fulfill his personal relationships in a deeply satisfying manner. He may grow up to marry "the boy or girl next door" with whom he has much in common in terms of essential character, background and ideals. His marriage becomes the center of his universe, as he experiences a growing comprehension of just what constitutes a truly functional love relationship. It is not uncommon for two first-stage Librans to come together in a love match at this stage of their development, often forging a bond which may last for lifetimes.

By the end of the first stage of Libra, the individual has come to be in love with love. Highly idealistic, he or she sees only the beauty in life, and innocently seeks to serve and uphold the values of true life harmony on all levels. Indeed he would find it difficult to imagine that others would ever truly feel or be essentially any different from himself, at least with regard to the values which he holds most dear. His world, however, is growing too small for him. Sooner or later he must reach out into a larger arena, and come to discover how truly innocent he has actually been.

First/Second-Stage Transition

As the transition begins, the Libran may grow restless. He feels the need to test himself against some form of obstacle, a desire to encounter new worlds, perhaps through travel, or the experience of a different form of social environment. He may begin to rebel against the harmonious circumstances in which he finds himself. He wishes to develop new relating skills and to achieve greater complexity of individuality.

These urges cause him to develop a desire for something more than the simple experience of natural compatibility. The realization that not everyone has had a chance to experience love as he has causes him to feel a great deal of compassion for others. He is drawn to share what he knows with those who suffer in conflict, isolation and loneliness. Yet he may sense that the road ahead will not be easy, and so may attempt to hold back from entry into the world beyond his little paradise.

Eventually the call of the unknown and the sense of compassion which he feels become too much, and he is drawn into the world of conflict and into personal relationships with those whose natures are perhaps far from naturally compatible with his own. Unconsciously he feels that these individuals possess a sophistication which he lacks, and his attraction is also an unconscious means of attempting to find himself through another. Ultimately he finds himself irresistibly drawn to the turbulent, mysterious stranger from the outside world, and so passes into second stage.

In an older soul the social or political arena may also have a profound effect upon the choices made during this stage of development, for he may feel more and more that the laws of harmony under which he lives need to be shared with the world at large. His experience causes him to leave behind the simple world from which he has originated, and to head toward the corrupt forms which society sometimes seems to take. He wants to show the world what it may be missing, through failing to abide by the laws by which he lives.

Unless he begins to make a transition into the third

stage, he will most likely find himself drifting into situations where he may haphazardly attempt to communicate his perceptions, or will most likely attempt to do so under the guidance of others, rather than making distinct plans and undertaking them with a sense of individual purpose.

Because he has not placed himself under Divine guidance, as he would have if he had made the first/third-stage transition, he tends to experience a greater or lesser degree of resistance to his ideals. The same aura of subtle conflict which permeates his newly chosen intimate relationships will inevitably make itself felt in terms of his social involvements. Eventually he himself will taste the bitter fruit of social injustice. And so, as he begins to make actual encounters with the world at large he, like his younger brethren, also passes into second stage.

Whether or not he may choose to take an active social role at this stage, he will without fail experience the personal aspects of the transition into second stage, as his choice of partnership inevitably makes a dramatic shift at this point in his development.

Second Stage

In the conscious or unconscious effort to share and further develop his relationship skills in the company of another human being, the second-stage Libran now selects as a partner someone with poor relating skills, with whom he is not naturally and innately compatible. He finds himself irresistibly drawn to this challenge. He is beginning to become subtly fascinated with struggle; even though he believes that he is seeking harmonious union, inner peace and tranquillity. Consciously he still wants peace at any price, because it is only in an atmosphere of peace and harmony that he feels secure and at home. Consequently he is constantly attempting to maintain the peace between two innately conflicting individuals—himself and his partner.

His sense of individuality is not as strong as that of other signs in the same stage of development, for he has always leaned on his partner and perhaps his community to give him strength during the first stage of his development. Because he stills feels in need of external strength, he will not want to rock the boat in his relationships. He may be inclined to attempt to please his partner even though it goes against himself. In order to avoid conflict or confrontation he therefore sometimes avoids standing up for the things he believes in, should such a sacrifice seem to be necessary to maintain the appearance of union.

On the other hand, he feels a strong need to instruct his partner, to give this other individual an opportunity to learn how to relate, and to experience the joys of love which the Libran, over the course of many lifetimes has learned to appreciate. In a sense he is trying to become an individual by assimilating the unique qualities of his partner. Unconsciously he wishes to exchange his relating skills for his partner's apparent sense of unique individuality. Part of him may tend to mistake an emotionally dysfunctional individual who refuses intimacy, for an independent soul who does not need to relate as deeply as he does, and so may choose to admire his partner for qualities which he or she truly does not possess.

He wants to understand the deeper ramifications of union, but cannot do so without a stronger sense of self. The difficulties and challenges to which he subjects himself may eventually provide him with ample opportunity to develop this. However, he must avoid suppressing himself for the sake of apparent external harmony if he is going to be able to use his experiences as keys to personal self-actualization. Because he may not yet be ready for Ultimate Union, he settles instead for struggle followed by reunion. He dreams of giving his partner the gift of love for the first time, while secretly hoping to absorb his partner's actual or fantasized strengths as he does so.

In the first part of second stage he is usually able to experience some form of union with another individual after much struggle and effort. He has managed to compromise his way into his partner's heart. With great tenacity, he has enabled another soul to change their patterns of relating, to the point where they may be able to experience a level of intimacy which they would never have allowed or understood before. Some might call it manipulation; and it is certain at this stage that the Libran has learned how to subtly, but firmly, and even at times unconsciously manipulate his partner into seeing his point of view. Of course he does it to serve his ideals of justice and harmony, and for the sake of the beauty of love.

He may manipulate others in an artfully persistent manner yet, in this case, little real damage is done. It is when he manipulates himself to please the dictates of another, or to maintain the appearance of harmony, that the real cumulative damage is done. Libra is under a great deal of constant stress, for on the one hand he is trying to uphold his ideals and fulfill the conditions which he desires from his relationships, and on the other hand he is attempting to please others, hoping thereby to keep them around, and also to maintain an atmosphere of peace. He is in a double bind, for he is attracted to conflict for the opportunity which it represents to challenge and discover himself; and yet he needs peace in order to feel that he still has a sense of security and can maintain contact with the original aspects of himself.

Living in a world based in many ways upon compromise and subterfuge (which is a very strange reality for one who is such a lover of justice and honesty to find himself in),makes it very difficult to be allowed the time and opportunity to come to know oneself. This is the source of the well-known propensity towards indecision which plagues most of the members of this sign. They are so used to taking their cues from the external world and attempting to please others, that it becomes very difficult for them to know what they themselves actually want. While hemming and hawing over the dinner menu, for instance, they are really waiting for some sort of tide to wash over them which will dictate the direction of approach, so that they will know which is the best step for them to take for all concerned. Seeking external cues becomes such a deeply ingrained habit, that it soon becomes a powerful form of security in and of itself.

Although early second stage has its stresses, in this phase the individual can usually be assured of reaching some form of personal fulfillment—at least by the end of his lifetime. However, with each successful conquest, the individual has a tendency to choose a greater challenge than the one which he had previously overcome. He hopes that his relating skills will be further developed with each successful attempt. He chooses situations of increasing difficulty, and since his choices are usually unconscious, he may not even be aware of what he is actually doing. He enters each new relationship with rosy dreams of romantic fulfillment. At the beginning of second stage for example, he may choose someone who perhaps has little experience of love, whereas by the end of second stage he may choose an individual who has deeply rooted psychological problems and perhaps a great deal of anger towards any potential partner and a resistance to the very concept of intimacy itself.

With each new relationship the Libran adapts and twists himself in response to his partner's demands and desires. Consciously or unconsciously his actions may become more and more strategic as he attempts to turn each new situation in his favor. He is unlikely to become terribly dishonest or overwhelmingly manipulative however, for he always retains his love of justice and his innocent desire for honest communication. One day he changes himself to suit his partner, the next day he is implementing his own strategy in an attempt to meet his needs, and the next day he is attempting to institute true communication in the hopes of being fair to both parties often not realizing, as he nears the end of second stage, that his partner has no interest in being fair at all. Poor Libra is trying so hard to please, and again and again finds that the door is simply shut in his face.

Because Libra is the sign which is attempting to perfect relationships, this pattern commonly also spills into his social or professional relationships as well. He comes into contact with increasing forms of injustice. He may be treated with abuse by his employer, or by his family. He may be ignored or taken advantage of by those whose friendship he seeks. He may experience or witness traumatic forms of social injustice.

He is unaware that it is his own unconscious patterns which have drawn him into these situations. He may feel helpless to change the larger patterns of injustice which he sees around him. This, coupled with the nearly constant abuse which he experiences in his personal life as he nears the end of second stage, may deeply damage his self-confidence and self-worth, which usually has had little opportunity to develop during first stage. He feels weaker and weaker as time passes, and his tendency to compromise with every person he meets seems to turn him into a chameleon with little or no real sense of self.

Because he does not realize that his experience is a result of his own inner pattern, he may gradually come to lose his innocent optimism and faith in life. It seems as if the world has turned ugly. A late second-stage Libran may become helpless, frightened and destructively self-abnegating. He is often likely to turn deeply cynical. He is usually very isolated. He may emerge from his isolation just long enough to attempt yet another destructive and unsuccessful personal relationship, and then retreat once more into his own little world of darkness.

At this stage he is understandably very angry. The anger may be suppressed because it threatens his inner and outer harmony. If this is the case, it may eat away at him or be expressed in self-destructive habits or actions. He may decide to become a misanthrope, feeling justified in defending himself from the outside world in any manner which he sees fit. He may abandon his earlier ideals and affect a resentful form of self-centeredness, seeking vengeance upon society by fulfilling his external needs without any thought of the affect his actions may have on others.

Some Librans at this stage become highly dominant in relationships, putting the shoe on the other foot as it were, and associating only with those who will serve them, while avoiding and disdaining the rest of humanity. He has no concept of what it truly means to love another. At least this is how he appears. In reality he is struggling against a feeling of helplessness, and the belief that loving another will only leave him open to pointless victimization. This response is somewhat rare, and really represents a way of overstaying one's welcome in second stage. It is ultimately a very difficult pattern, as it must indeed become very stale before the individual will consider releasing his stubborn stance of resentment and hunger for power and security.

Another response to late second stage occurs when the individual attempts to develop his or her individual strength, while fearing that a relationship may prove to be his undoing. He may become promiscuous, losing all ability to commit to a lasting relationship, or he may develop confusing feelings of ambivalence, feeling incomplete without a partner, yet feeling trapped when involved in an intimate relationship. This pattern is not without its value, for the individual will tend to develop certain personal strengths which will provide an easier transition into third stage. However, where it operates compulsively, this response can produce a great deal of frustration, which will eventually lead the individual involved to seek some alternative to the situation in which he finds himself.

Second/Third-Stage Transition

Eventually his life becomes too narrow, too painful, or just too darn ridiculous to continue in the same pattern any longer. He realizes that he must now seek some alternative to the life which he has been leading. When he comes to realize that there must be a better way, he begins an earnest search for the way out of his difficulties, and the transition into third stage has begun.

First and foremost he must realize that he himself has contributed to the difficulties which he has experienced. If he is to overcome the difficulties which he now faces, he must come to understand the subconscious motivations behind his present life choices. This may be difficult for him to do, for he can be very stubborn. He has learned to be tenacious in the past, as he attempted to master his personal relationships. By the end of second stage his tenacity often expresses itself in forms of self-protection which are not always completely constructive.

He must come to terms with his anger. He may be reluctant to do so. He may be reluctant to open up the Pandora's box of seething emotions which are stored just beneath the surface of conscious awareness. All he may have left in life is his self-control, with which he maintains his tiny little oasis of tentative and rapidly diminishing peace and harmony.

He needs to understand that part of his unconscious motivation has been the development of his personal relating skills, and that despite the mess in which he may find himself at the present time, those skills have been honed to a fine edge. He must learn that it is he who programs his subconscious, and that the present programming is no longer necessary, for it has achieved the purpose which it once served. He must now give himself his graduation papers and firmly decide that he deserves positive relationships, beginning with his relationship with himself.

He must learn to act consciously in his relationship choices, and to understand what his true motives are in being attracted to any given individual. As his relationship with himself improves, he can learn to look before he leaps, and avoid becoming involved in any relationship which may disrupt his new-found feelings of self-love and self-respect.

Although achieving the knack of reprogramming himself may be difficult at first, no one can change their relationship patterns faster than a Libra. It is common for a second/third-stage transition Libra to go from black to white when it comes to the form which their intimate experience takes. They have saved up many lifetimes worth of positive karma in the romance department, for they have truly given many people the gift of love. And when they are ready to have this gift returned, they are capable of attracting a truly positive individual to be their mate.

For some individuals the change in the pattern of intimate relationship occurs in two stages. The first stage involves attracting a much more positive and harmonious relationship than they may have experienced for lifetimes. They settle into what they believe is a happy state of romantic fulfillment, only to find that the old patterns begin to reassert themselves on a more subtle level. In time they may discover that they are still compromising themselves too much, and that their chosen partner, while usually a positive person in his or her own right, may still be too different from themselves to be a true life mate. Strengthened by the positive aspects of this relationship, Libra sets out once again, this time to achieve intimacy without compromise.

While some individuals in this transition will choose to attract a partner to aid in their reconstruction process, others prefer to learn to go it alone and develop the personal independence which will assist them in their search for self. This individual may delay or forego the experience of partnership, while spending a great deal of time learning to be their own best friend.

Some Librans who have refused relationship at the end of second stage may spend a great proportion of their time during this transition experiencing a state of independence which is of their own choosing. They will develop all of their strengths and skills and come to understand their place within the greater whole, all the while avoiding or doing their best to avoid relationships, perhaps becoming abusive towards their partners or being unable to fully commit to any relationship in which they do become involved.

Their behavior may be a mystery to themselves, as much as it is to others, but the answer to the dilemma lies in the fact that their pride has been wounded through so many lifetimes of abuse and rejection, and now they feel that they are fighting for the very survival of their own personal ego. For this kind of Libra the final piece of the puzzle before he can pass into the third stage involves the realization that he is capable of surrendering to love without losing himself, and that those exist who can love him in a just and nurturing manner. He ultimately learns that it is safe to share himself, and that doing so can aid and assist him in the fulfillment of his purpose.

It is very important for Librans to regain their strength as they pass through the second/third-stage transition, and to find out once again who they truly are. So many lifetimes of twisting and bending themselves in order to please others have made it hard for them to know what their true feelings and opinions actually are. Masters at the art of compromise, they are constantly considering how to adapt themselves to others, and can still quite easily sell themselves out for the sake of harmony or be led along by stronger personalities than themselves, unconsciously being led away from their true path in life.

Attempting to correct this imbalance may lead certain second/third-stage Librans to affect an outer persona which seems brusque, aggressive or overly egotistical. Whether they are aggressive or overly submissive, the fact remains that on a soul level they do need to learn to assert themselves and, in time, the balance point of the pendulum will be attained.

Achieving a balanced attitude towards the emotion of anger can be very valuable here. The average Libran at the end of second stage or during the transition to third stage contains literally lifetimes worth of repressed anger. This anger has been built up as a result of too much compromise, and through the unconscious realization that the individual has been violated, often due to the forms of injustice to which he or she has been subjected. Some individuals have suppressed their true feelings and opinions for so long, that this anger has built up to the intensity of a murderous rage. Libra may be scared to let it out for fear of completely losing control.

A great amount of this individual's stored rage truly stems from a feeling of helplessness. He or she has felt helpless and out of control in his or her relationships. He has also felt helpless in the face of whatever social wrongs and injustices he may have witnessed or experienced. When the feelings of helplessness have been removed, the rage does not have to be present as a compensation.

In all signs, as third stage approaches, the individual comes to understand certain universal principles. The first of these is that we are all unconsciously responsible for our own experience. When we become aware that this is in fact so, we can begin to become consciously responsible for the relationships and experiences which we attract to ourselves. To do so causes us to be freed from victimization, and so removes the feeling of helplessness which is always a part of the life experience of the second-stage individual.

Resentment, cynicism and the negative interpretation of events and circumstances must be released, as this behavior really represents a karmic attachment to difficult forms of relationship which needs to be left behind. This kind of life attitude is common at the end of second stage, and seems to form some sort of protection for the individual concerned. It is a safety valve whereby a certain amount of stored anger is released, and the individual also feels better prepared for life by feeling that if they see bad things coming, at least they will stand a better chance of being able to deal with them when they arrive. In reality they are reaffirming their feelings of helplessness and causing themselves to remain enmeshed in disharmonious surroundings and relationships, due to the fact that we tend to receive in life whatever we habitually focus our mental attention upon.

Many Librans feel that it is foolish to adopt a positive

attitude towards life, because they unconsciously recall having been too innocent and optimistic at the end of first stage. It seems to them as if this attitude completely failed to serve them, and in fact only set them up to suffer all the more. Yet the real cause of their suffering was being unaware of their true life motivation. Once they learn to become aware of this they will develop great personal strength and independence.

Once they begin to achieve freedom from those forces which have seemed to oppress them, they will find that they are not yet truly out of the woods; much of their internal rage also stems from the injustices which they have witnessed, not just those which may have befallen them personally. They need to understand that in the course of human evolution suffering is necessary, and that the apparent injustices which they see around them are a necessary part of each individual's development within the context of the greater whole. We all need to be asleep before we can be awake, and we only wake up when we are ready. The trials and tribulations to which we are all subjected help us to become ready to awaken. When Librans have resurrected and liberated their true selves from the chains which bind them, it becomes their calling to be one of the awakeners, and to demonstrate to and instruct humanity in the art of true relationship so that others can also become free of any unnecessary suffering.

In their earlier stages of development, Librans tend to feel that all anger is bad. However, they need to come to understand that anger is in many ways an instinctive force which, when properly attended to, has the capacity to assist the individual in maintaining or re-creating his or her sense of inner balance. In Libra it is often self-assertion in disguise. Anger can be transformed into a form of personal power which will in time liberate not only himself, but many of those with whom he comes into contact.

The key lies in realizing that there are two kinds of anger: a lower and a higher. Lower anger lashes out in frustration, reacting against a feeling of personal helplessness. It seeks to destroy, sometimes choosing to put an end to the force or individual which seems to oppress it, at other times acting even less rationally. It will destroy anything, even the self, just for some change in circumstance, whatever this may be.

While lower anger is destructive, higher anger is constructive and creative. It is the force of Divine Justice, which acts always in harmony with life, and seems to express itself as a higher power. It transcends the personal, and is capable of any accomplishment which is in harmony with the greater good. In the human world it must be accessed by an individual or individuals who are aware of and trust in its existence. It cannot really be understood until it is experienced. And for second/third-stage transition Libra, this seems to be the catch.

This individual may have difficulty believing in the power of the greater whole, because of lifetimes of negative experience which have usually left him somewhat bitter and cynical. But whatever our conscious opinion of life may be, there is always a part of us which remains in contact with the life power itself. It resides hidden within all, as a great source of power, waiting for just the right stimulus to emerge into active expression.

Higher anger is inspiring and transformative, for its true expression is Divine Justice as it acts through the medium of human interaction. When we decide creatively that "This cannot be so," and allow the power of the life force to act through us, a completely new set of alternatives are born which enable the necessary social changes to take place. On a smaller scale, positive anger allows us to set proper life limits upon ourselves and others, and this force frees the Libran from the apparent necessity of compromising his or her life away. Higher anger teaches us the undeniable truth. Lower anger is an instinctive form of self-defense, stemming from a belief in and a fear of personal helplessness. Higher anger always includes love, both of the self, and our apparent adversary.

Before this power of Divine Justice can be utilized, lower anger must be accepted and transmuted. It does exist for a reason, and this individual usually has a right to feel the way that he does. It is the destructive urges accompanying it which need to learn to bear a different fruit. The late second stage or early second/third-stage transition Libra can feel so trapped in a world he has not made, that he may sometimes feel an irrational urge to lash out and destroy whatever surrounds him, regardless of the cost to himself. Understandably, he usually suppresses these urges. He needs to recognize that in many ways, he does live in or amongst unjust circumstances, and that his feelings are therefore natural and understandable. But he must also recognize that he is not just a helpless victim or a powerless observer.

He has a responsibility, both to himself and others, and he must learn to interpret his experience differently, so that he can find his own inner power and personal capacity to effect lasting change. In late second stage he may have learned to contract emotionally and retreat into himself in order to protect himself from the negativity which surrounded him. Now he must consider, in theory at least, his mental responsibility in creating his own conditions, and begin to look always for the larger picture, the higher answer. He must expand his outlook, while simultaneously supporting and acknowledging himself.

Many of the changes which take place during the second/third-stage transition of any sign are accomplished as the individual learns to observe his or her habitual patterns of thought, and determination to transform his old way of approaching himself and the outside world. Libra must learn to value himself and his inner feelings once again, so that he can gradually release the internal pressure cooker, and learn to feel his anger without acting on it in a negative fashion. At the same time, he must avoid feeding negative energy back into his psyche in a way which will only fill the pot up once again.

By constantly seeking the larger picture, and by continually choosing to see all life as one, the Libran begins to access the truly spiritual aspects of himself and so loses his initial feeling of powerlessness. Spiritual power can accomplish what political or "personality" power never could. Libra nears the fulfillment of the third stage when he learns to allow a higher power to work through him to accomplish whatever social changes the soul may deem necessary.

Another important key to the transition between the second and third stages of Libra involves developing the self-knowledge which will allow him to resurrect his own unique powers of self-expression. Personal identity may be largely lost by the time he enters the second/third stage of his development. Because he has spent so many lifetimes focused upon the needs and desires of others, he did not have full opportunity to develop a true sense of self. Whatever small sense of identity he did possess was often shattered by the abusive relationships of second stage.

As soon as he is able to overcome his karmic attachment to negative forms of relationship and environment, he begins an extremely important phase of his development. At times choosing personal solitude but at other times often accompanied by a highly supportive mate whose assistance he has more than earned through the gifts he has given in past relationships, he retreats into a harmonious environment, where he can fully restore himself. In order to attain greater strength of character, Libra builds a stone wall about a beautiful garden and begins to discover who he is and where his true ideals and talents lie. He needs to be completely free from all external demands for a time, so that he can learn to follow the dictates of his inner being. He needs ample time and unconditional support while he explores his talents and interests and heals the last remaining wounds of second stage. He may require some encouragement in order to learn how to relate to himself, and to discover what his needs and personal strengths actually are, rather than succumbing to the temptation of pleasing others in the hopes that they will provide him with the personal fulfillment which he seeks.

The more he discovers who he is and what he truly stands for as an individual, the more confidence and inner stature he assumes. He learns that the world does not come to an end when he chooses to do what pleases him, rather than adapting to the demands and desires of others. He achieves the ability to express perfect balance in all of his relationships — both public and private. Once his true strengths as an individual have been discovered and resurrected, he is ready to leave the confines of his personal retreat and step into the world at large to share his message with others. Finally able to fulfill his true soul purpose, he passes into the third stage.

Third Stage

By third stage, the Libran is fully equipped for the fulfillment of his soul purpose. He understands himself to be an agent for the higher forces of social welfare and natural order. Saturn, the planet of responsibility, finds its highest expression in Libra. The third-stage Libran serenely surrenders to his or her role of natural responsibility within the larger community. Having experienced first hand the utter folly of attempting to fulfill or cater to the personal whims of isolated individuals, he is now free to listen uncompromisingly to the law of his own inner being. In doing so, he knows exactly his rightful place within the greater scheme of things.

No challenge is too large or too small, for he knows and understands the value and importance of all things, and realizes that of his own accord he can do nothing, but that the power which he may allow to move through him is truly invincible. He will instinctively act to provide the people with the teachings or concrete transformations which are timely to their needs. Like most third-stage individuals, he may lead a retiring life, allowing the people to come to him and be transformed as they will. Alternatively, he may assume a public role, perhaps appearing to enforce his understanding upon the world. In reality he is only acting as an agent for a higher force which spontaneously comes into operation as the hour of transformation nears.

He is content to be alone, for he is at last strong and self-sufficient. Nor is he ever truly alone, for he almost certainly experiences a deep feeling of oneness with all kingdoms of life, both seen and unseen. Yet third-stage Librans are still seldom completely solitary individuals, for their purpose is to demonstrate right relationships, often on many levels; and so the divine institution of marriage (spiritual if not necessarily legal), is often an important vehicle for the expression of their purpose. They most likely experience the profound support of their life partner as they go about the business of fulfilling their purpose within the larger community.

Libra is the sign of the harvest. Archetypally it represents a time of the year when the bounty has been collected, and the community pauses to share in celebration, during one of the most beautiful periods of the year. The harvest must be fairly shared, and there is time to spend with those we love, and to consider the needs of the less fortunate. It is quite clearly an image of fulfillment and perfection.

Every Libran holds within his or her soul this image of completion, beauty and harmony. In early third stage this may make him something of a perfectionist, overwhelmed with the power of his social mission. As he progresses, he will release even this; as he grows toward a deep capacity to trust in the way of all things. Simply doing his part, large or small, he helps to bring in the harvest which he knows shall in time feed the whole of mankind.

Libra at the Crossroads
First/Third-Stage Transition

Except in very old souls the first stage of any sign represents a natural state of innocence concerning the self and its patterns of personal development. Second stage generally tends to represent a state of somewhat willful ignorance concerning the self, as well as embodying a certain lack of desire or ability to take personal responsibility for the course of one's own life experience. Third stage is the only stage when an individual can truly be said to be consciously responsible for himself and his own life, and truly conscious of the greater reality which surrounds him.

Because innocence can lead to enlightenment without requiring ignorance as part of its path to fulfillment, every individual is offered the opportunity to sit at the crossroads at some point in the first/second-stage transition. If the individual continues to take a completely subjective approach to his or her life — following the path of least resistance — he will inevitably fall gradually into the illusions of second stage. Only if he maintains a constant vigil over himself, reminding himself to remain aware of his feelings and choices, will he be able to grab hold of the opportunities for self-awareness which are always presented at this stage. The first/third-stage transition begins very much like the second/third-stage transition, in that much of the wisdom which the individual encounters tends to be new, frightening and perhaps overwhelming. A second/third-stage individual is highly motivated to make use of this opportunity, for he or she is usually experiencing a great deal of suffering for which he is desperate to find an answer. The first/second-stage individual is only beginning to taste pain, and can easily retreat from it, without making any lasting changes in his life or attitude, should he or she choose to do so. Therefore, to take up the opportunity to move from first into third stage requires a high degree of personal will and determination, coupled with an unusual degree of foresight.

Generally speaking, it is only the older souls who have the capacity to make this kind of shift, saving themselves lifetimes worth of suffering in the process. While younger souls can also complete the first/third-stage transition, it might not be in their best interests to do so, for the second stage is not necessarily the waste of time which it perhaps first appears to be. Only by passing through the kind of suffering and ignorance found in the second stage can we develop the depth of insight and compassion, as well as basic humility, required for the ultimate development of our true Self.

Older souls have passed through the second stage of many other signs, and so have already developed this kind of understanding on a soul level. For them the first/third-stage transition represents a challenge to the cultivation and maintenance of true awareness. At this point in their development it becomes important to learn not to fall asleep in preparation for the responsibility of embodying their own eternal being.

For Libra, the crossroads may first be encountered as the individual begins to experience interest in the world beyond his own immediate family and surroundings. He begins to feel restless and is attracted, literally or symbolically, away from what seems like a simple rural setting toward the complexities of town life and the larger civilization of which he or she is a part. He begins to become attracted to individuals who do not relate to others or accept intimacy easily, and who may live in this greater, more complex and imbalanced, outer world.

At the same time this individual will find himself increasingly aware of certain social issues. Just coming out of the first stage of Libra, this individual tends to wear his heart upon his sleeve, and possesses an innocent sort of wisdom concerning right relationship in all of its forms. It is very easy for him to see what is wrong with society, and to do so in a non-judgmental manner, which is almost impossible for the late second stage or second/third-stage

Libran to do. First/third-stage Libra has not lost any of his or her idealism, and could easily commit to the dream of social change, were it not for one very large stumbling block—lack of personal ego strength.

The first stage of Libra is generally spent developing relationship skills, often at the expense of acquiring a sense of independence or awareness of one's own true individuality. As you may recall from our study of first/second and second-stage Libra, this individual is often attracted to the tall, dark and turbulent stranger, because he unconsciously interprets this individual's fear of intimacy as a form of ego strength which he wishes to emulate or absorb. He may fear that he will not have the necessary strength as an individual to begin to serve the collective in the manner in which his soul prompts him. And so he compensates by attempting to lose himself in this relationship, which appears so tempting. Most Librans fall beneath the surface and do not return.

However an individual in the first/third-stage transition who faces the crossroads will be given ample opportunity to see what it is that he is actually doing. First of all, if he is an older soul he will be unconsciously inclined to take larger leaps, and will therefore choose a partner with more severe problems relating, whereas a younger soul may choose someone who in all likelihood will be easier to reach. When the crossroads opens, the Libran will be able to see that he has chosen his relationship irrationally, and that it is unlikely to provide him with any form of lasting personal fulfillment. Yet, having experienced no hard knocks in life, and still filled with a great deal of vitality and an instinctive desire to know more of life, this individual will nonetheless be sorely tempted to see if he or she can meet the challenge.

If this individual is going to master the riddle of the crossroads, he must learn that this desire to be challenged is in part a desire for the personal strength which he could apply to the fulfillment of his social purpose. He can stumble about for lifetimes in an unconscious attempt to acquire these strengths, or he can begin now to apply himself consciously to the task of developing the strengths which will prepare him for his ultimate path of service. He can choose a path which will at first be terrifying in its immensity, as he steps forward into the unknown; or he can follow the path of least resistance as it leads him into a constant struggle for a union which will seldom ultimately be found.

If he succeeds in pulling himself away from what for him would eventually be destructive forms of relationship, his next step will be that of learning how to become a practical working partner with the forces of human evolution which wish to use him as their spokesperson to help to serve the cause of right relationship within the human world.

Having lived in an inner world of perfect harmony, and having experienced an early life of nearly perfect harmony (usually lived in relatively natural surroundings), this individual will be inclined to possess the great gift of trust. This ability to trust includes not only a spontaneous acceptance of most other human beings, but also extends into the natural world, endowing the Libran with a great feeling of oneness with the life which surrounds him. It is this spontaneous innate union with nature which first/third-stage Libra can draw upon in order to align more fully with his or her inner voice and gain, borrow or inherit strength thereby.

Libra's most natural tendency is to seek union, and at this stage of his development, he would be best served by seeking it first within himself. Listening to the voice of the wind, he will learn to unite with spirit, beginning to achieve the inner marriage with his true self which speaks to him of his ultimate destiny within the course of human evolution.

At the end of first stage he seeks a more challenging lifestyle and a new and larger experience of love. This need can be fulfilled by embracing the adventure of the larger life, dedicating himself to the cause which is dearest to his heart. He can dedicate himself to his dreams and let them live through him; for not only will he go astray if he attempts to go forward under his own power alone, he knows before he even starts that he does not possess the necessary strength to be able to do so. At this stage of his development, this individual needs to learn how to trust the process of life, and to learn to think big, while allowing his larger thoughts to take on a constructive life of their own, through which he can be guided, and from which he can draw strength.

The individual who fears to take this larger step will inevitably follow the slow and winding path of least resistance into the second stage, where he subconsciously believes he will be free from the responsibilities of his calling. However, nothing could be further from the truth, for this individual will face the same challenges in his personal life as he would otherwise have faced in the outer world. The only difference being that these challenges will be more hidden, more subtle and, for the older soul at least, slower to resolve, more complicated and painful. Nor can the soul who is truly called upon to conquer the challenge of this crossroads (and it is very important to remember that some are not) avoid this responsibility by crying indecisively, "I don't know what it is that I'm supposed to do!" For Libra is the sign of love, and there is always some aspect of life which this individual loves above all else.

Although the first inward step into the great unknown must be taken alone, he certainly need not undertake his greater quest in total isolation. Once the inner commitment to his cause has been made, he may find himself naturally a part of some larger group, all joining together to call upon the archetypal mind, perhaps with himself as their sometimes unwitting child-like leader. He is certainly capable of uniting with a cause which reflects his own natural idealism and innate purity of being.

Having pulled himself away from the temptations inherent in second stage, he need not sacrifice any intimate contact. The crossroads may present him with a soul with whom he has experienced deep intimate union in previous incarnations—otherwise known as a soul mate. This individual is usually in the second/third or third stage of development in his or her respective Sun sign, and may provide increased motivation to seek the high road into third stage. Life does not require the Libran individual to experience conflict and difficulty in his or her personal relationships. Instead, if he chooses the path into third stage, he will in time find someone to share the dream with and may also discover a group of individuals to share in his purpose.

Will is necessary in order not to fall into temptation. Faith is necessary in order to take up the banner, knowing that "It is not I that holds this banner but the Mother and

Father within me." This understanding having been won, serenity and completion are assured. From this point on, the Libran will be taught to develop personal strength by the Divine Source itself, which will then be able to use this individual as an exceedingly pure vehicle for the fulfillment of Divine Purpose. The Libran soul possesses the inherent ability to achieve Divine Union without having ever fully experienced separation.

Childhood Conditions and Relationship Patterns

The first-stage Libran is commonly born into a large family, closely knit tribe or small community. His early environment may be prosperous on many levels, and is certain to demonstrate strong values of interpersonal loyalty and family unity. While there may be difficult or negative events surrounding him in the world outside of his personal paradise, the trials and injustices of life seem to always pass him by. His early upbringing develops his idealistic nature, and gives him a strong love of justice and fair play. The ideals born in these early first-stage environments will never entirely leave him, and he will carry the dreams born during these early days with him throughout the many lifetimes to come.

Unlike most other signs, Libra is likely to be almost equally influenced by both parents. Despite this, he is likely to feel closer in spirit to his father than to his mother. In first stage he generally idealizes his father. He sees his father as a person who works in some way for the good of his community, and who stands for the values which inspire his Libran offspring who dreams of growing up to be just like his father.

Libra gains his philosophical and intellectual ideals from his father. Through his mother, he develops his emotional responses to life. His mother reacts more emotionally to life than does his father. In first stage she is strongly affected by her interpersonal relationships. It is from his mother that Libra acquires his romantic nature. The relationship between the mother and father is likely to be almost ideal, and it is as a result of their example that the

Libran is able to choose a highly compatible life partner.

While Libra admires his father and generally has greater respect for him than he or she does for his mother, he is likely to experience a bond of close friendship with his mother. She tends to relate to her child as an equal, relating to him at times as her closest confidante, instead of always adhering to the traditional parent/child model of relationship. As a result, he learns at an early age to relate consciously to another individual, cultivating strong social skills, when he should perhaps be exploring and developing his own individual identity. When he grows up he seeks a similar close bond with a partner whom he can emotionally support and be supported by.

By the time he reaches the first/second-stage transition, it is no wonder that he has become bored with all of the harmony and oneness which he has experienced, and that he comes to long for greater challenges. He does not realize how rare the opportunities which he has had actually are. And so he leaves his peaceful paradise behind to come to an understanding of the purpose of conflict.

As he enters second stage his desire to challenge himself and to share his knowledge of relationships cause him to be attracted to parents whose marital relationship is deeply troubled. He often finds himself in the position of family mediator. He longs for harmony in his environment, but may experience only strife. His desire to see his parents achieve a peaceful union is played out in his adult relationships, as he chooses an incompatible mate, subconsciously hoping that by achieving union and triumphing over all difficulty he can leave behind the scars of his childhood.

Whether he is born into first or second stage, his early environment over-emphasizes relationship. In first stage there is so much emphasis on harmony and togetherness that it is not always easy for Libra to develop a personal identity of his own. Instead he focuses upon pleasing others, which it is easy for him to do in such a nurturing environment. In second stage there is too much conflict for him to have the time to know himself. He is either trying to fix things, or running for cover.

In second stage he may have to grow up too soon, and take on too many responsibilities before he has had the opportunity to spontaneously discover who he is. He feels that he instinctively understands certain things about relationships and could help his parents, if only they would listen to him. He tries to find ways to make peace. Although this teaches him a great deal about human nature, which may become useful to him in his later years, he will generally find it to be a thankless task at the time. Each of his parents may attempt to get him "on their side", and their manipulative tendencies may cause him to feel that he is being torn in two. Alternatively they may neglect him, being too busy with their own problems to form a proper relationship with him. They push him away and want to be left alone.

Some Librans have spent so many lifetimes trying to please everybody that in second stage they find themselves with a demanding parent or parents who are almost impossible to please. His parent(s) do not allow him to act naturally. They want him to be something that he is not -- to act in accordance with their image of the perfect world, the perfect child, the properly functioning family. In essence he must subscribe to their idea of what creates perfect harmony. This kind of early experience will either set him up to be easily dominated by others, or it will prompt him to seek his own sense of individuality and not be so ready to surrender his own opinions for the sake of maintaining external harmony.

In late second stage or early second/third stage it is common for Libra to experience a great deal of conflict with one of his or her parents. For the male Libran the conflict is usually with the mother, for the female it can be either the mother or the father. This conflict corresponds to Libra's tendency to experience conflict with a love partner. The conflicts with the more difficult parent are likely to be reflected in the individual's adult relationships. Sometimes Libra will experience a difficult relationship with their more dominant parent and a more harmonious relationship with their more submissive parent. In second/third stage they will experience difficult relationships which conform to the pattern set by their relationship with the dominant parent, and as they begin to change their patterns of intimate relationship they will find themselves attracted to partners who express many of the traits of their less dominant parent.

Third-stage Librans are once again born into a harmoniously functioning family situation. Instead of expressing unconscious harmony, this family is consciously aware of the principles which create a well functioning whole. The relationship between the parents is mature and creative. The entire family is taught to relate consciously without losing their integrity as individuals. Independence and interdependence are encouraged — dependency is not. The family has a strong social conscience and encourages the young Libran to be true to his ideals.

Famous Librans

First Stage: Linda McCartney, Julie Andrews.
Second Stage: Britt Ekland, Oscar Wilde, Bruce Springsteen, Lenny Bruce, Arthur Miller, Charlie Brown.
Second/Third Stage: Bob Geldof, Peter Gabriel, Alistair Crowley, Confucius.
Third Stage: John Lennon, Margaret Thatcher, Bishop Desmond Tutu, Jimmy Carter, Lech Walesa, Mahatma Gandhi.
First/Third Stage: Eleanor Roosevelt.

SCORPIO
divine will

Astrology has always considered Scorpio to be a fixed water sign. Fixed signs are stubborn and enduring. Water signs place great emphasis upon their feelings. Scorpio begins by pursuing her desires with stubborn emotional intensity, and ends by transcending her lower emotions in an enduring manner. Because water is considered a feminine element, I use the terms "she", "her" and "hers" in this chapter as neutral terms which can apply to either gender.

No one has stronger, more insistent desires than Scorpio. Her soul has a strong desire to move the world forward in some manner. She may possess special talents and a karmic tie with a certain culture, nation or cause. Her love for her highest ideals is so strong that she may feel sent to Earth by God Herself. In a sense this is true of all of us, but no one knows this more profoundly than a Scorpio, whose soul purpose is to become an expression of Divine Will on Earth.

Readers should note in this and other chapters I occasionally refer to God as "He". This is only because most of the individuals in our society at this time refer to "Her" as such. Personally I tend to see Divinity as 'That", "It", "Us" and/or "He and She". We make God in our own image, and "He" is usually quite happy to respond, regardless of whatever 'handle' we may personally choose to use.

First Stage

Here is an individual who knows exactly what she wants, where she wants to be, and what it is that must be done. She is uncompromisingly dedicated to her purpose. Early in life she realizes her chosen goal, and marshals all of her resources in the pursuit of it. She may perhaps seem self-centered and ruthless to the casual observer, but in reality she is completely dedicated to some cause which goes beyond herself and her own personal concerns. She feels that her purpose, because of its potential effect upon so many important areas of life, must be of more value than just the petty concerns and feelings of any one individual, herself included. Therefore she possesses complete and undaunted courage in the pursuit of her ideals.

She cares deeply for life, and for those things which are important to her, and will do everything in her power to ensure that her purpose is fulfilled. In early first stage, she is strong, courageous and confident. She may be seen as arrogant. What others perceive as arrogance or pride is in reality a kind of instinct which this individual possesses and appears larger than life; for the concerns which she serves are certainly in their own way also larger than life. In essence she is putting on a show before the opposition, as she enters life's arena wearing all the necessary battle regalia. Her show is really only for herself, to assist in maximizing her own strength and courage.

Consciously or unconsciously, she feels imbued with divine purpose, and symbolically seems to have come from a spiritual world, the home or abode of God, into this material world, which is bereft of the blessings of spirit. She is like a one-woman army in the battle to enhance or defend what she sees as being of most value here upon Earth. Although most coffee-table astrology books tend to paint Scorpio as a bad guy, in reality this is far from being the case. This individual seeks to be a force for good, and has a horror of causing harm to anyone. Unfortunately she tends to play for large stakes. Her greatest challenge occurs when she encounters an obstacle to the fulfillment of her purpose which comes in the form of other individuals.

Because her commitment is often to a larger purpose or principle, the fulfillment of which will affect the fate of many, she may feel that there is no other choice but to deal with this obstacle in whatever manner may seem necessary. This may ultimately require her to make a decision which will lead to the harm or suffering of another individual or individuals. She feels that she has no other choice, and that she is actually choosing the lesser of two evils.

Each situation she is called upon to decide the fate of another seems an isolated event, and she responds to it as such. At first she has regrets, but she is able to leave them behind after a short time and continue forward. She may achieve a great deal of success in her chosen field, and yet may fail to fulfill her goals to the extent that she deems necessary. In time she begins to have subtle doubts about her ability to fulfill those things which she feels to be her true responsibility.

After a series of lifetimes, her doubts begin to nag her constantly. She feels that she has given her all, and yet has failed somehow to attain a complete conquest. Her self-worth is now in jeopardy. Her standards for herself and her desire to give to the world are so great that she threatens to crush herself under their burden. Her conscience is powerfully developed; as she looks behind herself and sees the long string of bodies, which she had previously tried to ignore, she begins to wonder if it was all worth it. Others have suffered because of her. Did she make the right decisions? Or was it all in vain. The question of her ultimate responsibility in these situations begins to haunt her.

Her fears may eventually come to overwhelm her, causing her to pass early into second stage with all of her ideals and standards intact. Or, in her horror of ultimate judgment, she may choose to run from this day of reckoning. Secretly she feels that she is unworthy, almost as though she has failed God. She did not fully achieve her purpose, and she has harmed others in the process. She is haunted by the waste. As she continues to run from the real truth of the situation, she will imagine for herself an image of a judgmental God. This process may be conscious or unconscious. She believes herself to be bad in the eyes of this God and, still struggling against ultimate judgment, chooses to pit her strength against it. She tells herself that she can somehow triumph over fate, and that her own personal will ultimately has more power than any force of good. Certainly her own good intentions seem to have failed time and time again, or so it seems to her. If she cannot be good at being good, perhaps she can excel at being bad.

She may use her powerful will to go about the process of fulfilling only her own personal desires in as sumptuous a manner as possible, while painting herself as a romantic sort of "bad guy". If because of past subconscious guilt, she believes herself to be somehow innately bad, she decides that she is now going to do a good job of it and be "damn bad". She almost makes a cartoon character of herself, and may be a somewhat self-centered individual who simply plays at being bad. Or she may become genuinely ruthless and destructive, attempting to annihilate anything which serves or symbolizes "goodness", for it seems to represent symbolic proof of her own failure to achieve the fulfillment of her ideals.

She may seek fame and worldly power as a substitute for true accomplishment; wealth and pleasure to compensate for a lack of true fulfillment. Whatever she does will only delay the final judgment. She can stay in first stage for as long as she chooses, but eventually her self-created haven will turn into a meaningless purgatory at which point she will find that she must go forward. She may choose to live without conscience, and can do so, for she is a powerful individual. However, conscience, while it can be silenced, will never die. Eventually she must face herself in the guise of her own judge and jury, and catching the course of her evolution as it reaches high tide, she must move on to the crossroads or make the transition into second stage.

First/Second-Stage Transition

There are essentially two different types of first/second-stage Scorpio. The first maintains a strong sense of purpose, but as she draws near to the end of first stage she becomes increasingly frantic and ruthless in the pursuit of its fulfillment. She feels the hour of greatest opportunity drawing to a close without the goal having been reached. Frantically she begins stepping on more and more toes. She is less content to do so than ever, but still continues to tell herself that it is indeed a necessary evil. Unfortunately, no one can live in a whirlwind forever, and in her quieter moments she feels profound regret stealing over her like a cloud. At last she grows tired and succumbs to the abyss of self-doubt, which has been gradually growing in the hidden recesses of her mind.

At this point she may continue for a time as though nothing has happened. Her life activities remain the same, but beneath it all she realizes that she no longer likes herself very much. The spark has gone out of her life. She is no longer a being of confidence and effect. Instead she begins to turn her once great powers in upon herself. Whatever her outer accomplishments may be, she feels that they are not enough. Certainly they do not justify the suffering she believes that she has caused in the process of attempting their achievement.

In her guilt and self-loathing she may destroy herself. She may simply lose her will to live and allow outer forces to overwhelm and dominate her to the point of extinction. She may end her life dramatically and suddenly through accident, suicide or violence at the hands of another. It is also possible that her self-destruction will be slow and agonizing. She may take action unconsciously for the purpose of destroying her personal life and worldly happiness. She may destroy herself financially, emotionally or physically through habits, addictions or impulses stemming from her conscious or unconscious self-hatred and her need to escape the pain of being herself. Of course, in trying to escape her pain, she almost certainly brings even more ruin down upon herself. This may seem to make no sense at all, but somehow the outer pain lessens the effect of the inner pain, for none could judge her as harshly as she does herself.

It may be interesting to note at this point, that many Scorpios have walked quite lightly through the world during the first stage of their development as compared to certain natives of the other 11 signs in their first and second stages. While some Scorpios are truly evil in their life-expression towards the end of first stage, many are simply highly idealistic and truly regret being an agent of suffering on any level.

The second path through this transition leads, unfortunately, to the same place. The starting point is all that differs. This kind of Scorpio has usually strongly resisted the transition before it came. She has lost her ideals, and has tried, perhaps quite successfully, to achieve great heights of destruction. At the very least she has lived a self-centered and self-indulgent life. This individual will go through the first/second-stage transition with the blinders firmly on. She will remain egotistical, self-centered and perhaps destructive, and yet from an unconscious level there comes a backlash.

She will find that wherever she turns, life somehow seems mysteriously intent upon giving her a very hard time. She attracts negative attention from those around her. Like her more conscious brother or sister mentioned above, she may find herself compelled towards certain self-destructive actions. She does not understand their source, and may not even acknowledge their presence. Slowly but surely, they will drag her beneath the surface of the water.

As the first/second-stage transition nears the end, Scorpio succeeds in completely annihilating her old sense of self. Her personal will, and the ability to know herself or create anything of lasting value has more than likely been completely destroyed. Poor Scorpio. Guilt, regret and feelings of failure are her traveling companions now. And it is with this load upon her shoulders that she enters the second stage.

Second Stage

An individual born into the second stage of Scorpio lives a life which is almost completely dominated by her self-destructive unconscious motivations. Eventually the urge to destroy the self will develop into an urge to transform and regenerate the self. Until this time, the road ahead is almost certain to be long and difficult, fraught with much fear and uncertainty.

Consciously or unconsciously, an individual entering into the second stage of Scorpio will have made a series of key decisions. She is likely to feel that she may lack certain essential qualities. Had she possessed these mysterious capabilities, she feels that this would have guaranteed the success of her soul purpose. Secretly she feels inherently unworthy, and may be consumed with frustration and self-loathing. If she became 'evil for evil's sake' during the latter part of the first stage, it was probably at least partly due to the fear that she lacked the essential power to achieve her true purpose. This underlying fear is what may lead to power hunger and cruelty in first stage.

The second-stage individual is consumed with regret at her actions of the past and will not allow these frustrations to be directed outwards. Instead, they are directed at the self. The tremendous burden of guilt which the second-stage Scorpio carries constantly expresses itself as a deep-seated need to pay for the suffering which she may have caused. She also desires to avoid causing future harm of any kind to any individual, other than herself.

Scorpios sit in condemnation of themselves more than almost any other sign during second stage. And whatever their crimes of the past may be, to this individual they seem to be perfectly heinous. No one has a spotlessly clean karmic record, nor is anyone meant to have, for it is only through error that we grow. Yet I have seen other Sun signs carry with them the glow of pride concerning their ill-doings in either past or present lives; while Scorpio, who may have one tenth the number of black marks upon the book of life, seems consciously or unconsciously unable to forgive herself.

This individual feels the need to pay, and pay in spades she does. The desire in their nature, through being honed and intensified in first stage, has created tremendous unconscious force, and now in second stage these same unconscious powers draw doom and destruction to this individual. Second-stage Scorpios are often the victims of violence, mindless destruction or freak accidents. They are subject to loss, plague, pestilence and betrayal. In addition, as second stage progresses, these individuals usually have no idea how it is they manage to draw these kinds of events and situations to themselves. First-stage Scorpios often feel that they must fulfill their purpose regardless of the cost to themselves. This pattern may continue into second stage, causing much suffering to the individual who must always end up paying the highest price in the process of helping her ideals to see fruition.

And so they suffer. But it is not enough. And so, unconsciously they feel that they must pay the ultimate price, and they do this through denying themselves the most precious thing in life which, of course, is love. Everywhere they go, second-stage Scorpios are rejected. They may choose parents who cannot love them, or who leave them abandoned through death or neglect. When they grow up they fall in love with those who will hurt or leave them. They attract abusive relationships.

Poor Scorpio. If only they could forgive themselves. The only problem is that, as their lifetimes progress, they usually become quite unaware of the massive amounts of guilt and self-hatred which they do in fact carry. It seems to them as though a mindlessly insane Universe is somehow bent upon their annihilation. And it would succeed, were they not so tough. The patterns experienced during second-stage Scorpio would certainly destroy an individual of any other sign!

To pay is one thing—to avoid further harm is quite another. Unconsciously this individual does not really trust herself. Because she has lost confidence in her ability to fulfill her quest or ultimate soul purpose, this purpose begins unconsciously to be associated with the ability to bring harm to others. If she had not been so determined to achieve her goals in the past, no one would have been hurt. And so, to prevent the unthinkable, her purpose must now be sabotaged.

This may take several forms. Some second-stage Scorpios are born with a vague feeling that there is something important that they must do, but they are never able to discover what that something may be. What you do not know cannot hurt you—or in this case anyone else. They wander vaguely through life, seemingly irresponsible, seeking answers that will not come. In other cases the individual knows exactly what it is that she truly dreams of, but try as she might, she finds that she is unable to accomplish it. One insurmountable obstacle after another rises up to sabotage the best laid plans. No matter how competent this individual may be, her dreams seem to always end in ruins.

Late second stage is seldom a picnic for most individuals of any given sign, but in Scorpio the suffering involved often seems to enter into the realm of the ridiculous. Scorpios are usually very strong people, and so most manage to survive. Eventually, however, even they must become exhausted and desperate to put an end to their unfathomable difficulties. When they decide that they simply must find a way to save themselves, and that truth must be found regardless of the misgivings or resistances of the individual, then they will enter the transition into the third stage.

Second/Third-Stage Transition

In order to resurrect herself, this individual must learn first of all to be gentle with herself. Usually Scorpios are quite unaware of how hard they actually are on themselves. They do not realize the power of their tendency to choose the difficult path through life, and are largely unaware of the ways in which they tend to berate themselves internally, demanding perfection and practicing self-condemnation whenever a mistake is made. It is a good idea for them to learn to watch their daily habits of thought and action, so that they can learn to cultivate new mental habits which are more nurturing to themselves.

Scorpios emerging from second stage contain powerful subconscious patterns of self-condemnation and self-destruction. These old, firmly entrenched subconscious currents surface into consciousness on a more or less steady basis. These patterns create the semi-conscious habits of negative self-esteem which Scorpios carry around, often without consciously realizing it. As far as they are concerned, they are hungry for fulfillment and for self-actualization. Choosing to form new habits on a conscious level will gradually begin to transform their old destructive subconscious habits.

Subconscious habits are built in one of two ways. The first of these is repetition, the second is emotional intensity. The pattern of self-destruction which Scorpio brings into second stage is born of intense feelings of guilt, regret and self-loathing. Over time this pattern is re-enforced through repetitive acts of internal self-judgment. There are also two ways to dismantle destructive subconscious patterns. One is to experience a flash of Divine Grace, which will be discussed below, the other is to reinforce a completely new pattern through acts of mental and physical repetition.

This second technique obviously takes longer to create a lasting effect, but it is usually the essential first step due to the fact that it assists the individual in achieving a greater degree of self-awareness. Developing the habit of watching our daily acts of thought and attention is an important step for individuals who are involved in the process of making the transition between the second and third stages of any given sign. At first, most people are inclined to dismiss the importance and value of doing so. For Scorpio it is essential to observe the inner attitude towards oneself, with a determination to reverse any destructive, demanding or self-judgmental behavior which may be discovered.

They must learn to be extremely kind to themselves under <u>all</u> circumstances. Negative thoughts and feelings directed towards the self need to be discovered and replaced with thoughts of nurturing compassion. A good example of the attitude towards the self which needs to be cultivated is expressed in the following situation which occurred when my older son (who has a Scorpio ascendant) was about three years old.

The two of us were grocery shopping one day when he discovered an enormous bottle of catsup on a shelf which he could just barely reach. Its size was fascinating to a child of that age, and so he reached up to attempt a closer examination. However, he was unable to maintain a firm grip on such a large object, and the bottle plunged to the floor and shattered.

"I hate myself now," he said, as he ran to hide behind me.

I told him that this was definitely not the time to hate himself, that at a time like this he needed to be his own best friend, and he sheepishly emerged from behind my leg. He was able to release himself from his automatic impulse to condemn himself, and we went on our way.

He was fortunate enough to have an understanding parent (at least in that situation) who could teach him how to relate constructively to himself on an emotional level. Scorpios entering second/third stage are seldom so fortunate. More commonly they experience parents who are just as condemning towards them as they are towards themselves, for such is the karma which they have created. To transform this karmic situation, they need to learn to 're-parent' themselves, and to develop the attitude of being their own best friend no matter what. This does not excuse them from taking responsibility for their own actions—the catsup must still be paid for—but it gradually begins to transform the deeper levels of their being, slowly dissolving those subconscious patterns which tend to attract destruction, rejection and obstruction into their lives.

Self-forgiveness and compassion for self are essential. In order to exercise these qualities with maximum effectiveness, they need to be applied to the individual's past as well as to her present. This may involve going through memories of the present lifetime and releasing guilt or self-judgment, by understanding that they were always doing the best that they could, at their stage of development.

Exercises which assist this individual to remember past life events can also be of great value. If the individual can recall her late first-stage and first/second-stage lifetimes in a spirit of compassion, this may enable her to discover the original source of the pattern of self judgment which she has been carrying with her ever since. Now that she is a somewhat older soul, it may be possible for her to view herself through different eyes. She may finally understand the forces which drove her, so that she can release old feelings of guilt. It will be of value for her to understand the positive nature of her own original intentions and to realize that she had never originally meant to cause anyone any harm. If a more complete series of memories can be recovered, this individual may also come to see that she has usually caused herself to suffer far more than she had ever caused others to, so that by now the debt has been more than repaid.

This earthly life is meant for self-development and self-actualization, and in order to reach our highest potentials, we must all start out as bumbling infants. We are _meant_ to make a mess of our playpens at first. It is the only way to learn certain essential life lessons. Not only are we meant to make a mess at first, we all also volunteer to take our share of lumps in the process. It is part of the larger game. Anyone who was harmed through the past actions of a Scorpio underwent such an experience as a part of their own path of development, and possibly also as a result of their own individual imbalances. The Divine Source, which sent Scorpio here in order to fulfill a certain purpose, watches all of us with incredible compassion—victim and apparent victimizer alike. To fulfill her life purpose, the Scorpio individual needs to learn to view all of life, including herself, through the very same eyes.

This awareness is not an excuse to return to the tendencies of first stage or late first-stage Scorpio, where the individual attempted to achieve her goals or desires regardless of the effect which her actions may have had on others. Instead the individual is now ready to operate from a much higher level of understanding. She is now ready to live according to the law of faith.

Faith is the second key to the transition between the second and third stages of Scorpio. In fact, if the individual had understood the true power of faith during the first stage of her development, she would not have taken any actions which she would later have come to regret. Her original error was her belief that she was here to achieve some important purpose by the power of her own unaided personality alone. When this was not possible, she felt like a worthless failure. In actual fact she was never meant to go it alone. She did not leave a spiritual world to come to a material world. All worlds are spiritual, and the Divine Presence has been with her always. This presence has been waiting for her to realize that her true purpose is to allow it to act through her. This can only be achieved through faith.

As Scorpio moves through the second/third-stage transition, she usually comes to learn certain spiritual principles. Until she understands certain aspects of Divine Law, she is inclined to be very skeptical. She does not like to trust to the unknown, because her life has been very painful and the stakes seem too high to leave anything to chance. And yet it is common for her to encounter obstacles in her life which cannot be overcome without Divine assistance. When she learns to understand that spirit is the greatest power, and that its principles can always be trusted to act in the highest good of all concerned, she is ready to look at these obstacles as potentially fruitful challenges. When she learns that the power of trust can bring about the necessary changes in her own life, then she is ready to teach others how to literally move mountains.

Faith and self-forgiveness are the two necessary keys to overcoming the riddles of the second/third-stage transition. These two qualities can be learned in any order. Eventually they must co-exist and support one another. Self-forgiveness cannot be fully achieved without Divine assistance—Scorpio's guilt patterns are too deeply rooted. Without a certain amount of self-forgiveness, the individual is incapable of believing that she actually deserves to receive Divine Grace.

Sometimes the only way for Scorpios to save themselves and to emerge from the painful circumstances in which they find themselves is to serve some greater altruistic purpose. Without something greater to dedicate themselves to, they simply may not feel that they are worth saving. They may have to save themselves for the sake of others. Perhaps their children rely upon them to emerge from their patterns of self-destruction. Perhaps they are able to re-discover some purpose which they seek to serve above all else, and realize that they must heal themselves in order to be fully worthy of the ideals which they seek to serve. Although the path which they must travel seems difficult at the best of times, and completely impossible at the worst of times, they have the strength to eventually emerge victorious. Having forgiven themselves and others, and having aligned themselves with the power of the infinite, they pass into the third stage.

Third Stage

The traditional symbol for the third stage of Scorpio is the eagle. The eagle flies above the Earth, her wings supported by the air currents she has learned to master. One meaning of the symbolism of air is the Life Breath—the Spiritual matter which permeates all things. Air is invisible, yet omnipresent in our environment. The Scorpion is the symbol for the first stage of Scorpio, and represents the soul's belief that she exists in a hostile desert-like world where she may be required to use her venom in order to survive. There she believes that she is alone, without any spiritual protection or assistance. By third stage she has learned to trust in the invisible, to learn to master it, so that it is able to uplift her, moving her beyond the earthly limitations to which most of us are subject.

The eagle has incredible powers of vision. From a great height, she can see the smallest object, descending almost instantaneously to capture a mouse which has made even the smallest movement. Eagles have been known to sit, resting in their perches, watching the sunspots dancing on the surface of the Sun. This is a potent symbol of the penetrating vision of third-stage Scorpios, who can see to the depths of any situation or individual. Their vision is as fearless as it is penetrating. They are capable of seeing the workings of spiritual law, which is invisible to others, or would prove too painful for most people to perceive. The

Sun is a symbol of the spiritual source of life, and the central laws of our solar system. Like the eagle they are capable of watching the interplay of these central forces.

The eagle is also a ruthless hunter, and when it is necessary the third-stage Scorpio can be uncompromisingly ruthless as well. However, she is never destructive. As a healer, or leader, or spiritual teacher, she knows when others require confrontation or challenge in order to move beyond their limitations. She is hard when it is necessary for her to be so.

However, she can also be incredibly gentle, and often possesses a very calming presence. This is another little known trait which she has in common with her animal symbol. Her strength is apparent to all who know her. Because she can see so clearly to the depth of their souls, she has complete unconditional acceptance of others. She is also very inspiring. She takes wing; she seems to do the impossible. Living by her powers of faith, her enthusiasm for life is highly contagious. Because she has accepted and forgiven herself, she is not vulnerable to the criticism or skepticism of others. She has been there, she understands them, and can smile acceptingly at their doubt. This means that they have no power to inspire doubt in her, and may find themselves transformed, seemingly in spite of themselves. Third-stage Scorpio never pushes these truths and transformations upon others. She simply goes about her business, following the dictates of her inner being, and life changes around her as a result. Of course I have been discussing the old soul in third stage. The young soul lives according to faith, and is self-accepting and humble at most times and truly compassionate towards others, but lacks the depth of vision and conscious spiritual power of the older, highly developed soul in third stage. Still she is a special individualwho brings many blessings with her wherever she may go.

Scorpio at the Crossroads
First/Third-Stage Transition

As the first stage nears its completion, Scorpio secretly begins to wonder if she is really a failure as an individual.

She may have achieved great things in the eyes of the world, but she may not have realized the things which she believes she ought to have accomplished. She may wake up one day to realize that she loathes herself for the lifestyle she has been living.

She may have a close friend or relative, or perhaps even a mate or a lover who is more mystically or philosophically inclined than she is. Or she may discover a new view of life through isolated self-analysis or a chance encounter. Something prompts her to reconsider her attitude towards life. It is extremely important that she find a way to avoid condemning herself.

Her self-loathing must be transformed into a desire to leave her old response to life behind forever. It is important for her to realize that she can never change her past. To hate herself or to feel excessive guilt will never help the situation. But if she begins living a new life now, positive contributions may be made through her which will more than make up for any past sins or omissions.

A religious or spiritual conversion is often part of the first/third-stage transition in Scorpio, for there is a tendency in these individuals to experience a sudden and dramatic change in their entire view of life. A sudden spiritual awakening allows her to fly above the desert world of the Scorpion, achieving empathy for herself and the faith and self-forgiveness necessary to enable her true purpose to begin to act through her.

She may then make a powerful impact upon the world almost immediately, for she does not have to deal with the tendency towards self suppression which is a part of the second stage. Her personality is powerful, and she surrenders this potent vehicle to a higher will, with often dramatic results. She may not quite possess the compassion of her third-stage brother or sister who has experienced the acute suffering of second stage. She knows how the impossible can be achieved, but sometimes she makes it look too easy, and may grow impatient with others who struggle under a greater burden than she has ever known. After her initial bout of enlightenment, she may still have periods when she attempts to impose her own personal will upon life, or when she may be tempted to take the crooked path in order to reach a certain destination more rapidly. However, in time these imbalances tend to correct themselves, as her vision and compassion expand to encompass the world.

Childhood Conditions and Relationship Patterns

Scorpio is the archetypal symbol of humanity's experience of separation from the Divine. Therefore it is no surprise that Scorpio's early life, in most stages, is characterized by experiences of separation or rejection. Powerful internal conflict often results from the upheavals which the individual experiences in her early home environment.

The early part of first stage may be less difficult. The family usually remains intact, although they may suffer due to external pressures. The father generally has a strong sense of purpose and instills feelings of honor and ambition in her offspring. The mother of a Scorpio has strong desires and a powerful will. She encourages her offspring to stick to their ideals and to follow up on their goals no matter what. She may expect them to be even more powerful than herself, often unconsciously hoping that young Scorpio will make up for all of her personal failings. She is strongly identified with her child, and young Scorpio may feel that she has no choice but to forge ahead. She cannot disappoint her parents, and besides, she is truly inspired by their example.

She may see her home as an oasis from a troubled world. The family does not have an easy life, and this makes it easy for her to acquire an unconscious belief that Divinity must be present elsewhere, and that It cannot be the ruling power of this world.

As first stage progresses, family tension and upheaval is likely to increase. It is common for the father to be absent as a result of death, divorce or separation. If she is present the child experiences very little personal involvement with her. Her physical or mental absence corresponds with Scorpio's increasing tendency to become alienated from her original feelings of idealism. Scorpio is a water sign. Water symbolizes the emotional nature. As cold and ruthless as some first-stage Scorpios can seem, they are primarily very emotional beings. Because the mother represents our first real emotional experience in life, she generally tends to be the dominant parent in Scorpio's childhood. With an absent father, this already powerful woman learns to take the reins with maximum intensity.

In first stage, the mother of a Scorpio child is invariably a tremendously powerful individual. She is either consciously or unconsciously destructive toward her child and those around her, or alternatively possesses great power to heal and transform others. The positive or negative nature of Scorpio's mother can also be associated with the amount of contact which Scorpio still has with her true soul ideals. Whether the mother's attitude towards life is positive or negative, she will almost certainly be very ruthless in her approach. Sometimes there is conflict between mother and child, often complicated by some form of disruption of the early bond between the two of them.

Scorpio's mother often has an aggressive and dominating nature. She tends to act on her emotions in an illogical and impetuous manner, and may fail to explain her actions to her child. Her behavior is a direct reflection of Scorpio's tendency to act upon her own convictions or desires without considering their effect on others.

Scorpio will react to the upheaval of her early experiences by developing a very rigid emotional nature. She will react with a fixed determination to enforce her will upon the world. In early first stage she tries to change the world for idealistic reasons. In later first stage she may be more concerned with surviving or achieving her desires despite the difficulties which she inevitably believes she must face. 'They' will never be allowed to get her. If need be, she will get them first. She may indulge her emotional nature, as her mother did, viewing this aspect of her being as her greatest strength.

It is also interesting to note how the child feels about her father's absence. If she blames her father for abandoning her, this is likely to correspond with a feeling that Divinity has abandoned her here upon this desert world. This may develop into an anger at God, which may cause her to overstay her welcome in first stage. To simply mourn the separation may indicate that her ideals will probably remain intact throughout first stage. Apathy and indifference most likely indicate that the individual feels little need for Divine contact. She has decided to be strong and to rely upon the power of her own personality to survive in life. Guilt indicates that the soul feels the Divine separation to be her fault, and that she may feel that some form of punishment is required in order to rectify matters. This latter response is more common in second stage or as the transition into second stage approaches.

As the transition into second stage begins, Scorpio may choose a mother who does not know how to nurture her, or may be born at a time when circumstances prevent her from properly doing so. If our mother is incapable of providing us with the unconditional love which should be the birthright of all, it is often an indication that the soul feels unworthy of or incapable of receiving this kind of unconditional support.

Sometimes a child born into the first/second-stage transition may choose a mother who is capable of giving her unconditional acceptance and who has herself developed at least a certain level of spiritual understanding. In this case, it is she who is presenting her with the crossroads. It is quite possible that Scorpio may reject a positive mother's influence upon her, at least initially, for she often feels that she does not deserve the love which she so badly needs. It may also be hard on her pride to admit how much she really does need her mother's love. She may be angry that it is even presented to her, for she is certain that it will soon be snatched away—this possibly having been her experience in previous lifetimes. Should she be able to overcome these conflicts to receive the wisdom of her mother, she will be fortunate indeed.

If the soul has been unable to master the crossroads, she will find as she enters second stage, that she is likely to undergo a painful experience of alienation from her mother. Alternatively her mother will dominate her in a symbiotic manner which may sap her will and damage her personal identity. The mother may manipulate her through attempting to instill feelings of guilt, or she may feel excessively guilty herself. The mother of a second-stage Scorpio may find that her child is easy to control by prompting her to feel guilty about behavior which the parents feel is unacceptable. She may not realize how damaging the use of this Achilles' Heel may be. The mother of a second-stage

Scorpio is often inclined to be abusive towards her child, or to feel victimized by life and therefore to retreat and become emotionally absent.

In second stage the childhood is tumultuous and difficult. The child may suffer abuse at the hands of strangers, parents and siblings. Father may still be absent, but he may once again be present and is rarely a constructive force. He may be overly demanding, with rigid standards, or he may be irresponsible, irrational and abusive. Sexual abuse is extremely common at some point in second-stage Scorpio. Whatever father is doing, in second stage his child is unlikely to understand him at all. In second/third stage there is often a great deal of conflict between the Scorpio individual and her father, as young Scorpio needs to acquire her own personal spiritual and philosophical understanding of life in order to master this transition.

Many Scorpios are born just after a death or major tragedy or disappointment within the family. The atmosphere of mourning which surrounds her birth reflects her feeling of a lost paradise. A second-stage Scorpio will somehow trick herself into believing that all of this suffering and upheaval is somehow her fault. Somehow she must pay, and so she goes through life doing just that, as she collects more and more guilt with each passing lifetime.

A child born into second/third stage is still likely to be born into a difficult situation. However, this is not invariably the case. Sometimes the attitude of the parents, and their relationship with their child, undergo a radical shift. This is likely in the case of an individual born into the latter part of the transition. The family may experience crisis and difficulty, but find that they are enhanced through the process of dealing with it. They look at difficulties as opportunities for growth. The relationship with the mother may be more positive, as she teaches her child to accept herself, and lives constructively according to her faith. The relationship with the father may also experience a healing. In general, the closer Scorpio's relationship is to her father, the closer she is to regaining contact with the omnipresent Divine Source.

Even in early third stage, things may not be perfect. However, a third-stage Scorpio will transcend her childhood experience through objectivity and compassion. Later in third stage the early childhood experience loses the darkness and intensity of the earlier stages. The parents uplift and inspire the child. The family secret is that the impossible is actually possible. Scorpio's innate courage is reflected in a family which embraces the adventure of life. Her upbringing may be unusual; the family may lead an unconventional lifestyle and may travel frequently. They appreciate the humor of life. Non-judgmental, her parents have great trust in life, passing on the gifts of faith and self-acceptance which her karmic history has earned her.

The late first-stage Scorpio will be likely to become involved in a battle of wills with her mother or the family as a whole in late childhood or early adolescence. The Scorpio female will attempt to prove that she is more powerful than her mother. If she can conquer her, she feels that she can rule the world. This attitude of conquest may express itself in her romantic involvements as well, as she may feel the need to test her power in an intimate setting. She may look down on men, as her mother was usually more powerful than her father, and she may have a hard time finding a man who can be her equal. She may be inclined to become involved in triangles if she was not completely successful in unseating her mother from the throne.

The late first-stage male is usually involved in a powerful love/hate relationship with his mother. This early relationship can damage his later ability to relate to women, as his feelings for them are likely to be contradictory and ambivalent. If his mother suffered at the hands of his father, he may be determined to be different. He will not wish to be like his father, and yet he may still have a strong subconscious desire to lash out at his partner to make her pay for the ways in which his mother has wronged him.

Scorpios in early first stage, and some Scorpios throughout the whole of first stage, may have a better time of it. They may be so busy attempting to fulfill their purpose that they have little need of a partner. They may also be so dedicated to their mission that they naturally attract a supportive mate. They may relate to their partner as an equal, as the two work together in complete dedication to their chosen project. Or they may be dominating and at times abusive, expecting complete unconditional support and total compliance with their will. In the first/second-stage transition they may be inclined toward infidelity, as they feel under pressure with a need to escape. Because they have such strong feelings of loyalty, their actions often leave them plagued with guilt.

A first/second-stage female often feels unloved and unwanted and seeks a partner whom she hopes will fill that gap. However, she is often suspicious and distrusting, having experienced the pain of abandonment or abuse in her relationship with her father. Her distrust puts her on the defensive, and this, coupled with her innate power as a person, means that few individuals have what it takes to be her partner.

A second-stage Scorpio may also experience conflict with her family as she matures. In this case she may become involved in a struggle to break free from the manipulative demands of her parent(s). Scorpio does not need to be fed any extra patterns of guilt or self-destruction at this stage, and may need to abandon ship in order to survive.

The Scorpio female may feel inadequate as a woman because her mother upstaged or dominated her. She may seek a partner who does not find her highly attractive, and who symbolizes her own lost knowledge and purpose. She may be abused or abandoned by this individual. Second-stage males often experience similar patterns.

Third-stage Scorpios can again find partners who share their vision. Life is no longer attacked with driving intensity; instead the eagle and her mate are free to soar. Scorpio's trust in life in this stage attracts a partner who shares her personal life philosophy, and the unconditional acceptance between the two of them creates genuine magic. They have the potential to uplift not only themselves, but also any of those with whom they come into contact.

Famous Scorpios

First Stage: Marie Curie, Dr. Jonas Salk, George Eliot, St. Augustine, Christopher Columbus, Nadia Comaneci, The Shah of Iran, Joseph Goebbels.

First/Second Stage: Richard Burton, Vivien Leigh.

Second Stage: Sylvia Plath, Bonnie Raitt, Marie Antoinette (despite massive press to the contrary), Prince Charles. (A somewhat unusual example — here the purpose dominates the person, so that he seems to have no choice. He is not in a position where he can cause much harm to others. Is his potential failing to be fully tapped? He may enter the second/third-stage transition in this lifetime.)

Second/Third Stage: Roseanne Arnold, k. d. Lang, Art Garfunkel, Linda Evans.

Third Stage: Carlos Castenada's Don Juan, Da Free John.

First/Third Stage: Martin Luther, Billy Graham.

SAGITTARIUS
natural truth

The third fire sign, Sagittarius, is considered the fifth masculine sign of the zodiac. This does not mean that Sagittarians are necessarily more masculine than feminine, although it usually indicates that they possess a strong tie with their father, whose early example is a powerful positive or negative influence. Because Sagittarius is a masculine sign, I have used the words "he", "him" and "his" as neutral terms in the following description, which refers to either gender.

Sagittarius always retains at least a hint of a memory of the spiritual world which he dwelt in before rebirth. There he found the pure joy of being which now forms the foundation of his soul's understanding. He knows that he will always be loved and supported by the Creative Source from which he came.

As he draws closer to the material plane, he develops a great desire to share the spontaneous joy which is now a part of his being. His innate knowledge must be tested and tried in the material world. Self-awareness must be developed, as well as some form of mental understanding. What exists as pure potential needs to be made real, and so the soul is once again reborn.

In traditional forms of astrology each sign is symbolically associated with one of the four elements. Sagittarius is a fire sign, and fire is symbolic of the spiritual and philosophical urges of the individual. Each sign is also considered to be either goal-oriented, stable-stubborn or mobile and changeable. Sagittarius is the latter type, traditionally known as mutable. Mutability represents adaptability or personal transformation. Therefore this combination of mutable fire produces a soul with the urge to merge itself with the spiritual source, or negatively, to dissolve itself and its life due to an undeveloped sense of spiritual understanding. It may represent an urge to mold oneself according to a certain spiritual or philosophical ideal, a desire to mold the world according to one's own spiritual or philosophical ideals, or the presence of unformed spiritual or philosophical aims which change according to the winds of circumstance.

Sagittarius's purpose is to discover the essential truth of life and to live in accordance with its laws. He is born to live out of and demonstrate Universal Truth to Humanity.

First Stage

The first-stage Sagittarian is born with a feeling of complete trust in God and in the life force which surrounds him. He instinctively knows that he is a cherished and nourished child of God. He is so aware of his Divine inheritance that he does not even question it. There is no sense of ego involved in this realization; instead he exists in a constant state of deep humility and reverence. He is aware as well that every other being is also completely loved and supported by this Divine Source of Being. Without really being intellectually aware of it, he instinctively lives out the most essential aspects of spiritual truth.

And yet he is a very simple soul who feels that he has actually very little knowledge and perhaps very little inherent power or skill with which to make his contribution to humanity. This realization does not disturb him; instead he goes about immediately attempting to be of service and to develop whatever skills may be required in order to do so.

Because he is so trusting, everything which he does comes easily to him. He is immersed in the feeling of eternal playfulness which is an essential aspect of Divine Being. He never loses his optimism, and never ceases to enjoy life. Even adversity is accepted and approached in a simple but philosophical manner. He is untouched by the things which cause his neighbors endless anguish and concern. He works hard and with great honesty and sincerity. But because he enjoys life, regardless of what he may be doing, he appears to many to be irresponsible and perhaps even lazy and impractical.

In truth, his innate trust in and contentment with life are subtly unsettling to others, for they wish they could surrender themselves to life in the way that he does, but are afraid to do so, believing that they will suffer in some unpredictable manner if they do. This being the case, they may feel the need to see him as being somehow inferior or dysfunctional. They criticize him for being irresponsible or self-centered and attempt to reform him.

He feels rather saddened by the fact that he sees so much suffering around him. He has little intellectual understanding, although he may have some practical skills. While not necessarily lacking in intelligence, he has no way of understanding what it is he knows that others do not seem to know. What makes his life so different from others? He is very innocent, and begins to feel subtly guilty about his own personal happiness, wondering what gives him the right to lead a charmed existence while others must suffer.

Because what we concentrate on is what we tend eventually to attract to ourselves, gradually his reaction to the lack of acceptance which he experiences in the presence of certain individuals tends to draw more and more of this type of experience to him. His feelings of guilt begin to increase, and unconsciously he allows himself to become their whipping boy. It is very common for later first-stage Sagittarians to attract a critical or abusive life partner. Sometimes being belittled or abused by others seems to roll off his back; at other times it temporarily relieves some of his guilt. He appears unconcerned or at worst helplessly resigned in the face of a hostile environment. Gradually feelings of self-doubt tend to creep over him, and his self-worth begins to erode. His sunny countenance begins to fade as he becomes more and more frustrated and confused. He begins to lose contact with his natural faith in life, and the transition into second stage begins.

First/Second-Stage Transition

The first/second-stage transition Sagittarian generally has a low sense of self-worth, reacting emotionally very much like an innocent, rejected child. He feels deeply isolated, but what weighs upon him most is the feeling of having made no contribution to society. When he is accepted by others and left to his own devices, he still knows that he possesses the key to lasting happiness. But being unable to find a doorway which he can unlock and free those around him, he feels truly inferior and useless.

He may also begin to recognize that he has been persecuted unjustly. This realization may prompt him to a certain amount of righteous anger. It motivates him to prove himself to others and therefore redeem himself in the eyes of society. He decides to seek a means of understanding and expressing what he knows to the people around him. He will seek truth, and the right way to live, and bring his knowledge back to the world to free those he loves from their burden of suffering.

His wounds cause him to move further and further away from his inner self, and to be increasingly less trusting. Because of this he will easily fall prey to the temptation of second-stage Sagittarius, which is the belief that truth lies outside of oneself.

Second Stage

The commencement of second stage shows a renewal of outer self-confidence, as the individual sets out upon his noble quest. He seeks to find some sort of philosophy which he can utilize in order to discover and express ultimate truth, or at the very least find a way to demonstrate to the people a workable way of life which will redeem them from their suffering and forge a pathway to fulfillment. He wants to catch It, whatever It may be, almost as though he were a biologist with a butterfly net, to bring It back where It can serve the greater good of all.

If the criticism he has suffered in first stage causes him to be angry enough, he will be tempted to shove whatever he finds down their throats, where it will still forever their taunting cries. Feeling by this time secretly weak and fragile inside, he also seeks something which will give him a sense of security and personal code by which to live. By seeking truth not only for its own sake, but also to secure and redeem himself, he walks blithely and unwittingly down a path of serious error.

He may become a traveling philosopher, who lifetime after lifetime will become a student and a devotee of religious and philosophical thought. Because his quest is so intense, and the mysteries of life seem such *mysteries* to him, he assumes that truth must be complex and difficult to find — especially since he is looking for a concrete, intellectually explainable and truly livable form of truth. His search may take him all over the world, and expose him to the most extreme forms of discipline.

Because he secretly feels that he must not be adequate

as he is, he is attracted to practices which attempt to recreate and transform the self in some extreme and possibly unbalanced manner. He tries to re-arrange his parts. One philosophy may declare that sexuality is the enemy of the spirit. Sagittarians tend to possess a very strong and natural form of sexuality which is their gift from the Gods. Bedazzled by the guru or the preacher, he or she may attempt to slay this aspect of his being. Attempting to extinguish or suppress the sexual aspect of one's being is one of he most effective means of losing contact with the core of inner truth which we all possess.

Or he may be taught that the rational mind is the enemy of his progress. Certainly to be aware of the "higher realms," we need to be able to release our hold upon the lower mind, to let go for a moment and still the inner chatter. But early second-stage Sagittarius is always the innocent extremist and often sets out to totally destroy or invalidate this aspect of his being. He may live the life of the ascetic, punishing his body in the quest for truth. He may deny his emotions as being illusory, attempting to fit all of his responses to life and, often the responses of others as well, into the pre-conceived molds of his chosen dogma.

This is not to say that the philosophies and practices with which he concerns himself are untrue or without value. It is simply their more extreme or dogmatic forms which he often finds himself attracted to. Certainly he may learn much of great value as his quest progresses, but he always does so at grave cost to his inner being. His experiences may leave him with mental, emotional and sexual dysfunctions which may follow him for lifetimes. They are certainly not guiding him toward the recognition and expression of his own truth.

In his search for the truth, he may seek social or ideological answers to his questions. He may come upon or create a political philosophy which he comes to believe must be imposed in a universal manner. His philosophies may be in direct opposition to the social norms of his time, which is quite understandable, for he does possess inborn knowledge of certain life truths which few around him can comprehend. As he experienced much criticism from others during his first-stage lifetimes, it is now understandable that he should find himself easily feeling like an outcast or an outsider, and that he should therefore decide to become something of a social iconoclast. Because within he is such a natural being, it is easy for him to see what is wrong with society and to decide to become a one-man or one-woman army out to extinguish all injustice and inequity.

If he seeks to discover the answers for himself, in second stage he will attempt to do so in an overly rational manner. He does not know how to integrate his own personal perceptions with the true underlying forces of human evolution. The philosophy or lifestyle which he may create or discover is therefore lacking in some essential quality which will enable it to have an enduringly positive impact upon the world. His life and discoveries may be exemplary but, during his lifetime at least, they will fail to provide the answers or fulfillment which he himself is seeking.

Because his search for truth is partly motivated by a need to compensate for personal insecurity, he often becomes highly defensive or opinionated concerning the formulas which he has claimed as his own on his journey to ultimate truth. He may loudly expound his life philosophy and see his perspective as the only valid way to view life, as he attempts to impose it upon any individual fortunate enough to get within earshot of him.

Or he may silently and stoically attempt to demonstrate his truths through the adoption of a personal lifestyle which demonstrates what he has found. This may mean taking on a vow of poverty or living some extremely abstemious lifestyle, while living in accordance with the values he has been taught or has come to formulate for himself, no matter what the cost to his own sense of personal well-being. As he continues through early second stage, he may find that he becomes attracted to early home environments which reflect this extreme tendency to dogma. At first he absorbs the dogma of his upbringing, taking to it like a duck to water; but as he develops, he finds he must often make a somewhat traumatic break with his past.

If he has less trust in himself, he may choose some established aspect of the social order or some aspect of the philosophical norms of his society and cling to them as foundations of the social truth which he is seeking. He can make business his religion. Conventional politics may attract. He may become extremely right-wing in his politics or lifestyle, as always assuming that all about him should follow his example. Or he may be prone to following the latest mystical fad, which promises the fantasy of truth, enlightenment or a sense of belonging. This form of second-stage Sagittarius may be a compulsive conformist, for he is tired of being criticized and tired of being on the outside.

Eventually he comes to realize that there may be no simple solutions, no easy formulas in the quest for peace, happiness or enlightenment. As he reaches the midpoint of second stage, something within him comes to rebel against all the rigid external structures which he has absorbed. He reaches a crisis in faith, and how he responds will depend upon which aspect of his psyche first comes to realize that the external forms he has attempted to rely upon for so long are indeed empty of meaning.

For some individuals, it is the inner voice which cries out from beneath the sea of illusion in which the soul has enmeshed itself. This experience may lead directly into the transition into third stage, or it may result in a relaxing of the rules, providing a certain flexibility in his basic ideology, while life in general continues as it was. Eventually the individual will reach second/third-stage transition through a process of gradual awakening.

If it is some aspect of the personal self which rebels, the journey may not be so smooth. The individual may begin expressing himself in a manner over which he has very little control, as the sexual, emotional or mental energies spill out beyond the bounds he has created for himself. He may still live by the rules he has set for himself, (perhaps without truly realizing that they are actually self-imposed) while experiencing serious outbreaks of irrational behavior. He may be subject to fits of rage or cruelty, or uncontrolled outbursts of sadness and despair. His sexual expression may from time to time take on a life of its own. Or he may be subject to periods of mental confusion, as he gradually develops a complete inability to observe life in an objective manner.

If he identifies with the aspect of himself which is seeking to rebel against all restraints, he may choose to live outside of the bounds of conventional society. Having released himself, his life expression may appear to be more healthy than it was before. However, he still must live with the results of the damage he may have done himself in his previous attempts to fit some kind of mold, which usually stretch back several lifetimes into the past. His personality lacks cohesion. In the past he may have rejected so many parts of himself that he now finds his psyche cannot function in harmony. Various aspects of his self-expression may be blocked, suppressed, or controlled by the irrational levels of his being. He is in a state of free-fall and may spin through life, experiencing frustration and confusion, and perhaps leaving a trail of chaos in his wake.

Nor has he completely left his past beliefs and attitudes behind. He carries them with him, where they surface from time to time to complicate matters even more. He usually possesses a judgmental streak which he applies with equal fervor to himself and the world beyond. Although he may have chosen a conscious stance of superiority towards the outside world—he is beginning to remember once again that he knows something which most of them do not know—though secretly he still struggles with feelings of inferiority. He may loathe himself for having lacked the strength to achieve the perfect standards he had previously set for himself, which he attempted to live by during the more rigid phase of his development. A part of him feels guilty for leaving the past behind, and he is also aware of never having redeemed himself in the eyes of the people.

He may also feel a frustration, rage or resentment towards humanity, for he feels that they have backed him into a corner. He may feel great remorse at times for having failed to explain himself to them, while at other times he wonders why he ever should have needed to in the first place. When this attitude surfaces he is inclined to blame them for all of his suffering. These feelings may cause him to be cynical, judgmental, apathetic or destructive towards the outside world.

His tendency to attract a critical mate during late first stage may continue throughout the second stage with disastrous results as far as the flagging confidence of the individual is concerned. Or this tendency may transform into more subtle forms of rejection and a life pattern which tends to somehow manage to sabotage all intimate relationships or the possibility of attaining intimate satisfaction. On a deep level this individual does not believe that he or she will ever be accepted or understood. Instead of realizing his own inner responsibility for this pattern, the second-stage Sagittarian may develop the tendency to see himself as a helpless victim of circumstance, feeling as though he has been randomly or unjustly wronged.

Or he may attempt to turn the tables, once again turning rage and resentment upon the outside world, and tending to be overly judgmental and suspicious of his or her mate and the opposite sex in general. On a subconscious level every mate symbolically represents The Mate. This means that emotionally speaking the Sagittarian (or anyone else for that matter) sometimes cannot differentiate between the present partner, whatever his or her attributes may be, and the past partner or partners who may have been abusive or lacking in understanding. Many times the present lifetime-partner will pay for the crimes of the previous partner(s), whether or not the present situation seems to warrant it.

As he nears the end of second stage, Sagittarius may grow more and more tired, and less and less certain of himself or indeed of anything which life may have to offer. He may feel that he has lost himself in the complexities of the world which he has come to be a part of. Or life may force him to re-evaluate, as he reaps the sometimes sudden and dramatic consequences of is own frantic and volcanic temperament. Neither rebelling nor conforming holds any meaning for him anymore. He finally comes to admit that he is completely lost; his spirit broken.

Ready truly to surrender, but not to a dogma, he begins to seek truth in its most simple form. He begins to look around for some alternative which will allow him to resurrect his true self once again. For a time he no longer feels that he has something to explain. He simply wants to be free to contact the source of inner peace and well-being which he vaguely and dimly remembers to be his true inheritance. Willing at last to perceive, rather than to discover or build mental or spiritual structures, he passes at last into the second/third-stage transition.

Second/Third-Stage Transition

It is difficult for many Sagittarians to enter the second/third-stage transition. In order to do so, they have to admit that they truly do not 'know'. It is also important for them to accept themselves in spite of the fact that they have realized that they truly do not understand the great mystery of life. Their old attitudes, beliefs and values all need to be questioned. Many of the things which they hold to be true may in fact be so, but the attitudes which they hold concerning these truths may still be personally limiting. Much of their mental attitude may not even be theirs at all. Or they may have given up attempting to pose as someone who knows, and instead surrendered to a morass of negative emotion, experiencing great hopelessness concerning life and their place in the world.

The Sagittarian needs to learn to release his old mental and emotional attitudes and to listen within himself in a new way. He may have to pass through a period of great darkness before he is able to solve the mysteries which his life presents him with. As time passes, his life often becomes increasingly colder, darker and more of an experience of solitary futility. However long it takes to reach the point of release, he eventually comes to his deepest, darkest hour of despair, and in a moment of almost alchemical transformation comes to realize that love is the only truth, the final answer to all of life and the eternal mystery of existence. At this point he realizes that the underlying spirit of life is truly loving, purposeful and meaningful, and that the answers to all questions can indeed be found within the self.

This realization may seem obvious and may be taken for granted by the vast majority, or may not seem to be a realization which has any real strength or impact at all. However, most of the deeper mysteries of existence are indeed deceptively simple and surprisingly optimistic. Were we to believe in them as concepts without having truly experienced or realized (in the full definition of the term) them as living realities, we would indeed be living in a dream world. Many of these truths are well-known on a rational and collective level, but are once again enduringly transformative when experienced as living realities.

Having begun his reunion with truth, the Sagittarian now possesses a new foundation upon which his ideals can be rebuilt. A trust in the guiding force of nature becomes manifest within him, and he also gains new confidence in his inner being and the power of the still, small voice within himself. The arrow aimed for the heights so many lifetimes ago has at last begun to find its mark, and he can finally begin the process of rediscovering his true selfhood.

This surrender to love as the greatest truth in all existence has relieved a great deal of the pain and pressure he had previously experienced, and now forms the basis for his spontaneous retrieval of inner truth. This stage of his development inaugurates an entirely new phase of exploration, in this case, an inner exploration with the Self as the guide. He rediscovers those truths which were always innately his to express, discovering at the same time an ability to achieve conscious insight into their meaning, purpose and value. As he begins to develop insights which are truly his own, he finds himself guided by the life force itself as he begins to develop a balanced perspective upon all of his life experiences. He is now able to start retrieving the basic elements of eternal wisdom which he has gathered through his previous lifetimes of training and suffering. No longer weighed down by dogma, he is able to extract the true gems of his experience. He begins to distill the most important elements of whatever spiritual or social systems he may have studied in previous lifetimes.

He can now place his spiritual history into proper perspective, for he is learning once again to trust himself. He enjoys exploring the insights he has received throughout the centuries, as his past knowledge surfaces from the archetypal mind. He may find himself drawn once again to the study of certain disciplines, which he seems able to understand almost instantaneously. This is because he has studied them in the past. He may actually recall those past lifetimes, consciously retrieving all of his previous understanding as he does so. Or he may be unaware of his past knowledge and experience, while still finding that a certain intuitive understanding of the principles of life seems to come to him from almost nowhere.

However, he is now capable of being detached from

these ideas and principles, using discrimination as he goes about the process of deepening his understanding. He learns not to allow these concepts to distort and dominate him, through constantly weighing them against their true source, the source of all being, which is universal love. He may choose to become a spiritual student once again; this time under the guidance of a tutor who will help him to evoke the truth from within himself, rather than imposing it from without. He finds the source of the rainbow (an old traditional image for the sign Sagittarius) through becoming fully enveloped in the heart of the universe.

In time he comes to realize that, although there are mistakes, at the same time there truly are no mistakes. In entering the house of mirrors in search of himself, he has seen perhaps every distorted image that there is. Now he finds, as a result, that his view is totally comprehensive. He cannot be fooled and exists once again in his natural state of innocence and simplicity. A wise innocent this time, he stores within his soul the wisdom of the centuries, and has at last, as he had originally intended, the power to open the door to the world of spirit and to a larger, more comprehensive view of life for all who seek to make the journey. He no longer feels he has to change the world. But for those who seek to change their worlds and enhance their lives with the tools of wisdom, it is his great satisfaction to possess the keys to pass along into their waiting hands.

Having achieved the conscious wisdom which was his original goal, his new sense of self-confidence releases his previous susceptibility to criticism. No longer karmically attached to experiences of rejection or miscommunication in his personal life, he is able at last to attract constructive experiences in his personal relationships. He trusts himself and is now capable of truly independent thought. He does not have to conform to society or remain cynically at its fringes. His mind falls back into the natural state of balance which it possessed during the first stage of his development. He responds to the material world with integrity, and to his own sexuality with reverence, recognizing its power to evoke natural truth. Working in harmony with the Divine Mind, he can once again smile at the world, and so enters the third stage of his development.

Third Stage

The third-stage Sagittarian has regained his childlike joy in the spirit of life. He is no longer naively innocent. Instead he has innocent wisdom. The Source of Life has revealed its simple truths to him. Now he is able to review the knowledge which he has gathered over the centuries, spontaneously allowing it to surface as he gives it meaning within the larger context. He is able to pass on the wisdom of the ancients in a way which has perfect relevance to the time and place in which he finds himself. At last he is able to help the people. He also knows why they suffer, and that it is not always wrong that they do so. He holds the truth for those who are ready to receive it, allowing the rest to travel whatever path they must. Because of his love and the attractive simplicity of his joy, he is able to assist many.

He lives life with little attachment, and yet he embraces the world. No longer concerned with those who cannot understand him, he has perfect confidence in his inner contact. He goes his own way and allows others to go their own, his patience stemming from his knowledge of the power of evolution. Eventually he knows that all others will find the Source which he has found within himself. If he can join with them in that discovery, he will feel himself truly privileged. If not, he has all of infinity to explore, and all of time in which to do it.

Sagittarius at the Crossroads
First/Third-Stage Transition

Poor Sagittarius. Everywhere he turns, he is criticized needlessly. His family may not understand him. His mate seldom does. At the end of first stage the individual usually chooses a partner who is far from satisfied with his or her basic nature. His wife feels that he doesn't take life seriously enough. He is always friendly and smiling, when there must be more important things to do. She is left to fret and worry all by herself. She feels that he is exasperating when he tells her not to worry, he is sure that everything will work out fine. When it does, this is still no proof he is right.

Sagittarius's husband wishes she were not such a free spirit. He does not know what it is that she knows, but secretly it threatens him. He is concerned that she may be dangerous in some unknown way, and he seeks to keep her under his thumb by knocking her down and destroying her self-confidence.

Rejected and misunderstood, she retreats by the riverside. Why does no one understand? She is just going about her business in all sincerity, and it seems to upset others. There is something which she needs to say to the people, but she can barely articulate it. It is at this stage that the crossroads presents itself. Here the individual can become overwhelmed with feelings of guilt, anger and insecurity. To attempt to justify oneself to the world at any cost would be to fall. To take responsibility for the suffering of others and to frantically seek an answer will lead into illusion.

The only key to mastering this transition is maintaining one's spirit of trust. First/third-stage Sagittarius needs to spend a certain amount of time alone with himself. Even if circumstances do not permit him the necessary periods of physical isolation, he must learn to be alone within himself. This does not mean that he must be lonely, but he must learn to give himself the inner support which will enable him to pass through his time of personal trial.

The truth is within him. If he can trust and listen in the silence, he may find that his innate knowledge will be explained to him. We all walk with God, most without even realizing it. First-stage Sagittarians are closer to discovering this truth than many others. Turning to the solace of nature, remembering to trust in the process of life and the power of his own integrity, this individual can discover that which he has never completely forgotten. No one can make so pure and non-dogmatic an inner contact with the Source of Life than an individual at this crossroads.

Sitting by the water's edge, after many visits and much time spent expectantly waiting, suddenly he Knows. Nothing is out of order, nothing is out of place. He need explain himself to no one, but now he has something which he can reveal. He returns quietly to the world, prepared for those who are ready; a pure, enlightened wise one.

Childhood Conditions and Relationship Patterns

Sagittarius is a Fire sign. In all fire signs, the father is usually the dominant parent, and represents the spiritual and philosophical ideals of the individual, while the mother is less dominant and may be inclined to be rather sensitive and perhaps victimized. She represents the individual's emotional nature and his relationship with his earthly personality.

In early first stage, Sagittarius has a supportive and enjoyable relationship with his father. His father is inclined to have a youthful attitude towards life, and is open and flexible as a parent. He seeks to learn from his offspring. As a child the early first-stage Sagittarian usually has a lot of freedom, which enables him to explore life and develop his own unique perspective on reality. His father makes life look easy. He may be financially well off, or he may lead a materially simple life, while truly enjoying and being thankful for all that life has to offer.

His mother is a sensitive individual who seems to live in a romantic world of dreams, fantasy and magic. From her he learns to trust life. He is never taught to question himself, and does not develop the ability to be objective about his beliefs and feelings. He is too busy having fun, and making his own loyal contribution to the welfare of the family and the world around him.

Sagittarius is the only sign which can continue to have a positive relationship with one or both parents throughout all three stages. However, certain distortions in these relationships may also surface as he progresses in his development. In late first stage some difficulty with the father may emerge. His father may lack the interest or ability to be a proper parent to him, and may leave him to his own devices or be critical, demanding and abusive of his offspring. This kind of early experience can hinder the development of the child's self-confidence, making it easier for him to question himself under criticism.

As he develops he may find himself involved in a conflict with one or both parents, concerning his choice of life direction. They may want him to live a certain way, playing upon his innate feelings of loyalty in an attempt to manipulate him into living the life which they have chosen for him. Though they are rarely successful, he may be left with lingering feelings of guilt as well as an increasing tendency to doubt himself in his quieter moments.

Towards the end of first stage his mother may grow less trusting of life and more victimized by her circumstances. Sagittarius often feels great empathy for her, and would like to help her if he could, but there does not seem to be any way to do so, and this may increase his feelings of impotence. She may be part of the circumstances which motivate him to seek answers which he can use to help the world, while any difficulties with the father are more inclined to prompt him to seek the truth in order to justify himself.

Children born into late first- or second-stage Sagittarius are often given inadequate care. They are often born to young, inexperienced parents, old and tired parents or as the sixth child in a family of nine. In early first stage this would not be such a problem, for their trust in life makes them largely self-supporting. Later on they need more support and they need more answers, and often neither of these are forthcoming.

In second stage, mother may be absent or may respond to her child in an irrational manner. She may fail to provide the unconditional support which he or she requires. To make matters worse, Sagittarians often end up as the black sheep of the family, often without really trying.

In second stage the family may begin to reflect the karmic results of his or her past spiritual or philosophical response to life. The family may practice repressive spiritual or philosophical disciplines. His father may be dogmatic and dominating. He may be told to have a 'stiff upper lip' and that he must fit in and follow the rules no matter what. Or he may suffer as a result of his family's rejection of society's present social values. He may be born into a sexually repressive environment, or grow up being told that he is stupid.

As second stage progresses the family may reflect his increasing tendency towards irrationality. His father may be subject to fits of irrational violence. His mother may be unstable. There may be a family history of drug or alcohol abuse, and he may be sexually abused or raised without being given any real values in this area.

Individuals born into second/third stage will generally begin to experience positive family relationships once again. While some of the traits of second stage may still be present, the qualities of third stage will also begin to make themselves felt. His mother is regaining her trust in life. His father is learning how to be a father, and may discover himself through his child.

In third-stage Sagittarius the parents often have similar traits to the parents of a first-stage individual. The difference is that they consciously possess more wisdom. The child may inherit a spiritual tradition through his family, which forms part of his greater karmic heritage of ripening wisdom.

The relationship patterns of Sagittarius have been mentioned above, and so I will only discuss them briefly here. In early first stage, partnerships may be reasonably harmonious. There may be an instinctive rapport between this individual and his mate. However, there may also be a certain amount of distance. Each partner lives in his or her own world, and when they meet they may share intimately, but at other times the Sagittarian is left to his or her own devices, just as their parents may have them on their own a good proportion of the time. They are used to experiencing a certain amount of independence. But with time they may also grow increasingly lonely.

As first stage progresses they long for someone to understand them, and so become more vulnerable toward their mate. The relationship to the partner often reflects the relationship with the parents. Women in first stage who have been criticized by their father will be inclined to find the same conflict in their relationship with their partners, who may attempt to dominate them, and who may fear what they stand for in the same way that their father (or sometimes their mother) also did.

The late second-stage male may be quite close to his mother, and is likely to feel a great deal of empathy for her. He sees her suffering, and grows up with a desire to save or inspire the woman he loves. She may not realize that she needs saving, however, and may be more likely to believe that she requires serving! Before he realizes what has happened he is likely to find himself with a dominating partner who is never quite satisfied with his behavior or his accomplishments.

A tendency to become involved in difficult relationships tends to follow Sagittarius into second stage, as I have previously mentioned. This individual easily feels alienated and misunderstood by his or her partners. While second-stage Sagittarians can easily become divorced from their sexuality as a result of their involvement with restrictive philosophies, they can also indulge in a form of hypersexuality as a means of compensating for their lack of intimate fulfillment. This can become just as much of a habit as repression can, and for Sagittarius these two patterns can even co-exist.

In late second stage their erratic behavior combined with their tendency to lash out at their mate makes them often quite difficult to deal with on an intimate level. Some Sagittarian males in second stage have been raised in such a strongly male dominated environment, that they truly prefer the company of men. This is not necessarily an indication of homosexuality, instead it often indicates that male Sagittarians may separate their relationship with their partners from their 'real' life, or may be subtly condescending towards women.

Women raised in the same kind of environment are often inclined to be incapable of following the usual 'rules' of behavior which society, and often the men with whom they become involved, may expect of them. They are not consciously rebellious, they just see no reason not to be themselves. They may compete with men, while secretly doubting their desirability as a woman, which may make them somewhat defensive and hard to get close to.

At some point in second/third or third stage these difficulties become resolved. As the individual begins to accept himself, he or she then naturally attracts the supportive mate which he has always longed for; and may even have given up hoping for. We are often attracted time and time again into the same sort of negative situation because we subconsciously believe that this is the only way to resolve the problem. But it must be resolved within; it can never be worked out in a relationship. The third-stage Sagittarian has realized this, and no longer becomes attracted to those who will criticize and misunderstand him, because he no longer feels the need to resolve his internal difficulties through a mate.

Famous Sagittarians

First Stage: Unlikely to become famous, except by 'accident'.

Second Stage: Alexander Solzhenitsyn, Francisco Franco, Bhagwan Shree Rajneesh, Richard Pryor, Jimi Hendrix, Jim Morrison.

Second/Third Stage: Tina Turner, Mark Twain, Keith Richards, Walt Disney, Bruce Lee.

Third Stage: Dyhani Yawahoo (First Nations North American spiritual teacher), Lao Tsu (my guess — I do not know if there is any record of his birth date).

First/Third Stage: Enoch (biblical figure from Genesis).

CAPRICORN
visionary integrity

In traditional astrology Capricorn is a cardinal earth sign. Cardinal means goal-oriented. Earth signs seek to apply their talents in a concrete manner. Because the element of earth is considered a feminine element, in describing Capricorn I have used the terms "she", "her" and "hers" as neutral terms meant to apply to either gender.

On a spiritual level Capricorn is dedicated to the Earth and all of its inhabitants, and seeks to better the lot of humanity within the material world. Eventually she will fulfill the goal of transcending all earthly limitations.

She possesses a special form of x-ray vision, and understands the fundamental manner in which certain aspects of life are structured. She has an innate capacity to understand the natural course of evolution, and to assist its forward progress in some specific area or areas. Her inner vision inspires her greatly. On a soul level she is certain that she can aid humanity by teaching them how to make the best use of the structure of their own minds and bodies, or some part of the physical, material, political or spiritual world which surrounds them.

First Stage

The first-stage Capricorn wishes to influence humanity as a whole, or at least to bring about some form of fundamental change in the culture to which she was born. She has strong powers of intuition which allow her to see how and why certain mass changes should occur. Because she is a practical reformer, her first task upon arriving in this world, is to learn to master the material plane, or at least place herself in a position of worldly power and influence. She seeks to affect others en masse, and to make whatever changes in the structure of human society may be necessary, by instituting her values from a position of social or political influence. She knows how things work, and she wants to show others how to make use of that knowledge in the way that will bring the most benefit.

In order to achieve this goal, she will adopt one of two

approaches. She may choose to be born into a position of wealth and influence, where she has immediate and ready access to the people, tools and resources necessary to the fulfillment of her purpose. Or she may choose to be born into obscurity and work her way into an influential position. Each alternative presents certain distinct advantages, as well as certain disadvantages.

If she chooses to be born into a position of power, this gives her ready access to the masses. She saves herself the trouble of having to struggle to the top, and can begin to institute reforms more rapidly. Her visionary capacity will also be more likely to remain intact, for she will not be subject to the stresses and the potential for disillusionment which she may encounter if she attempts to achieve eminence through the use of her own personal powers alone. Instead she has ample time and resources to allow her the luxury of exploring and developing her spiritual visions, allowing her to keep most of her ideals intact.

In early first stage, Capricorn still tends to possess a great deal of innate spiritual understanding, and maintains her conscious contact with the Divine Source from which she stems. In comparison with other signs, this is somewhat unusual, as spiritual vision is not generally a part of the nature of most other signs of the zodiac during the first stage of their development.

The drawbacks to being born into a high position include the risk of relying too heavily upon the comforts of one's own personal fantasy-world, while remaining in a state of naiveté concerning the realities of life as it is lived beyond her 'palace walls'. Being too innocent of the ways of the world may cause her to be easily taken advantage of by others, and may also result in a tendency to fall out of step with the ways and needs of other people, so that she is unable to present her ideas in a way which will guarantee their acceptance among the populace. She may seem weak and ineffective in her role as leader and teacher. Her ideals may be too far ahead of their time, causing any reforms she may attempt to instigate to be poorly received and lack staying power.

If Capricorn falls prey to the traps of her position, this reduces her personal effectiveness, causing her self-worth as an individual to be threatened, and perhaps tempting her to retreat even further from reality. He may then choose to immerse herself in the temptations afforded by the luxury which surrounds her, or to indulge in flights of fancy which enhance a false sense of ego, creating the illusion of personal superiority. She may easily become quite lost in herself.

Being born into royalty may cause her to assume that she is superior, as so many others in positions beneath her may actually believe. If she feels inferior due to a lack of fulfillment of her true purpose, it may be easy to slide into the trap of believing herself to be better than others. She can justify these feelings by virtue of her social position and the power of her personal vision, which is above and beyond the general norms of the society in which she lives. She may feel that because she is special, the rest of the world really exists only to serve her, and may become addicted to luxury and pleasure, expecting that life be served to her upon a silver platter.

Souls who choose this path exclusively may ultimately become severely handicapped in terms of their capacity to be self-supporting and self-motivated. They may tend to feel subconsciously that they are still living in the state of passive universal oneness from which they originally came. Beneath their sense of privilege lurks a vast feeling of personal insecurity which constantly threatens their self-esteem as an individual.

Should Capricorn choose to be born into a position of obscurity, she then has the opportunity to develop great strength of character. This presents a contrast to those born into their position, who may possess the character flaws and weaknesses mentioned above, as well as having cultivated a certain tendency toward personal dependency. The Capricorn who must work her way to the top tends to develop unbending determination, practicality, strength of will, and a certain flexibility and humility. The stresses of making this climb, however, may also tend to take their toll.

This individual runs the risk of losing touch with the purity of her original vision. In order to get where she is going, she may find that it seems necessary to scale her dreams down, perhaps making them overly practical, in order to conform to the realities of this world. While the

Capricorn who is born into wealth and privilege may run the risk of becoming too naive, this individual may become too hardened, believing that she must compromise many of her most important values in order to get into a position where she may have some effect. She may find, as a result, that her social impact is lessened. She may be outwardly successful, but perhaps not in ways which are truly meaningful to herself.

She may grow somewhat cynical and world weary as a result of having to deal with so much corruption in the process of having scaled the heights. She may have had to suppress her own sensitivity in order to cope, for she has encountered much competition and opposition to her purpose. Few truly desire that she succeed as an individual, and many may seek a position of power for their own ends. Few individuals who seek the heights do so for the sake of the world in which we all must live.

In time she may find herself grown into an automaton with little personal feeling or awareness of the inner self. She may develop tunnel-vision and feel forced to become personally ruthless in the pursuit of her goals. Or she may experience persecution as a result of her stubborn unwillingness to compromise. Perhaps then she will begin to make little compromises in the pursuit of all which she holds dear, and as one compromise easily leads to another, she gradually becomes absorbed in the corruption which surrounds her.

Each soul will choose their own individual combination of the above alternatives. Some will choose always to be born into the position they feel will allow them to make the greatest difference. Others will choose each time to make their own way there after having been born into a position of obscurity. Many souls will alternate; and most will experience at least one lifetime upon each alternative path of first-stage development. Whatever choices they make, for better or worse, will be certain to leave their mark.

Whatever her life path may be, at this stage she will develop her internal and external powers to their utmost. She will most likely become the master of some trade, skill or channel of cultural power through which she will attempt the improvement of mass human consciousness. She may also attempt to perfect Man by developing herself into a perfect specimen of humanity. The first-stage Capricorn is a reformer of life, who changes things from deep within the halls of the hallowed. In this culture, a first-stage Capricorn may become an architect, social scientist, priest, doctor, lawyer, politician or a master of technological or military science. Alternatively she may be an artist, or even an athlete, yet always expresses the underlying theme of her purpose, beneath the role which she has chosen to play. He exists on the crest of the wave of forward movement of the upper classes.

However, at this stage, she may not yet be fully prepared to deal with the world which she seeks to serve. Her approach is still too materialistic. She attempts to institute social change, but without individual transformation the larger social fabric cannot be reformed in any lasting manner. The difficulties which she faces are bound eventually to become too much for her to bear, and so the fabric of her personality begins to crumble beneath the stress, and she passes into the first/second-stage transition.

First/Second Stage Transition

As the transition from first to second stage begins, the individual finds herself experiencing the strain of the responsibilities which she has taken on. She begins to lose confidence in her own power to triumph for the greater good of all. The corruption which surrounds her threatens to overwhelm her individual resolve and idealism. She has spent many lifetimes attempting to institute the desired changes, and is beginning to believe that the entire process may actually be far more difficult than she could ever possibly have imagined. Between lifetimes, the soul looks back upon her own past history and discovers that even when she has successfully transformed the fabric of society, the changes have seldom been of a permanent nature. In fact, they have usually failed to outlive the individual by much more than a single lifetime.

Frustrated in her purpose, her self-worth plummets. She struggles constantly with a deadly form of insecurity which haunts her quietest moments and threatens to undermine whatever strength she may now possess as an individual.

236

She is often locked into a private prison of her own making, and tends to feel that she must somehow learn to master her insecurities in isolation. She now finds it extremely difficult to trust other individuals, having experienced the results of their jealousy as she attempted to reach or maintain her position of worldly power.

Few, if any of her competitors have ever understood her ideals or shared her level of integrity. There are those who envy the position she holds, which they feel they may never be able to achieve for themselves. Because of the structure of human society at this time in evolution and for many years before the present historical period, most of their difficulty has come from men; and many Capricorns, male or female, may develop an instinctive distrust of men as a result.

She no longer believes that she may be able to remain true to her ideals or have the power to implement them. In this transition the individual struggles with the overwhelming opposition which she experiences. The ground crumbles constantly beneath her feet. She may experience some traumatic form of betrayal, or simply run up against a stone-faced bureaucracy or an uncomprehending populace one final time too many. When she comes to the conclusion that the corruption of the world is greater than her power as an individual, she passes into second stage.

Second Stage

In second stage, Capricorn's frustration and lack of fulfillment creates many difficulties, and the soul may choose to respond in a number of different ways to the confusion which she experiences. Believing that she has lost the power to implement her ideals, she now begins to assume a new attitude towards society. Will she choose to remain a part of something which she senses to be innately corrupt? "If you can't beat them, you may as well join them," choruses the little devil on her left shoulder. Or will she choose to step outside of society's confines, relinquishing her position of personal importance as she does so? Many Capricorns will express both of these alternatives at different points in their evolution, or perhaps even combine them within the course of a single lifetime.

Corruption is her enemy, and yet it is easy for her to absorb it. Because her self-esteem is low and her hopes may be shattered on a deep level, she may feel that she must compensate for the pain which she feels by fulfilling the apparent needs and desires of her personality. She has had much opportunity for pleasure and may lose herself now in all forms of self-indulgence, feeling perhaps that there is little else which she can do. If there is nothing she can do to change the world, she might as well enjoy what it has to offer. Perhaps doing so makes her feel once again like the pampered prince or princess who is worthy simply by virtue of her position in society. Perhaps she can dream that she has indeed accomplished something of value.

She may be highly ambitious to achieve externally recognized success in some form, as the appearance of achievement may be a substitute for the recognition gained through acting in alignment with her true wisdom and idealism. If she cannot be true to herself, she will settle for being important to others. She can become an ego-maniac, compulsively seeking outer importance in order to compensate for an inner feeling of failure.

As second stage progresses, she may lose contact with her natural intuitive ability and so forget what her true dreams really are, knowing only that she is restless and is vaguely seeking some height. She confuses material with spiritual height. Her soul will not be satisfied until she has achieved both in a balanced manner. At this point her inner insecurity may make her ruthless in the pursuit of her goals. This kind of second-stage Capricorn is highly competitive, partly because she may have once experienced a struggle to reach the top and partly because she feels that if she can show herself to be better than someone else, or perhaps better than everyone else, she will have finally proven her worth as an individual.

She may become a cruel self-indulgent despot, turning the self-hatred which she cannot face, as well as her frustration at society for failing to heed her deeper message, upon those around her and feeling temporarily consoled by the abuse of power. In short, she comes in time to resemble everything which she had once hated in society.

Perhaps she retains her integrity, while lacking confidence in her ability to reach the heights. Instead she may serve in a smaller capacity, doing her best to assist the people with whatever knowledge or personal effort she may be capable of providing. She accepts the status quo and becomes a hard-working contributor in some quiet arena. She may be satisfied with her lot in life, as she can attain true satisfaction from serving the people, but she may also feel trapped in some form of slave labor and long for a better life which she believes may never be possible.

Alternatively, she may suffer from enormous laziness and inertia. She may drown herself in sensation as a way of dulling the pain which comes from failing to respond to her true calling. Pleasures, possessions and entertainment make her feel good, so therefore she feels that she must indeed be happy. She is putting off the day of reckoning, by telling herself that she truly has nothing to reckon with. Perhaps she is waiting for someone to rescue her, for she may subconsciously remember a time when others supported her and raised her to the heights from which she shone.

If she refuses to absorb the corruption, and instead rejects society and its conventions while holding firmly to her ideals, she may seem for a while to have attained greater satisfaction than her more self-indulgent brother. She may lead a band of rebel followers. She may live in isolation as an angry philosopher shaking her fist at the powers that be. Her freedom may give her a sense of fulfillment for a time, and yet it is not her nature to remain on the outside.

If she rejects involvement in the material world, seeing it as too evil a place to be worthy of her ideals, she will never be satisfied; for it is her nature to make manifest her ideals. Her spirit ultimately is capable of embracing the whole of life, and to separate herself from any aspect of it is to be more than lonely. Once she proves that she can live and flourish alone and free in alignment with nature's true laws, she must then find a way to bring this truth back to the people, or else suffer great feelings of futility. As good as she may feel about her rebel spirit, the time comes when she needs to bring her discoveries back into town, and if she feels that she lacks the power to do so, her self-worth will inevitably suffer.

Her frustration will most likely be taken out upon herself (she will punish herself severely if it is taken out on others) as acts of self-destruction or extreme forms of self-indulgence. Alternatively she may attract victimization or persecution. She may also take excessive responsibility for those around her, unconsciously feeling that if she can save other individuals at great cost to herself, she will in fact make up for not having influenced the underlying fabric of her culture. Instead of saving many, she will have saved a few very profoundly. In reality this choice is often destructive both to herself, as well as to those in whom she cultivates excessive dependency.

Rather than attempting to save the people one by one, she may instead be angry at them for what she feels is their refusal to accept her gifts. She may view them with disdain and treat them with cruelty or neglect, perhaps becoming the ultimate opportunist and a lawbreaker, either in social or natural terms (as she may be a perfectly law-abiding citizen and yet twist the laws of man to her own ends in an evil and destructive manner).

She may come to experience such a state of despair and frustration that she abandons both society at large as well as any form of personal ethics or morality. At first she may exult in the feeling of power which she has achieved through becoming a law unto herself, but eventually the wind will drop out of her sails and leave her to hover useless and impotent about the fringes of the society she has rejected, which she may now feel has rejected her as well. Her self-worth may reach an all time low at this point, and she may conduct herself as one capable only of menial labor and little else of any enduring value. She seems to others, and perhaps to herself, to have little purpose or impact as an individual. She feels unequal to her true goals, and therefore incapable of accomplishing anything.

By the end of second stage, Capricorn is truly lost. Within herself lie deep feelings of guilt and lack of self-esteem as a result of her refusal to face the issues which she knows to be her responsibility. Yet she does not know how to create the improvements or find the answers to the riddles which her soul presents her with. To compensate, she may have leaned too heavily upon the earthly or material side of her nature. She may have sought adulation and acquisition, becoming a self-serving despot. Conversely her guilt and confusion may have dominated, causing her to feel lost in the material world and stripped of all personal power and a sense of importance as an individual. She has judged herself or the world to be inferior and therefore unworthy of the love or grace of God. She has either rejected the world as being too corrupt to meet her standards or rejected herself for being too weak to make a difference.

When she grows tired of compensating and wearies of the feelings of personal failure which dog her every footstep, only then will she be ready to seek a true alternative. Only then will she be ready to begin the transition into the third stage.

Second/Third-Stage Transition

The second-stage Capricorn who has sought little more than personal power has come to the top of the mountain and now experiences a need to go beyond. However, she may at first refuse to consciously acknowledge her deeply rooted desire for transformation. To move on to the next level usually requires that she come to understand the value of experiencing and living by spiritual principles.

Tired of living on the outside and being denied a meaning or a purpose, and unable to withstand the emptiness which accompanies the lack of impact which her values seem to have upon society, the idealistic and rebellious second-stage Capricorn begins to seek an alternative to the life which she has led. She begins to look for a way back in. She needs to expand her horizons, for she is now ready to drop her rigid stance of rebellion, which she knows is growing old. When she learns that she must seek the answer to her questions within her deeper self, she is ready to begin to resolve the old difficulties and obstructions which have plagued her, consciously and unconsciously, for so many years.

If she chose to remain on the mountain while abandoning the true heights of spirit, she now finds her life to be achingly and unbelievably lonely. The emptiness of her life haunts her and drives her to a frantic search for alternatives. Her indulgences have completely isolated her. Her denial of the promptings of her spirit have alienated her from her emotions. She no longer knows herself and can only look with loathing upon the face which she sees in the mirror. She is deeply wearied by the life of corruption and compromise which she must lead daily. This individual feels more than anything else like a sleepwalker lost in a dream which has by now ceased making any sense at all.

Her physical health may be poor, for she struggles under the burden of several lifetimes of self-abuse and over-indulgence. Many individuals, regardless of the sign which they are born under, find themselves entering the transition into third stage as a result of a health breakdown, for certainly the stresses of second stage are likely to take their toll upon the physical body. Some signs are more likely to do this than others, and Capricorn is one of them.

The individual who has abandoned society as well as her ideals and personal feelings of self-worth, now finds that the pain of living in limbo is too acute. She may have clashed with society in some extreme fashion, perhaps eventually causing her to break down on every level. She may have experienced imprisonment or total failure. An individual who has managed to maintain her idealism throughout second stage, leading a rebellious, though possibly fruitless lifestyle, may also have lost her spirit and enthusiasm by this stage, and may feel completely beaten by the powers that be. Regardless of her situation, she now finds that her creativity and her passion can no longer endure oppression. She struggles to resurrect herself, but the effort required is great and progress seems at first slow and disheartening. Few people realize at the start of this transition that they are in fact dealing with the inertia, scar tissue and residual traumas of several lifetimes. The going seems heart-breakingly slow at times, and yet an enormous amount of ground is actually being covered in a very short time.

To move into third stage, Capricorn must learn to look at life from an inner level. For those who have absorbed the corruption which surrounds them, this means letting go of old, destructive habits and going through the painful process of learning how to feel again. This individual may find that in a very short period of time her opinions about just about everything have gone through a radical transformation. For the sake of her own survival she now

242

allows herself to dream again, not yet considering what she shall actually do with those dreams once they are resurrected.

Once this individual can feel again, she must struggle with her feelings concerning the world beyond herself. The only way to resolve these feelings, and to find the key which really will make a difference in society, is to continue following the path which leads deeper within the self. She has learned to care about life again, and instead of succumbing to her old feelings of impotence and futility regarding those things which she cannot change, needs to learn to understand the structure of life from an inner, not outer, viewpoint. As she comes to know her deeper self, she rediscovers her natural visionary and intuitive ability. Now she knows why things are the way they are, and how she can make a difference by sharing her perceptions with the world.

The underlying structure of the universe reveals itself to her, and if she begins to listen to the powerful sources of inner guidance which she has discovered, she will be guided to a new level of understanding concerning all which she holds dear. In time she learns to view life from a spiritual rather than a material level. Her great mistake has been to attempt to change things from a mundane, and material level, mistakenly believing this aspect of life to have the greatest power. Now she has the opportunity to know better. This does not mean that there is anything inherently wrong with the material world. Nor is the material world un-spiritual in any way. This world is sacred, and is not to be ignored or escaped in any manner.

Having discovered the inner source of reality does not invalidate the importance of physical evolution or the need to improve our life conditions. What it does indicate is that externally instituted changes can never have a lasting effect. In order to make a truly lasting impression upon reality, change must first occur on an inner level. Then, any external transformation which is instituted in response to a collective or individual change of consciousness must surely endure and bear lasting and beneficial fruit for all concerned.

As she learns to study life from an inner level of being, she learns to see how the process of evolution is progressing and what its next step must inevitably be. In her first-stage lifetimes she may have been ahead of her time, attempting to enforce a change which the people truly were not ready for. Now she learns that she cannot do it for them, for to do so would not only be ineffectual, it would also rob them of the opportunity for growth. She realizes that there are times when just holding the wisdom is enough. The people will seek her out when they are truly ready, and she makes her greatest contribution by allowing the truth and wisdom which she is able to perceive to flow through her unhindered to those who need it most.

As the transition progresses she learns to approach life from a mostly spiritual and intuitive viewpoint. At first these moments of insight into the true nature of reality are few and far between. Once she first becomes committed to this new perspective, she may tend to place too much emphasis upon certain newly discovered theories, which she views at first from too much of a mental level. Having not yet achieved true feelings of self-esteem, she may at first be inclined to view her spiritual life from a curiously materialistic perspective. During this phase of development she may therefore be prone to a form of spiritual one-upmanship.

Secretly she is reaching for something which she has not yet quite mastered, and this causes a feeling of insecurity which threatens to draw her back into her older patterns of destructive self-doubt. Again and again she is pulled back towards second-stage values, as she loses and then regains the vision which is leading her toward third stage. She may feel that being spiritual and being practical are two different things. He may experience a confusion of values, and at times may take materialistic approaches to spiritual issues.

To compensate for her feelings of insecurity, she may imagine herself wiser and more knowledgeable than others. At this stage she often tends to emphasize the value of knowledge, unconsciously considering its pursuit to be more important than achieving a feeling of oneness with life. Knowledge does have its value. However, it is intended to be used as a tool to serve the greater good of all, not as a possession which is collected as an end in itself or as a means of inflating the ego. Without actually realizing it, she may make spirituality a competition in which there can only be one winner. She may become self-righteous, domineering and dogmatic.

In terms of her greater evolution, this phase is unlikely to last very long, for her desire to learn more will eventually lead her beyond this particular illusion. The less she knows when she first enters this phase, the longer she will be inclined to continue thinking and behaving in this manner. All tendency towards competition will cease, once she resurrects her true spirit of integrity and realizes that fulfillment can only come from service, and no one form of service is greater than any other. It is not how much we know that counts, but how deeply we love that is truly important. Nor does our capacity to love and serve determine our essential worth as an individual. The essential worth of each individual, expressed or unexpressed, is incalculable. When Capricorn can see this truth reflected in herself as well as in others, then she will finally be ready to enter the third and final stage of her development.

As she progresses, she begins to feel herself truly cooperating with the current of evolution as it moves through her life and the lives of those who surround her. She learns to listen within on a daily basis, and so receives further knowledge and guidance which leads her steadily along the path of liberation. She discovers that she now possesses the ability to relax and enjoy life in the moment, while finding that much of truly practical import can gradually begin to be accomplished.

Freed from the pressure to accomplish the impossible, she uncovers some startling and highly relevant new forms of understanding, which will eventually allow her to make a truly valuable contribution to the society in which she lives. He resurrects her innate talents, simply for the joy of reclaiming those aspects of her basic nature.

No more is she self-deprecating and insecure; nor is she conceited and competitive, holding a false image of herself as somehow superior to those who surround her. She denies no truths to herself and lives a life of deep humility coupled with simple, enduring self-respect. When she has achieved this lasting form of inner peace and true self-confidence, she passes at last into the third stage of her development.

Third Stage

The third-stage Capricorn is a crystal clear channel of divine wisdom, exercising itself in perfect humility. Within her mind lie the keys to the structure of the cosmos. In astrology Capricorn is the traditional ruler of the tenth house, or midheaven of the natal chart. This portion of the horoscope is the highest point of the birth chart, and represents the constellation which is directly above us at the moment of birth. In the early stages of Capricorn the soul tries to 'reach the top', and become the best expression of herself which she can possibly be. Her interpretation of 'the heights' changes in third stage to produce a truly celestial nature which reaches beyond all limitations to achieve the heights of perception. By third stage this individual has completely rejected a materialistic interpretation of life. She has no attachment to material existence, but nor does she reject this world and all which it has to offer. She understands that spirit and matter are truly one and therefore indivisible. She also comprehends much of the higher purpose of physical incarnation.

This individual listens deeply to her inner voice. Certainly the capacity to do so is inherent in all third-stage individuals, regardless of the Sun sign in question. In Capricorn the inner voice speaks often of and from the highest levels of being. Truly it can be said that this individual can hear the music of the spheres. She waits on and serves the understanding she receives.

Relaxed and childlike, she is at the same time mature and serene. She possesses a calm, enduring sense of personal dignity which no one can take away, for she understands that she and no one else is responsible for the state of her inner being at all times and in all situations. Knowing what it feels like to experience self-doubt, and having relinquished any illusory feelings of personal superiority, she is highly accepting of others and easily approached by people. This is a good thing—for she has x-ray vision. A third-stage Capricorn often possesses the ability to look within another individual and see how that person is built. She can see the seed potentials which may lie dormant or suppressed.

She always relates to each person in terms of her ultimate potential, and yet is never fooled by the illusions into which each individual may have fallen. In the presence of a third-stage Capricorn, one always experiences a feeling of enduring contact with eternity. This individual seems to somehow know the answer to the ultimate question: "Why?". Living a transpersonal life, she acts as a Divine repository of eternal wisdom and knowledge, and is capable of intuitively weighing any individual situation against the perspective of the greater whole.

Like a universal switchboard operator, third-stage Capricorn can plug others into an experience of union with ultimate reality, showing them their true place and potential within the greater scheme of things. This individual teaches others to view their personal struggles within the greater context of overall personal and universal evolution. Where I have gone, you shall go too, yet in your own unique way. This is their message. Whether operating on an informal or professional level, this individual is well-suited to counsel people on a collective or individual basis.

She is not bound, however, to be a counselor. She may instead choose to become a visionary, or to spend her time expressing her inner contact by working as a gifted artist, scientist or technician. Although often willing and capable of taking an active part in instituting physical changes in the world which surrounds her, she never seeks to impose her will, having learned the lessons of first and second stage. Life must be allowed to evolve as it needs to. She is only there to assist when necessary. And so she waits, and when the time is right, she allows herself to be placed in the spot of greatest need. She has no burning drive to change the world, yet impact it she does, for the quality of her vision is so acutely expressed that it proves to be transformative in its own right. She cares little for the acclaim which this might easily bring her, as she is busily engaged in creating and discovering, always actively involved in pursuing the next stage of her vision.

Her natural inclination is to lead a somewhat retreating lifestyle. However, as often as not she finds that the world will not let her alone. She may be drawn to speak or communicate to a large audience concerning her discoveries and unique brand of personal understanding. The power of the life-force, expressing itself as compelling external circumstance, may draw her into a public or political arena. She never seeks to impose her understanding upon a world which may not be ready for her, but when the call sounds at the appropriate time, she follows through with total dedication. She may often find herself utilized by the forces of evolution to create profound change in the world around her, upon whatever personal collective or individual level may be necessary.

Still and silent within herself, she watches the pageant fulfilling itself within and about her. Knowing that time is infinite, she has complete trust in the process, living each moment in its entirety. Knowing that all are one, she attends effortlessly to her true responsibilities, whether they express themselves within or beyond herself. Having little or no attachment to the process, she nonetheless fully enjoys the experience!

Able to see the underlying structure of some incredibly important aspect of human or natural evolution, she spends her time enraptured with observing and serving the process of its unfolding, sharing her own personal vision with any who express a need or interest in doing so.

She stands in wait, an ever-patient servant of life, looking with one eye at the world of Man, while her inner eye constantly scans the essential structure of the cosmos. She knows that all possess within themselves the keys which can unlock all truth and wisdom. Knowing this she feels no urgency to impose what she may see upon those who surround her. Instead she watches from the heights, assisting all who seek to climb the peak upon which we shall all stand united in the end.

Capricorn at the Crossroads
First/Third-Stage Transition

At the end of first stage, Capricorn feels helplessly isolated in a crumbling tower of decreasing prominence. She may be filled with feelings of futility and self-loathing. Tempted to fall back upon the pleasures that surround her or to eschew the heights altogether and live in ragged nobility, she begins to believe that the power of society is greater than that of her own individuality. Of course she is correct, if by the power of her individuality she is referring to the unaided strength of her ego alone. But to believe that the world has the power to conquer the soul, its vision or the ultimate fulfillment of its purpose, is to live in a seductive illusion which will eventually lead down the path of least resistance and into the difficulties of second stage.

If she is to triumph at the crossroads, she must not lose her power to dream, nor with it, her ability to trust. While the ruler languishes in her tower, the bard may visit to reinspire her deepest dreams and realign her with her most potent values. At the end of first-stage Capricorn, the individual must not lose contact with her inner voice, which is the doorway to her own Divine power. Her inner voice will guide her to take certain actions which shall in time prove that the cause has not been lost. Capricorn is the first sign after the winter solstice, when the Earth has had Her darkest hour, but it is also the time when the days inevitably begin to grow longer once again. Patience is a most important quality for every Capricorn to cultivate; for it is natural to long for spring, but we shall only reach that part of the cycle by cooperating with and trusting in the natural order. Capricorn must learn to build with what is, and must therefore learn not to attempt to instigate life before its time.

If she can choose to trust in her inner voice, to believe in the dream for just a little while longer without weakening in her resolve in any way, she will come to learn that there are those whom she can still trust. Not everyone seeks power, some still serve the cause of truth. He may know at the end of first stage that she has failed in some manner, but she must learn that this failure is no reflection upon her value as an individual. Instead it is a challenge designed to prompt her to develop the ability to express true humility. For once she has made the decision to become a student of life, she will gain the power to become a guide and teacher to those who seek, of their own free will, to ascend the heights to which she is heir.

True humility embraces the mystery of life. One says to oneself: "I do not know, yet I am always willing to learn." Humility honors itself and yet maintains openness. And so the king sits in her tower and listens to her bard. And as she looks out of her window, she begins to see the countryside with completely new eyes. If she can avoid condemning herself or others, if she can avoid shirking her responsibilities or seeking illusory forms of power, and finally, if she can keep from immersing herself in worldly pleasure to dull her hidden pain, then she can come to learn that the inner world is actually much more enduringly powerful than the outer. And if she is to truly change or touch this world, it is there that she must begin. With this knowledge comes freedom. And so tonight, there shall be great dancing and feasting upon the green.

Childhood Conditions and Relationship Patterns

Consciously or unconsciously this individual possesses extremely strong ties to the Earth, which is our home and the field upon which the great game of life is played. On a soul level, she experiences a deep fascination with the underlying laws of life, as expressed in this worldly arena. She tends to have more physical energy than most other people, partly because the nature of her desires is directed so strongly towards the things of the Earth, and partly because she is so strongly motivated by the service of its inhabitants. Capricorn is an Earth sign and because this archetype of the Earth dominates her psyche so powerfully, she tends to gravitate toward a very strong mother figure. In childhood her mother subconsciously represents her tie to the Earth, while her father subconsciously represents her spiritual and philosophical nature.

In first stage, her mother is generally quite strong-willed and ambitious. Her outlook on life is forward looking, if rather simplistic, and she is inclined to project her own worldly ambitions onto her child, spurring her onto further accomplishment. She is also her child's best friend and most supportive ally, standing behind her in every possible situation. As first stage progresses, the child may find that her mother is supportive of her ambitions, without truly understanding her ideals. She may also over-indulge her desires, making it more difficult for her to avoid succumbing to the temptations of her position.

In early first stage, the father is often an individual with a great deal of personal integrity and idealism, although on a personal level, he possesses less impact upon his child than Capricorn's mother does. He may also be a dreamer, and some of his dreams may have no practical application within the world as it is. However, the father's values give meaning and purpose to the Capricornian individual's inclination towards personal ambition.

As first stage progresses and leads on into the second stage, the Capricornian develops an increasing tendency to be distant from or experience separation from her father. This pattern reflects the soul's increasing tendency to become separate from her deeper values and spiritual ideals and its tendency to lean towards a feeling of helplessness or impotence within the material world. Even if her ideals are retained, she may feel that she has no guidance or support in making these ideals real, and so is inclined to flounder.

Some Capricorns may encounter certain male figures who attempt to play something of a paternal role to them, without actually being their father. In second stage these individuals will often reflect Capricorn's present ideals and attitudes (or those cultivated during the most recent incarnation)—often expressing the fears or distortions which she may have recently acquired. Alternatively, this individual may symbolize the corruption of society which Capricorn feels she must struggle against. In this case the relationship may not take a positive form, especially in late-first stage or early-second stage, where Capricorn may experience defeat and a feeling of powerlessness in relationship to her father figure or father substitute. Sometimes a second-stage Capricorn or early second/third-stage Capricorn may make life rather difficult for a step father through projecting these traits upon her, regardless of whether or not they are actually present.

As her development progresses, Capricorn is inclined to become attracted toward more and more powerful mother figures. By second stage the mother is often inclined to be actively involved in the pursuit of her own ambitions. She is a strong individual, and is likely to be a powerful force of great benefit or great detriment to her child's development. Capricorn's mother signifies either the best or the worst traits of her own earthly nature, and is therefore an important source of basic life lessons and a signpost of where or where not to go in terms of the individual's own personal development.

Capricorn's mother leaves a lasting impression on her child and will advise her (or attempt to advise her) about her future, sharing her own personal wisdom (if evolved) or her strong biases and opinions (if unevolved) concerning the ways in which young Capricorn should or should not live her life. On a subliminal level she represents either the power of the material world—in first and second stage- or the spiritual essence of the Earth itself—in third or first/third-stage transition. Third-stage Capricorn is influenced by a mother who possesses great spiritual and practical wisdom.

In second stage, the earthly or material plane may gain such power over the individual that she may come to experience strong relationships with other female members of her family as well as with her mother. She will be surrounded by women, possibly indulged, almost certainly overwhelmed. There may be many sisters, aunts or grandmothers, all with a strong involvement in young Capricorn's life.

Another pattern which may also be evident is the splitting off of the mother influence. The individual may experience the struggle between two mother influences or mother substitutes, one representing the negative aspects of her relationship to the Earth and the other the positive ideals which this relationship embodies. At first/second-stage transition, when the crossroads stands before her, this pattern may be particularly evident, for one mother influence represents the patterns which will take her into second stage while the other represents the patterns which will take her into third.

As I have said earlier, the father's presence in Capricorn's early life is not likely to be very strong. He may leave his child's life before the individual has reached maturity. This causes most Capricorns, both male and female, to secretly or openly long for their father, or for a father figure who can supply them with what has been lost. This longing for the father is designed to eventually trigger a parallel longing for the spiritual principles which appear to exist outside of the confines of the material world. The presence or absence of a father influence is directly related to the level of spiritual contact and commitment which the individual has achieved in her most recent lifetime. Capricorns born into the third stage will experience a very close and fulfilling relationship with their fathers, who will most likely have strong spiritual inclinations of their own. Those in the second/third-stage transition, as well as those who have successfully navigated the first/third-stage transition, may experience a joyful reunion with their father or a positive relationship with their step-father or father substitute.

In the earlier stages, because this individual usually wants to be her mother's co-pilot, she may be inclined to be rather suspicious or jealous of the father. The father or any other male influence is often seen as a rival consort to her mother, the Goddess. She feels as though her mother has power. Power is what she wants, and so she wants to take the throne at center stage beside her. She may begin to make herself indispensable, just to be important and be near her. This is especially common when young Capricorn lives with her mother in a fatherless household.

The relationship with the mother tends to spur her on to accomplishment or possible ego-inflation for if she is her ally, it will seem to her that she can do no wrong, and she may constantly indulge her and compliment her upon her strengths. If she is her oppressor, she will develop a tremendous feeling of ambition, as her will struggles to overcome the powerful handicap to her self-esteem which their relationship represents. Where the mother is extremely negative, she may be living under the karmic results of her own previous lifetime's negative personality.

Because of her early relationship with men, she will be inclined either to compete strongly with men in her adult life, or to attempt to find the figure who can be placed upon a pedestal as the ideal father substitute. Sometimes both patterns can operate at the same time within one individual. Male and female Capricorns easily perceive the innate power of the feminine psyche, and will tend to view women as powerful individuals who can or must be cultivated as allies. In second stage there may, however, be an inclination to make use of women as tools simply for the furthering of their own ambitions, tools which may ultimately be ruthlessly cast aside.

Male Capricorns may have deep feelings of ambivalence

towards women, due to the overwhelming influence of their mother in the early childhood, often accompanied by the lack of a strong male influence to pattern themselves after. They may feel that all their strength must come from the woman in their lives. Or they may fear being dominated or overwhelmed and having the weakness of their ego challenged or revealed in their relationships with women.

It is important for Capricorn, as it is for any sign, to become objective in terms of her early childhood. Consciously or unconsciously she may be tied to her mother in a way which is destructive to her greater good. If she has been negative, she must learn to forgive her and release any negative compensatory behavior which she may have acquired. If she has been spoiled, she must begin to build a foundation for her own personal strength which does not rest upon the easy external support she has become accustomed to relying upon. Ultimately this may be the only way in which she can salvage her true sense of self-worth.

The relationship with the father should be viewed as a reflection of the individual's relationship with Divinity and her own personal ideals. If Capricorn feels unhappy with her relationship with her father, perhaps the inner void can be filled by achieving a deeper understanding of the Divine Source from which we all emanate. This re-unites Capricorn with the Cosmic Father force, and will in time create changes in her earthly experience of the father, as well as all other male influences in her life. Whatever the childhood conditions, once Capricorn is able to unlock their inner significance, she will then be able to build a new foundation for her future success as a true individual.

The female Capricorn may search, perhaps unsuccessfully, for a father in her adult relationships with men. She may choose men who abandon her or wound her in some way similar to her father or the father substitute(s) of her childhood. She may give up her freedom in the face of a strong male influence, or feel compelled to enter into competition with him, while secretly wishing for his nurturing and loving attention. She may choose as a partner a man of great worldly success, from whom she seeks support and whose character traits subtly remind her of her mother, while her life lacks the feeling of romance which the search for the missing father figure would seem to provide her with.

Alternatively she may disdain men, feeling them to be 'the weaker vessel', for she has experienced the power and wisdom of the feminine, but may have difficulty understanding the true positive power of the masculine.

Capricorn is a feminine Earth sign, ruled by the planet Saturn which is usually, though not always, portrayed as a masculine symbol of ultimate wisdom. Individuals of this sign must learn to balance their masculine and feminine potencies. Once they are able to accomplish this, they will ripen into true individuals, and will find the key to true romantic fulfillment.

Famous Capricorns

First Stage: Benjamin Franklin, Louis Pasteur, Horatio Alger.

First/Second Stage: Egyptian Pharaoh Ankhenaten, Joseph Stalin.

Second Stage: Richard Nixon, Elvis Presley, Robin Hood, Howard Hughes.

Second/Third Stage: Rudyard Kipling, David Bowie.

Third Stage: Carlos Castenada, Johan Kepler, Sir Isaac Newton, Joan of Arc, Alan Watts, Gurdjieff.

First/Third Stage: Martin Luther King, Jr.

AQUARIUS
cultural transformation

Aquarius is the last of the six masculine signs, ruled by the element of air, which denotes communication and mental mastery. Because air is considered to be a masculine element, in describing this sign I have used the words 'he', 'him' and 'his' as neutral terms in a description which can apply to either gender.

As we prepare to enter the Age of Aquarius, we need the Aquarian now more than ever, for he can teach us how to live. His soul has been waiting a long time for the coming period in history when humanity shall begin to realize the need to work as one.

Before being reborn it seems that the Aquarian listens to the music of the spheres. Impressed by this experience of universal harmony, he approaches the human kingdom. The Aquarian may spend time observing humanity even before he is born. He develops a great love for the human spirit and perceives its highest potentials.

Aquarius is naturally drawn to groups of individuals, large or small, who express the power of universal harmony through some form of brotherhood. The soul may assist some group, tribe, culture or nation on a spiritual level before being born into the first stage. When he finally chooses to be reborn, it is often to the same people he has forged an inner bond with prior to this incarnation.

First Stage

The soul must first immerse itself in an experience which teaches it how to lead a harmonious life here on Earth. While perfect harmony is not possible until mastery has been achieved, it is possible to experience what it is like to live in a culture which understands and promotes certain laws of nature as well as certain values of communal relationship. So the first-stage Aquarian will spend his or her initial lifetimes living somewhere in a state of earthly paradise. This existence is usually what would be termed primitive by the standards of our modern world-view. The Aquarian is born into a culture which attempts to live in harmony with nature and where every individual is charged with promoting the welfare of the whole society.

Many modern North Americans in second to third-stage Aquarius have lived as Native North Americans during their first-stage lifetimes. Through being able to perceive the previous incarnations of some of my clients, sometimes confirming their own memories or perceptions, I have also seen past experiences in early Celtic culture, certain African cultures, what seemed like a Polynesian culture, and even lifetimes spent in early Christian communities. Perfection is not to be expected. While most first-stage Aquarians live in peaceful societies, I have encountered a few second to third-stage Aquarians who have lived in war-like cultures during first stage. And it is possible, though rare, to find first-stage Aquarians absorbing the best which our present society has to offer, despite its imbalances and its lack of proper relationship to nature. In general, however, the culture which spawns the new Aquarian is inclined to have strong interpersonal values, and is also likely to live in harmonious relationship with the Earth and those societies which may surround them.

He or she learns what it means to exist in right relationship to others. His thoughts, as he goes about his daily existence, are not so much of himself as they are of his people. He develops the habit of constantly considering the needs of all, as he makes his decisions or plans his activities. He learns to heed and work in alignment with the laws of nature. The plant, animal and mineral kingdoms are also his brothers and sisters. His bond with nature is strong, and he may serve some time as a healer within his society.

At first he is a student of life, learning the laws under which his people live, serving in whatever small capacity he can. But as lifetimes pass, he grows in skill and wisdom, until he becomes almost an expert in the art of living in simple natural alignment with the lifestyle of his people. The soul may remain with one society throughout first stage, or he may choose to incarnate into more than one culture in order to develop the practical and social skills necessary to his greater purpose. Whatever his choice, as time passes he finds himself becoming less of a student and more of a teacher. Yet he still retains a certain quality of humility and an essential attitude of loving service. He respects and understands the ideals of his society perhaps more than many of the individuals who surround him.

As first stage comes to a close, he finds that the love and wisdom which he has attained during his sojourn in paradise have become indelibly stamped upon his heart. Once he makes his first encounter with those who know nothing of how to truly live, he will begin his transition into second stage. For all men are his brothers, and those who live in ignorance truly need his wisdom more than do those who live in paradise.

First/Second-Stage Transition

The love of this soul for his people has become larger almost than the tribe itself. Instinctively he seeks a larger purpose. He begins seeking new horizons and begins to prepare for what he senses will be a great undertaking. He still loves and serves his land and people and is known for his love and his wisdom; yet he waits.

The turning point of his lifetime will come through an important encounter with a culture which is not his own. He may have lived in isolation, unaware that there existed any other way of life beyond the one he has led for so long. If so, then this encounter will come as a great surprise. Or he may have been dimly aware of those who have existed in another world and lived in another way, yet may never have considered their importance until some major event brings the two cultures into contact with one another.

His first encounter with these outsiders causes him to wonder at their ignorance. This is quickly followed by a great feeling of compassion. He can see that their lifestyle causes them to suffer. And what is even more awe-inspiring, they are often unaware of exactly how much pain they are experiencing. His heart goes out to them, and yet at first he will return home to his people, for his primary loyalty still lies there. He is destined, for a time, to be torn between two cultures.

As time passes he may develop a bond with one or more individuals from the new world of the outsiders. Perhaps they are individuals with whom a bond was forged in a previous incarnation or a previous cycle of incarnations.

Whatever the case, he may find that they are in need of his wisdom, and so they constantly draw him outward and into deeper involvement. If there is a peaceful interplay between the two cultures, (which is unfortunately seldom the case) he may find himself naturally drawn further and further from his home.

With time he may find that his commitment is to the world as a whole and not just to his land of origin. This can be a lonely realization, and one which is not often well understood by his nearest and dearest. He spends more and more time with those who require his knowledge and understanding, until he reaches the point at which he realizes that the interests of his highest ideals can only be served through fully entering into this world of the outsiders. He becomes inspired to take an active role in restoring the balance of their society as a whole — quite an ambitious undertaking!

More commonly, the initial interaction between the two cultures is less than harmonious. This causes a great deal of strain for the first/second-stage Aquarian, for he is always inclined to see every man and woman as a member of the greater human family of which he is a part. He may form certain initial bonds with various individuals, only to find his loyalties becoming traumatically divided as conflicts begin to escalate.

He may live to witness the grave wounding or utter destruction of his way of life at the hands of those who seem to have less wisdom, yet more power than his own people. Throughout it all, he will attempt to be strong for the people — all the people — and play the role of peacemaker when he can. Should he fail, and the forces of destruction hold sway (as they often do), then he will carry the scars of this battle with him through many lifetimes, making it difficult for him to avoid conflict on either a social or personal level, even though his goal and ideal is always harmony. Those who make the transition in this more traumatic manner will still choose to take the same steps and decide to become a part of the 'foreign' culture in order to heal and realign it, but these individuals may do so in a more intense, passionate and fearful manner.

Occasionally Aquarius may make the transition from first to second stage along with his culture. This may have occurred, for example, in a rural European culture of several hundred years ago, or in a modern community in rural Asia, as the society itself gives way to the forces of evolution and 'progress' and decides to modernize itself. In this case he watches the 'insiders' become the 'outsiders', as individuals in his culture go through the process of gradually losing their state of natural balance with themselves, each other and the world which surrounds them.

Aquarius seeks what is best for the people as a whole, while most individuals mistakenly believe that their best course of action lies only in the direction of apparent self-interest. Not wanting to devalue what is new, in case it does prove to be of some benefit, Aquarius still finds himself in the position of trying to defend the old ways to a people increasingly less inclined to listen to him. His rank in society may gradually change from that of revered elder to outdated crank, and yet he *will remember* the past, as he passes into second stage determined to heal and realign his people.

Second Stage

Keywords: "You're just not listening to me."

In second stage the individual's purpose is completely directed towards the new culture with which he has aligned himself. Because a new stage can begin at any point in a lifetime, he may begin the second stage in the midst of a single lifetime, often relocating to a completely different culture from the one in which he was born. Alternatively, he may begin this next stage of his development at the beginning of a new lifetime, having ended his previous life, perhaps as the result of violence or suffering brought about through cultural invasion or decay.

Whatever his situation, at the beginning of the second stage, he finds himself still armed with the wisdom and knowledge acquired in his first-stage lifetimes. Even if he is now living in a completely different lifetime, he will awaken to find that the old wisdom simply will not die.

Idealistic, hopeful and determined, he begins to attend to the process of cultural transformation which he feels must now take place. He might as well be a visitor from another planet for all the understanding which he receives.

Still his purpose burns within him, and cannot be denied. In early second stage, he may be alone, but he is never lonely, for he still feels the support of his ancient culture deep within his being.

He often takes on a political role, or a role as a healer, albeit a somewhat controversial one. His position in society may expose him to certain dangers, and so it is extremely common for the early second-stage individual to decide that he must walk his path alone, for he would not wish to subject family members to the dangers which he may face. Occasionally he may have to witness the suffering of his family before such a choice is actually made. After several lifetimes lived in this manner, the cumulative effect of these decisions begins to act as an automatic inner vow of solitude. Lifetimes later it may cause difficulty in achieving a fulfilling partnership, while the Aquarian may remain at a loss to explain this situation on a conscious level.

He may be an ambassador or a peacemaker, and learns to adapt to and understand human nature in a way that few individuals are capable of achieving. Yet as time passes he may experience enormous frustration, for the changes which he attempts to implement do not seem to stick, no matter what tactics he may employ. His values are just too far away from the level of understanding of those who surround him. They are for the most part incapable of perceiving the truths which he stands for and embodies. Although he may touch a few individuals, he does not create the large-scale transformation which his ideals would have him realize.

As each lifetime passes he draws further and further away from his original source of understanding and the innocent optimism which fueled his purpose at the beginning of the second stage. Feeling a sense of mounting frustration and futility, he may begin to lose confidence in himself and his abilities. If he loses touch with his most basic values, he may become a lost soul indeed. When what he stands for is not acknowledged, his self-worth plummets, and he may come to fear for his personal survival.

In reaction he may reject society, becoming increasingly misanthropic, cynical and suspicious. He may become an outsider, perhaps deliberately challenging human or cosmic law, or becoming violent and vengeful. He may simply surrender to his feelings of powerlessness, becoming a very little person who is lost in the shuffle, perhaps hardly capable of relating to others.

Or he may feel that if he cannot beat them, he may as well join them; and because he believes at this stage that society has an enormous power over him and his destiny, this decision may prompt him to become a fearful and compulsive conformist. In first stage he or she was a spokesperson for his society, upholding values which had the capacity to nourish all, now he may rigidly defend the values of the society which he has adopted, believing that he must do so in order to ensure his personal survival. He may be bitter and unhappy and tends to secretly hate himself for becoming everything which he once so stridently opposed.

As the individual nears the end of second stage a terrifying feeling of impotence may exist at the conscious or unconscious level of his being. He often responds to others in an emotionally or intellectually rigid manner. In many cases he still feels that he is trying to tell people something extremely important and that no one is listening. What he has to say may by now be little more than gibberish, or his ideals may have remained somewhat intact, and yet he develops a stubborn attachment to those who refuse to listen to the insights which he offers.

There has never been anything wrong with his deepest, innate life values, but his means of approaching life require drastic change. When he truly tires of the pain of alienation, and is finally ready to stop pounding his head against the wall and being mastered by his fears, he will begin to look around for a true alternative. When he gives up trying to tell the world and those who do not wish to listen to him how to live their lives, then he begins to become ready to enter the second/third-stage transition. For some the latter portion of this stage will endure beyond all necessity, for in a futile effort to fulfill what he once believed his purpose, he has developed an incredible amount of stubbornness.

It is quite common for the late second stage or second/third-stage Aquarian to experience a personal relationship with someone whose values clash with his own. All attempts to enlighten this individual are destined to come to naught. This relationship is a gift, offering him an opportunity to release his rigid stance. It is not that his ideas are wrong, only his way of presenting them, and his choice of whom to present them to which is mistaken. In the process of undergoing lifetimes of struggle against a corrupt society, he has lost the ability to understand another person's point of view. Until he has walked a mile in someone else's shoes, he cannot help them to untangle their shoelaces. The ultimate truth is that the second-stage Aquarian is in the right place at the wrong time. Most people simply are not ready for him. Only as he passes through the second/third-stage transition and comes to a true understanding of the forces of evolution, will he find the key which can be used to transform the world around him.

Second/Third-Stage Transition

When the loneliness and frustration which he feels become overpowering and he is finally ready to admit that he might not have all the answers, he eventually realizes that he must seek a solution to his dilemmas, and so he enters this all-important transition phase. Perhaps he has driven away everyone who loves him. Perhaps he has lost himself in a sea of conformity and now, deeply oppressed, needs to find the key to the resurrection of his true self-hood. Perhaps he has destroyed himself by rebelling fruitlessly and destructively against society and needs to reclaim himself from the bottomless pit of alienation into which he has fallen.

The list of his enemies at this point is large. They may include fear, cynicism, despair, helplessness, distrust, stubbornness, resentment and self-hatred. He should never include himself or others in this list, for if he does so, he will only be falling into illusion. His self-worth is low, as consciously or unconsciously he feels like a failed reformer. His childhood was most likely difficult, as he usually entered the world expecting alienation and perhaps feeling that he deserved abuse because he had not contributed as he should have. He needs to learn to understand (especially on the emotional level—for some things are easy to understand mentally, but difficult to absorb emotionally), that it is not his fault that others were unwilling or unable to listen to him. Whoever coined the saying, "You can lead a horse to water, but you can't make him drink," must have passed through the second stage of Aquarius.

Many times the difficult personal relationship or relationships which he experiences will ultimately assist him in understanding this truth. When he releases himself from his unconscious burden of failed responsibility, he will be half way there. He has to step out of the fray and know that he has a right to pause and take care of himself. At some point it is important for him to resurrect his innate spirituality, and instead of using all of his powers in a fruitless attempt to change the world, he must gradually learn to let go and allow a greater power to heal and transform his inner being. The more he becomes involved in a healing contact with spirit and nature, letting others go their own way, the more he feels himself gradually returning to his true identity. He spoke with spirit during his first-stage lifetimes, and once he decides to do so again, he finds it a relatively simple process to re-establish the original bonds which were forged within his soul.

The more he speaks with his spirit, the more it instructs him in his day-to-day life, and he realizes that he must never allow himself to get so caught up with others or with the outside world that he neglects his own growth. His contact with the spiritual forces of life and his own inner being also teaches him the truth about human evolution. He learns that there is indeed a purpose for all of the imbalances which he sees around him. To change society before it is ready to be changed often robs individuals of their need to learn enduring lessons which the soul will always remember. He must learn to let them come to him. As he heads towards third stage, he comes to a second important realization which will truly set him free: while it was not his fault that they did not listen to him, it was not their fault either! Everything in nature requires time to ripen to fruition.

This understanding frees his soul from any attempt to force or will a change in the world around him. As he learns to let evolution take its natural course, he frees himself to attend to the cultivation of his true inner self. Gradually he removes the old psychic scar tissue which has resulted from his clash with an unwilling and unwitting society. Anger is released, and he comes to realize that he really has nothing to fight against. Fear is released, and he no longer feels compelled to surrender to anything which is not in harmony with who he truly is. All of his original knowledge and wisdom returns with much greater depth and maturity of expression. He finds his true life inheritance.

In this process of healing and resurrecting himself, he must deal with any forms of imbalance concerning relationships which he may have acquired in the past. He must learn to trust again, and to know that others will accept him on an intimate level. It is important for him to be able to release any unconscious vows which he may have made to remain single and/or childless. He needs to experience a fulfilling relationship with a mate, and perhaps also to create a family of his own.

As he learns to allow others to come to him when they require the fruits of his wisdom, he begins to honor himself as an equal working partner with the Divine force which enfolds all things. Feeling himself accepted and supported by this central aspect of life itself, he knows that he is worthy of acceptance by others, and that all of those whom he loves can be cared for while he lives at-one with this presence. In time this knowledge leads him to form close bonds with other individuals who share his level of understanding.

He must untangle his ties with those who do not seek his level of evolution and understanding. While it is certainly right for him to love and serve all to the limit of their capacity to allow him to do so, he must learn not to seek love and acceptance from those who are incapable of giving it, no matter how strong his tie with them may be. Many late second-stage Aquarians develop an attachment to one or more individuals who do not honor or listen to them. This represents an unconscious attempt to make up for the fact that society at large did not accept or recognize them. This does not work, as the individuals he chooses do not accept him either, and these relationships only cause him much personal pain and suffering. To enter third stage, illusions such as these must be overcome.

Although they may have to leave certain individuals behind, they must also know that true love can never be lost, for as their loved ones emerge eventually from their own waking dream, in their own time they will all ultimately reunite. Each must be allowed to tread his or her own path. Beyond the natural concern which we may all express for each other, or the parent's concern for his or her child before that child reaches maturity, we all need to learn to allow those we care for to experience their own necessary allotment of personal suffering. For without each of us being able to forge our own paths through life, no true progress can ever be attained. Letting go is hard, but mastering the ability to do so gives Aquarius the gift of true freedom, and reveals a deeper level of meaning, allowing the Aquarian individual to give aid where it is really needed.

Many Aquarians in second/third-stage experience a conflict between urban and rural lifestyles. Although the life purpose of some third-stage Aquarians requires them to create a home for themselves within the city gates, most second/third and third-stage Aquarians do not belong in an urban environment. Simply stated, this transition requires Aquarius to turn and walk away from "The People" and from all of the ties which bind and limit, all of the unresolved desires that no one else can fulfill, to claim the freedom of being himself.

By the time he reaches the second/third stage the society to which he has formed his 'negative bond of compassion' will in all likelihood be experiencing its decline. Instead of adding to the destructive chaos which surrounds him by attempting to cut the old form loose by its roots, or clinging himself to those roots, as they shudder in the whole tree's death throes, he must turn and forge a gateway from an old world into the new.

As he does so, he will gradually come to gather his tribe about him. Many of the souls with whom he forged close ties during the first stage of his development, as well as some who have been touched (often after the fact of his passing) during the second stage, return to aid in the great undertakings in which he is involved. With full support from those in his personal, social and professional (for these read tribal) lives, he passes into the third stage of his development.

Third Stage

Third-stage Aquarians have learned to release the impossible task of attempting to change a world which does not want to be changed. Now they begin the process of cutting a doorway from an old world into a new one. First-stage Aquarians are born into an already existing harmonious society. In second stage they enter a corrupt society and suffer the burden of attempting to change it. In third stage they begin the process of founding a new society which will finally be able to express all of their soul's ideals.

They may do this on a large scale or in an apparently very small arena. Whatever they do will ultimately have a lasting impact, however, for their actions are perfectly timely. At last they can relax and truly enjoy themselves. They have a great love for humanity and are capable of understanding almost anyone, regardless of their station in life. They truly live and let live. Their creativity has been liberated, and forms a very important part of the process of building a new world.

While barriers to self-expression dissolve, so do all the old barriers which in the past may have prevented intimacy with others and his own personal acceptance of himself and the world. He now enjoys close friendship and intimate love. His community is very important to him, for he cannot build a new world all by himself. It is built through him and through those he is closest to. In this stage he enjoys the adventure of discovering new ways to express his innate knowledge, while he also enjoying the satisfaction of being able to build a fulfilling family life for himself and his partner. His microcosm and his macrocosm both reflect the values of the truly harmonious life, as his soul expresses the purpose which it has always longed for.

Aquarius at the Crossroads
First/Third-Stage Transition

At the end of first-stage Aquarius the soul encounters a new and unfamiliar society. Through invasion or evolution the world around him is changing. He may be asked to move to a new world where his talents may be required. Whatever the process, he finds himself about to enter new and unfamiliar territory. He sees corruption and imbalance, and he wants to help his new people to change. But can he?

To master the first/third-stage transition Aquarius must make a leap in perception. He is able to see the strength of his own personal values and the weakness of the society which he is about to enter. What he now needs to see is the purpose for it all to exist just as it is. His knowledge is more powerful than the imbalances which surround him. If he enters second stage and tries to enforce a change for the good of the people, he will be overwhelmed, not by their sheer numbers alone, but because he will unwittingly transgress a cosmic law. It is not his place to interfere. This is very hard for him to understand. Change can only happen when the people are ready for it.

Instead of binding himself to a world he believes is wrong, he must maintain his freedom and begin to work to build a world which he knows is right. Instead of staying with his old society (if this is even possible by now) or joining the ranks of the new world which has confronted him, he must set off on his own to explore and create new worlds. If he stops to listen before he speaks he will be guided by an inner understanding which will help him realize that the people must learn from their own mistakes. There is no other way. Those who do not seem to need to learn from these mistakes have only made the same ones in a different place and time.

He is far better served by laying a foundation which will serve those who have already learned the necessary lessons. It takes courage to set off in a completely new direction, vision to even perceive that it is possible, and understanding to know that such a course is in fact valid. An Aquarian at the end of first stage can develop this kind of understanding if he remains flexible and open to the voice of Divine Guidance as it expresses itself in his life. In the long run he will do far more good by creating a new way of life for those who long for an alternative than he will by attempting to tear down the foundations of corruption in this world.

If he is able to perceive and act upon this understanding, he will no longer run the risk of losing touch with the truths which he has spent lifetimes gathering. Instead he will bring them into a new arena where they can be freshly interpreted. The seeds gathered at the harvest which completes first stage can be planted immediately. They do not need to weather a long hard winter, when there are always new worlds in which they can flower.

Childhood Conditions and Relationship Patterns

Aquarius is an air sign. The element of air rules the intellect and social values of the individual—the part of a person which allows them to think and to relate. Because this aspect of the psyche is more strongly influenced by the father than by the mother, Aquarius also tends to be more strongly affected by his or her father or to view this individual as the dominant parent.

In first stage the Aquarian is born to parents who have strong feelings of loyalty and commitment to the culture in which they live. They define themselves according to their people and their society and are completely immersed in fulfilling certain responsibilities within their social environment. The young Aquarian is raised to do likewise and feels a great deal of pride in his society, enjoying the adventure of developing his skills in order to make a shining contribution to his world.

Aquarius's father is a law keeper. He is strongly involved with some important aspect of society, and as first stage progresses the Aquarian's parents seem to take more and more of an important position within their culture. The young Aquarian admires his or her father and would like to grow up to emulate his qualities. He is in awe of the man and wonders if he can ever be equal to his stature as an individual. By the end of first stage he finds that he triumphantly masters the culture in which he lives and can finally feel proud of himself and his personal contribution.

While Aquarius' father represents the abstract ideals of the culture into which his child has been born, Aquarius' mother embodies the same values translated into human terms. She truly cares about people as individuals and expresses the personal side of human unity. She knows that we are all one, not because it is written in the constitution, but because she can feel it. While Aquarius admires his father and seeks to emulate him, it is through his mother that his heart becomes completely committed to the cause. She can see her child's ultimate potential and believes that he or she can do anything. Aquarius is not always so sure. Nor is he always particularly ambitious in early first stage. However, her encouragement spurs him onward in his quest to live up to the ideals which his father has presented to him.

In early second stage the father is also deeply involved with the values of his culture. To his child he represents the powers that be. However, in this stage Aquarius is not always in harmony with the powers that be, and therefore he or she may experience a certain amount of conflict with his father. It is his natural tendency to want to look up to his father, and yet the ideals and values of the two individuals may clash. The father may have rigid attitudes, and may lack in understanding of his child, seeing his differences as weaknesses. He may become hostile towards Aquarius in order to toughen him up, or because he is frustrated and confused about his own life and fearful of the valid alternatives which he senses his child may have the potential to present.

Aquarius's mother often sympathizes with her child and tries to protect him, but may not have the power to completely counteract the influence of the father. Her example shows her child that his ideals are still important but that they may not ultimately have much power in the world. She still believes in him as an individual, however, and this may prompt him to courageously attempt to bring his ideals out into the world.

As second stage progresses his father may become more rigid, more authoritarian, and possibly somewhat violent and abusive. Aquarius's experience with him and other male figures in his life may not be very positive. The influence of the mother may also become somewhat negative as second stage progresses. If he feels that his personal values have no place in the world and that he is therefore bereft of support, he will be inclined to be drawn towards a very cold mother. Perhaps she cares more than she lets on, but feels that she is preparing her child for the difficulties of life or helping him to somehow cope with his father's influence by being cold and secretive towards him.

Later in second-stage Aquarius's relationship with his mother may deteriorate further. She may be neglectful and abandoning, or she may be irrational and abusive. Neglect is more common in the conformist phase of second-stage Aquarius, abuse more common for the non-conformist.

In later second stage the father may also abandon the child, leaving him to feel that he has no source of guidance to look up to and no ideals to determine his path in life. Alternatively he may reflect the individual's own response to society, by being extremely rigid and conservative or irrational and destructively non-conformist.

In second/third stage the relationship with one or both parents may balance itself and assist the individual in his or her process of self-healing. If the relationship with the father is positive, he is likely to be a creative non-conformist who strengthens his child's resolve to be himself. Aquarius's natural tendency is to be closer in spirit to his father than to his mother, and a constructive father influence at this point will ultimately be of much benefit to him. His father inspires him to seek alternatives, and helps him to renew his personal ideals. He may grow up to contribute new ideas to the world which are of great benefit to those who are seeking the 'doorway' which Aquarius has the potential to create.

If the relationship with the mother is positive during the second/third-stage transition it is an indication that the individual requires more assistance in healing his personal emotional response to life. He needs to feel that there is a place for his deeper values. He may need to remember what it is that he has forgotten, whereas the individual with a more positive father influence has not forgotten his ideals, he only needs some encouragement in expressing himself.

A child born into third stage often returns immediately to his tribe. His parents may be actively involved in some form of social change, busily building their own version of a new world. Even if they are not, the child often finds that he receives much support from a father whom he greatly admires. His mother is a very caring individual who encourages him to be true to himself. Even if the family is not perfect, the third-stage Aquarian will find that he or she gravitates toward other individuals who provide much in the way of personal support and encouragement as he or she matures. He may not be as deeply affected by the negative experiences of his childhood, for he knows that it is his destiny to create alternatives which will be deeply needed and appreciated by those who are ready to receive them.

In first stage most individuals have little difficulty locating a compatible partner. Female Aquarians at any stage are often inclined to seek a partner who subconsciously represents a father figure with qualities similar to their own father. In first stage they are likely to have a constructive and harmonious relationship with their father, and so it is easy for them to attract a partner who will be a great source of inspiration and support to them. In early first stage they will seek a strong and protective partner, whereas in later second stage, when they are often taking on greater positions of responsibility and leadership, they will seek a partner who is more of an equal or who provides a sort of back-up support system.

The male Aquarian in first stage has similar experiences. He is likely to choose a woman whose emotional strength and understanding reminds him of his mother. In early first stage she is undemanding and supportive of his potential, some of which is not yet realized. By later first stage she may assist him in his purpose or provide some form of personal support and refuge when he comes home to relax. The only difficulty which may emerge during first stage is that these individuals may sometimes be inclined to be rather neglectful of their mates, as they are so busy with their own careers, community projects or social involvements.

By second stage certain relationship difficulties may emerge. In early second stage the individual may still be able to attract a supportive mate. The two may attempt to change the world together. However, as I have already mentioned, the early second-stage Aquarian is often involved in dangerous undertakings, and may live to see his mate or family suffer as a result. This can lead the individual to avoid becoming deeply involved in personal relationships.

Another difficulty may emerge: the male Aquarian in second stage may be too controversial for his mate. She wants a quiet life for the two of them where they can raise a family and live out a long and happy life together. He knows that he cannot rest until certain things have been attended to. How can she ignore the needs of the world? The female Aquarian may have a similar difficulty. Her partner cannot understand why she feels a need to be so different and so controversial. Why doesn't she settle down and be quiet and stop embarrassing him?

Mr. Aquarius chose his mate because she was so sensitive and supportive. Mrs. Aquarius (she would probably prefer to be called Ms.) selected her husband because she admired his strengths, his calmness and his protective qualities. But it is as if they have each married someone from a different culture. Subconsciously they may be confused, for the criteria which they used to choose a mate in first stage, where everyone shared the same values, often do not work in second stage, where they have entered another world. Philosophical conflicts are therefore common during second stage.

As second stage progresses the female Aquarian may still subconsciously seek a father figure. Her own father may have been absent or abusive in some manner, and she feels compelled to compensate by seeking the image of the first-stage father figure which she still subconsciously remembers. However it is easy for her to delude herself, imagining that she has found someone who corresponds to the image she is seeking, when in fact she has only found someone who will treat her very much as the father of the present lifetime probably did.

The male Aquarian may once again experience a similar pattern. If his relationship with his mother was negative, he may find himself involved in a relationship with a woman who abuses or abandons him, or whose behavior is extremely irrational and disturbed. If his relationship with his mother was positive, he still may have become aware of her vulnerability in a disturbing manner during his childhood. This may cause him to avoid commitment as an adult, for he feels that he must protect his mate, as he should have protected his mother, and somehow make up for her suffering, and he may feel that he does not have the power to do so.

By late second-stage Aquarius has chosen either to conform or to rebel. Whatever his or her choice may be, this individual usually tries to select a mate who supports it. Unpleasant surprises seem to be a natural part of his experience in this area, for he may find that his mate once again is unable to live up to his expectations. The partner does not conform enough and conventional Aquarius is embarrassed. Or he turns out to be a living embodiment of some form of corruption which the rebellious Aquarian feels compelled to take a stand against. The mate could easily be one of the people whom Aquarius tries to change but cannot, as he or she comes to the end of second stage.

The relationship patterns of second stage may carry over into second/third stage or even into early third-stage. Or they may change almost immediately, as the individual enters the transition. The key is in learning to release the emotional attachment to making the world change, and beginning to embrace the natural changes which seek to act through Aquarius as an individual. Is Aquarius seeking a mate to compensate for something, to fill an emptiness or some sort of emotional 'need'? If so, he or she is inclined to attract the old pattern once again. When he becomes involved in the joy of discovery, and treasures any unexpected opportunity to share it, then he will be able to find a partner who is on his wavelength.

Partnership is an important part of community, and is automatically fulfilled once third stage gets fully under way. the Aquarian and his mate share the satisfaction of building a new world along with the tribe which they have gathered along the way.

Famous Aquarians

First Stage: Wayne Gretsky. (I used to think that there were no first-stage Aquarians in our culture, but now I believe that this was just own my bias. We do uphold certain important values as a society. This individual has come out of a closely knit environment, has learned a lot about teamwork and is certainly expressing many of the highest values of our culture. At the end of first stage, he has triumphed in this world. Is he approaching the transition?)

First/Second Stage: William Burroughs.

Second Stage: Alice Walker (old soul), Ernest Borgnine, James Dean, Germaine Greer.

Second/Third Stage: Lewis Caroll, Wolfgang Amadeus Mozart, Jules Verne, Alan Alda.

Third Stage: Paul Newman, Evangeline Adams (famous astrologer), Yoko Ono, Bob Marley, Abraham Lincoln.

PISCES
inspired visionary

Pisces is the final feminine sign of the zodiac. Because of this, while desribing the characteristics of this sign I have used the words 'she', 'her' and 'hers' as neutral terms which can apply to either gender. This does not indicate that Pisceans are more feminine or less masculine than members of the traditionally masculine signs of the zodiac.

Pisces is a special sign which has a different origin from the other 12. The Piscean is a true outsider. Many Pisces individuals are quite new here. Yet they are not young souls. They have already developed a certain amount of sophistication before entering this earthly realm. They are in the difficult situation of being an old soul, with an old soul's sensitivity and perceptiveness, while at the same time being relative newcomers. Because they can absorb and perceive more than others, their adjustment can at times be difficult. They have enormous compassion and a great desire to contribute. From the beginning theirs is not an easy path. However, they are often stronger than they realize, and are destined to triumph creatively in the end.

First Stage

According to esoteric teachings, the human soul does not just spring into being from out of nowhere. It takes many billions of years for a soul to develop the individuality necessary to become human. Some traditions teach that there are different paths towards the goal of becoming a human being. Generally speaking we begin in the mineral kingdom, move to the vegetable kingdom, then the animal kingdom, until we finally reach the human realm. But, as anyone who has spent a great deal of time with animals knows, even within the same species all animals are not created equal.

Pisces is one of the two most common signs that people tend to first select when becoming human. Some Pisceans have entered the human world from the animal kingdom. The usual last step on the path to becoming a human is to spend time as a domesticated animal. (Be nice to your dog, he might be your mother-in-law one day!) But the Piscean soul who comes from the animal kingdom has not been your average animal. He or she was often quite highly evolved and aware of things which most animals were not. For many souls the process of becoming human is rather unconscious. They gravitate in that direction slowly and steadily and wake up one morning with a mortgage and a VCR. The animal soul who is destined to enter the human world as a Piscean watches humans with a sense of purpose. She is fascinated with humanity, and develops a great love and admiration for them. He feels great compassion for their difficulties and longs for a way to contribute to their world.

I had a cat once who was born under the sign of Pisces. I'm sure that she was preparing to enter the human world one day under the same birth sign. We had a busy household and she positioned herself where she could watch people coming and going daily. She had very wise eyes and was enormously sensitive. She seemed to be studying us. She was very attached to me and followed me around like a dog. The other cats did not like her, sensing that she was different. She was completely unaggressive with them, even when they attacked her outright. She was very caring and affectionate toward everyone and no longer lived under the rules of a cat, but rather studied the rules of the human world.

There are other forms of life on this planet which do not have a physical existence such as ours. They are known all over the world, and in our culture they are called faeries, nature spirits or Devas. It is also possible to evolve through this kingdom before becoming human. Like animals, most Devic spirits are concerned with their own realm of life and do not spend much time concerning themselve with humans (although our present rate of ecological destruction does concern them.)

Some devic souls do develop a fascination with humanity, however, and may become human as a result. In the process of preparing for this passage they develop a greater emotional capacity than is usually common with the denizens of their realm. They learn to think independently, observe developing humanity and become inspired by our goals. They often become attached to religious buildings and sacred places and may thrive upon human emotions of spiritual devotion. Some less fortunate souls may become attached to an overly emotional human, with the result that they developand their own emotional imbalances once they themselves enter the human world.

Some Pisceans do not come from the animal kingdom or the fairy kingdom, but instead come to us from other worlds. This always sounds like science fiction to many people, but it is only logical if you look at it realistically. The Universe is a living intelligent being, with a tendency to evolve and develop increasing complexity and greater forms of intelligence. This cannot be the only world in a vast Universe to have evolved human life. In fact there is much scientific evidence for the possibility that life was seeded on Earth from outer space. (See Fred Hoyle's "The Intelligent Universe.")

The Piscean who comes to us from another world was not beamed down by Scotty. Instead she chose the easy route of reincarnation. According to yet another esoteric tradition, human life on this planet is extremely emotion-based. On many other worlds the civilizations are much more rational. They are peaceful and productive and do not suffer the same agonies we do but, accordingly, do not share the same ultimate potential. The planet Earth represents a sort of cosmic crash course (doesn't it feel like it sometimes!), and the soul coming here through Pisces is fascinated with the challenge. She has already developed more of an emotional nature than her fellows and is therefore a bit of a renegade. She has also developed a tremendous intuitive ability which allows her to become aware of the alternative which the Earth represents. She is greatly inspired by the potential of this world, and feels tremendous compassion for the suffering of the earthly souls which she has come to admire. And so she is drawn to rebirth upon this world.

The Piscean soul's origin always influences her subtly. Having entered through the animal kingdom she approaches life in a simple earthy manner and is comfortable with her physical being. She has great loyalty and is compassionate and non-judgmental. A soul coming from the Devic kingdom always seems somewhat ethereal. She may have a deep love of religion or a strong bond with a certain spiritual path. She is likely to be quite creative and mystically inclined. She may have trouble controlling her emotions and may be somewhat amoral, especially in first stage. The Piscean soul who has come to us from other worlds is always a unique individual. She may have unusual talents. In second stage she is often inclined to become overly rational, and may be uncomfortable with her physical body. If she is at first unsuccessful in her quest, she may feel very inferior to humanity and may never quite feel able to fit in. She may compensate through becoming something of an elitist.

It is possible for a soul to combine some of these origins, for example to begin her study of humanity as an animal and complete it in the Devic kingdom. Or she may come from another human world and make her adjustment to Earth life by spending time in communion with the elements. She may even choose a brief period of time in animal incarnation to help her adapt and become more grounded.

Whatever her origins, she is inclined to possess certain characteristics as she enters the first stage. She is inspired by the dream of the Earth. To become human means to experience a feeling of separation from the rest of life. This creates loneliness and a deep need to experience love. Becoming a true individual is hard enough without trying to do it in such emotionally oriented bodies. The only way in which we can end our pain is to learn to generate love — to create it within ourselves, rather than seeking it from without. Not only are we attempting to become consciously self-aware and aware of our independent powers as unique individuals, we are also attempting to become independently creative sources of love itself, thus attempting to do two things at once, so to speak. The crash course which Earth life represents offers a much greater creative opportunity, but also provides a much rougher ride as we go about the process of attempting to achieve the goal which we have set for ourselves. Attempting to achieve this high ideal takes great courage, and Pisces admires this. It also entails great suffering, and Pisces feels tremendous compassion for these courageous souls who must suffer so much in their quest.

Pisces is a water sign, ruled by Neptune, who in Roman mythology was god of the ocean. Pisces is drawn to this water planet, being profoundly affected by the struggles and potential triumphs which it represents. It is interesting to note that on a physical level this planet is very unusual due to the fact that it contains so much water, a substance which is comparatively rare on most other planets. It is the water-based nature of our environment which allows us to experience the form of evolution we are presently undergoing. This is one of the reasons why this planet is so precious.

Human emotions are based upon the endocrine system, which is made up of hormones carried in a bloodstream which is nine-tenths water. In this world we seem to be trapped in our emotional bodies, feeling the pain which results from our seemingly eternal state of separation. We are constantly seeking the eternal bliss and oneness which we instinctively know we have lost. We remain in more or less constant pain as we search for the love that we have lost. Until we are individualized enough to return to the greater whole, having the capacity to generate that love within us, we are trapped. We will never find love outside of ourselves until we have learned to find it, and our true being, within ourselves. The Piscean feels for this struggle. She is attracted to the adventure which it represents and wishes to assist others in reaching the goal which has been set. These desires draw her into incarnation.

Unlike other signs, the first stage is not an easy one for Pisces. She wants to contribute and assist those who suffer so much. Because she is naturally very empathic and intuitive and already more emotionally oriented than those who have surrounded her in her realm of origin, when she arrives upon the Earth she finds it a much more difficult undertaking than she ever possibly imagined. Her powerful sense of empathy and highly sensitized emotional nature, coupled with her poorly defined sense of self and its limits, causes her to absorb far too much of the suffering which surrounds her.

First-stage Pisceans are natural psychics and easily experience the pain of all those within a symbolic mile of themselves. Often they are completely unaware that the pain they experience is not just their own. They tend to identify strongly with others, feeling their pain and struggles as though they were their own, and at times becoming completely overwhelmed by their compassion. They naturally perceive the collective mind and emotions of Humanity and find that they are not prepared to cope with the impact of all this suffering upon their own psyches. Although they have nothing but the best of intentions, they find that their sense of inspiration and their high hopes and ideals are not enough. They wish to help, but do not know what to do in order to assist, and so feel helpless to do anything about the mess which things seem to be in everywhere. They may rush into situations with good intentions and find that they are overwhelmed by opposition from the forces, situations or circumstances which surround them. They may find that all they end up doing is harming or destroying themselves in their efforts to care for others.

They also experience difficulty in attempting to develop and express their own individuality, as it seems that even their emotions are not truly their own. Any personal pain which they experience is immediately magnified as they automatically contact its corresponding wavelength on a collective level. Stability is impossible. Understandably their life becomes almost impossible to cope with and tends to degenerate into chaos.

Being an old soul who is new here makes it very difficult for them to adjust on an emotional level. They are able to perceive more of what is wrong here, and they have had no time to adjust to it all. They are not accustomed to the hardness and cruelty that they see around them. They do not know how to cope with the defense mechanisms of others. Again and again they are drawn into caring for others in a very undiscriminating way, which often ends up causing them much pain and suffering.

Eventually they can no longer cope with their life experience and are forced to withdraw from the field. They can no longer remain trapped in the agony from which there seems to be no escape. They must leave this world and, consciously or unconsciously, this is exactly what they do. If their decision to leave is a conscious one, they may choose to commit suicide as the only way they know to relieve themselves of pain and suffering. If their choice is an unconscious one they may attract or manufacture some form of disease which ends their life prematurely. Their subconscious is literally saying, "This world makes me sick."

It is also possible that they may attract a violent end, perhaps having bitten off more than they can chew in an attempt to help another who is suffering in a self-destructive way. Or they may begin to feel that they are victims in this world, and this tendency may cause them to attract meaningless violence. When this pattern exists it always represents a personal choice, even when it is an unconscious, and may often represent a form of passive anger at the self and the world, stemming from the feeling that the individual's entire purpose is being thwarted.

Again and again Pisces tries, entering the world with great dreams and a spirit of hopeful optimism, and again and again she fails, until at last a change must occur, and the transition into second stage begins.

First/Second-Stage Transition

As this transition is reached, the individual develops an overwhelming feeling of despair. She is deeply aware that her mission just is not working. She is in danger of losing all sense of self-worth. She feels that she has come here with the intention of helping, but has only added to the mess instead, and all despite all of her own best intentions. It is crippling to live with the feelings of uselessness and futility which constantly threaten to overwhelm her at this stage.

Although she may fear that her failures indicate some deep lack of inherent worthiness, just as often she wonders if her failures may be the fault of the outside world. Slowly the innocent purity of her ideals begins to die, as a deep sense of insecurity replaces the natural, giving, optimistic spirit of blind faith which she once possessed.

She becomes self-doubting and suspicious of life. The outside world begins to seem dangerous and destructive. She is frightened of or disillusioned with too many aspects of the earthly reality in which she finds herself. She tries to trust and tries to care. She does not give up her mission or her attempt to live by the deepest values of her inner being without a battle; but eventually she just gets hurt once too often. She truly cannot withstand the pain of being anymore. For a time she may express the traits of both first and second-stage Pisces. She may become cold and power hungry, but still meet with an early end. She may be filled with compassion for others at certain times, while ultimately acting in a very self serving manner. Eventually she must choose what for her is the path of personal survival.

To attempt to remain open, to attempt to give to life is fruitless, for it only ends in self-destruction. She makes a decision to stop caring, to stop trying to make a difference in this crazy world and focuses instead upon surviving and, perhaps, even thriving. She will stop caring if she has to; and is certain, with some regret, that there will be times when she will have to. But from this time forward, whatever the cost, she will take care of herself alone. She may carry on struggling to endure or become determined to overcome but, either way, with this resolve she passes into second stage.

Second Stage

Pisces is the sign of the ocean. It could be said that when any part of the chart falls in this sign, the part of that individual's basic nature is symbolically thrown into the ocean. Since the Sun represents the soul, the Piscean's soul experience is that of having been flung into the depths. In first stage she will struggle and drown. In second stage, she looks for, and finds, a life raft or a desert island to cling to in order to save herself.

She seeks refuge, and may protect herself through some form of dependency. This dependency may take the form of drugs, alcohol, sexual experience or some other form of addiction. Substance abuse, addiction or obsession tend to form a buffer between herself, her own feelings, and the rest of the world. This response to life allows her to live in a fantasy world, where she can perhaps imagine herself as the savior she still secretly longs to be. She may have delusions of grandeur which help her to compensate for the feelings of personal inferiority which she has acquired during the first stage of her development. Or she may simply choose to imagine the world to be the beautiful place which she longs for it to be, while choosing to ignore the harsh realities of the environment which surrounds her.

Some Pisceans in second stage may not require addictive behavior to reinforce their escape from reality. They may create a quiet little retreat for themselves where they can imagine that all is well, enabling them to ignore the suffering which surrounds them in the greater world. They still hold high ideals but purposely choose to live in a fairy tale world, where they can lead a harmless life of peaceful simplicity.

Alternatively she may look for another individual upon whom she can depend, to buffer the cold winds of life and to nourish and protect her. Her love, of necessity is self-seeking. She is looking for refuge and a guaranteed sense of security. There can be a hard edge to second-stage Pisces, for she may feel that she gave the world the best she had to offer, and was destroyed in the process. Now she may feel that the world owes her, and secretly look upon others as being somewhat alien and not quite human. If this is the case, she may be ruthless in attaining and maintaining her refuge; and if she seeks this refuge through partnership she may be cruel, cold and demanding towards her mate.

While some second-stage Pisceans blame the world for their misfortunes, others blame themselves and feel guilt, regret or helplessness in the face of their apparent personal weakness. They may still seek to depend upon others, but in this case they will be inclined to do so at a high cost to their own personal well-being. They may endure abuse or allow themselves to be made into someone they are not, all in exchange for the illusion of security and protection from a world which is too large and overwhelming for their taste.

Second-stage Pisceans may also choose to seek their security in money, fame or power. Personal wealth allows them to build a physical world which is apparently separate from all that could harm them or make them vulnerable. The illusion of external sanctity and security may be a substitute for inner protection. Wealth gives them access to many forms of distraction which also assist them in avoiding the deeper aspects of their own feeling nature.

All Pisceans are blessed with the gift of personal charisma. While this special magic they possess will come into its full flower during the third stage of their development, in second stage it may be lost, hidden, or abused by being turned into a survival mechanism. An individual who responds to second stage in this manner may use her powers of attraction and persuasion to gain fame and power for herself alone. This response to second stage ensures that the individual will achieve and maintain a position at the top of the mountain where she will be in control, seemingly invincible and invulnerable in the face of all which might seek to bring her harm. The achievement of a high worldly position may also appear to compensate for the lack of personal worth which Pisces may feel at this stage, due to her initial apparent failure to make a valid contribution to the world.

Another means of protecting the self during second stage is through the excessive development of the intellect. This type of second-stage Piscean stands separate from life within her own consciousness, viewing reality coldly, cynically or mechanistically. Unwilling to admit or surrender to her own feelings, she chooses instead an ivory tower of abstraction. She may study life in the attempt to master it, overcome its dangers, and solve the unknown mystery which will somehow provide her with the answers which her soul is seeking. But because she searches with the intellect alone, she will be unable to find what she seeks until she learns once again to surrender to the emotional and intuitive aspects of her being.

Pisces is the only sign which experiences truly serious difficulty during first stage and so, it seems to me, they do have a right to seek some form of peace of mind or personal fulfillment during second stage. Because of this, it is possible for certain second-stage responses to be somewhat healthy, when not taken too far.

For instance, it is possible to learn how to master that big, bad concrete world, and "not let the bastards get you down", so long as one does not allow the urge for power to get totally out of hand. In like manner, the intellectual form of second-stage Pisces may become a brilliant scientist or social commentator. A positive urge during second stage is the urge to develop a more practical approach to life. Some second-stage Pisceans do not fit the classical image of the 'coffee-table astrology book' Pisces at all.

These individuals have learned how to survive in this world through efficient life functioning. They do not need to seek fame and power, but instead devote themselves to living sanely, practically, concretely and perhaps conservatively among their fellow human beings. They learn to plant their feet firmly upon the ground. The only danger here, as with any other response to second stage, is that they may go too far, becoming too controlling or obsessive compulsive in their need to compensate for the underlying fears and insecurities resulting from their first-stage experiences. To prove that she can survive in this world is the goal of second-stage Pisces, and this individual will be far from the wispy dreamer which conventional astrological images conjure up. This response to second stage ensures that the individual will be able to maintain psychological balance when the higher centers of the self open up in the transition into third stage, enabling her to make the most of her potentials.

In contrast to the above reasonably well-adjusted response to second stage, the individual may instead fall into such completely irrational rage and paranoia that she becomes almost completely dysfunctional. She may become immoral, vengeful or cruel, believing that she is justified in breaking all of the rules of society because she really does not belong here anyway. She may remain passive, in which case she will depend upon others or society at large and make no attempt to contribute positively to anything. This individual feels that the world owes her, and feels justified in taking whatever she wants, without ever considering the effect she may has on others.

If she is of an aggressive nature, she tend to blame the world for her suffering and take vengeance upon any real or imagined slight, perhaps acting toward others in a cruel or sadistic manner as a means of coping with frustration, and compensating for her lack of self-worth or contribution to society. Secretly she still wishes she could have given the world what she senses it needs. Knowing on some level that she is spinning her wheels, she may eventually lose complete control, for she has never learned how to master her powerful emotional nature.

Even if the individual is not actively aggressive during second stage, she may still possess a tendency to lose control of her emotions. In fact it is extremely rare to see a second-stage Piscean who has a properly balanced attitude towards her emotional nature. She is either out of control emotionally or too much in control, leading a highly repressive or overly objective lifestyle. It is even possible for a given individual to swing between these two polarities within the course of a single lifetime.

In fact the emotions themselves may form a means of escape during second stage, as the individual becomes overly melodramatic and self-indulgent, building a false image of herself as the beautiful or noble martyred victim. There is no room for an overwhelming feeling of compassion to destroy her, for she is completely involved in her own life- drama of real or imagined woes. It is no wonder that Pisceans often make such good actors; many times their entire life takes the form of a powerful drama which they have staged for their own benefit alone.

As the Piscean wanders through many different lifetimes during her second-stage experience, she may attempt more than one of the above forms of response. Eventually, however, those responses which afforded safety and security begin to feel boring and confining as the individual senses that life is passing her by. All escape routes are found to be dead ends, which in themselves ultimately create more pain than they are ever able to relieve, and so an alternative is sought. The soul feels a calling to the ocean and must enter the true waters of life once again.

Second/Third-Stage Transition

During second stage this individual proved that she could survive despite the sorrows of the world. Now she must learn to thrive through embracing and understanding those sorrows. If she is afraid to feel pain, she will be unable to taste true joy. By this point she wants to be alive again, and so she must confront the power of her own emotions.

She may not know why she is dissatisfied, but her dissatisfaction will not leave her alone. All her feelings are surfacing and she does not know where to put them. At times she attempts to face them, at times she tries to suppress them. At first she does not know why so many parts of her feel deadened. She searches for inspiration and for a way to be all that she can be, not just in terms of external accomplishment, but also in terms of her internal capacity for experience. She wants to feel free, and to fix the mess that she has created in denial and defensiveness.

She must remind herself that if she has already learned how to survive, then she really has nothing to fear from the ocean of feeling. She can get out of her life-raft, metaphorically speaking, and begin to paddle around in the water. If she feels threatened, she can always retreat back to the safety it affords her. Into the water she steps, and back onto the desert island she races, back and forth until she has learned how to float.

In real terms this means that she may be prone to eruptions of powerful emotion, which inspire her, touch her, overwhelm her, and then threaten to drown her. She may fall deeply in love and be inspired and terrified at the same time. One day she is in love, and the next day she is defensive or cold. She may be assailed by powerful fears, or by feelings of deep despair and hopelessness. She may feel for all of the suffering of the world, and then become terrified that she will not be able to survive.

She is attracted to mystical experiences: religious, spiritual and occult. She takes to it like a duck to water, and then panics—frightened that she will sink like a stone as she feels the waters close over her head. If she learns not to panic about her panicking she will do much better. When things get to be too much, she might need to bury herself in mundane distraction for awhile. If she realizes that she can control the experience, and take it a step at a time, she will begin to settle into a better approach to the whole situation. She may become afraid she will hide her head forever, but this will not be the case. If she tries to force herself back into the water, even on a subliminal level, she may freeze into the greatest procrastinator of the entire zodiac.

Certainly she must learn to be honest with herself. An understanding of her overall pattern and purpose throughout all three stages may help her to have compassion for herself, and not feel so embarrassed about her failings. Until she can understand why she responds the way she does, she may not wish to admit her fears to herself.

In discussing second stage I mentioned that when Pisces is the Sun sign, it is as if the entire soul were thrown symbolically into the ocean. In first stage, she panics, struggles and drowns. In second stage she saves herself by finding a life raft or a desert island on which to rest. To enter third stage she must finally learn how to float.

To float you must first understand and practice the technique, and must also learn how to relax and trust in the laws which enable you to do so. The more Pisces learns to be open to her natural, emotional and mystical self, the more she will begin to develop the ability to have access to certain spiritual truths which will help her understand why others suffer as they do.

Her original 'mistake' if mistake it was, was to use her natural intuitive and empathic abilities to perceive too strongly the present suffering of humanity. Consciously or unconsciously she drew upon the collective consciousness at the mass level as she passed through the first stage of her development. Now she must open up those same parts of herself, but learn to use them in a new manner. Instead of simply perceiving the suffering which exists everywhere around her, she must begin to make contact with the Divine Mind — the Higher aspect of collective consciousness. Instead of simply feeling the agony which surrounds her, she will begin to communicate with the Source of Being which will explain to her the purpose of life and the value and ultimate outcome of all human experience. It is far more difficult to see the suffering which exists in the moment than it is to see the final outcome of the process and ultimate kindness of the overall pattern of existence. As she begins to understand how life really functions, she begins to be able to embrace it, and returns to herself, as she learns to express all of her hidden potentials, now that she no longer needs to fear her inner depths.

Her new understanding comes at first in flashes of inspiration which allow her to express her pure joy of being. Soon after each flash she returns to her island, or finds herself struggling in some deeper waters of emotional confusion. In the early part of this transition these times of confusion and hopelessness may overwhelm her so much that she despairs of ever finding her source of inspiration again.

At first she may doubt that it was really a true experience at all. Each time she goes back to the water it seems more turbulent. She may face her desire to put an end to herself once again. But she has already walked that path and is unlikely to ever do so again.

Eventually the understanding she receives becomes clearer and more rational. She begins to know her way around the inner world, and begins to show others how to get there as well. Her earlier patterns of second stage are transforming. If she chose to become overly rational during second stage, she now becomes capable of recognizing this response as a defense mechanism. She can see herself beginning to rationalize a situation, distancing herself from her emotions or using her intellect to feel superior to others. She calls her own bluff and discovers the part of herself that she has been hiding from. Instead of being destroyed by that aspect of herself, as she had once feared, she now finds that her life loses a certain quality of obstruction which she may have once blamed on external events and situations. Now she can use her intellect to help her to understand the higher truths she is beginning to perceive. Her new found vulnerability is like a rebirth.

The soul who has relied upon her charisma to dominate in a self-seeking manner has come to realize that this response does not bring lasting satisfaction. Her life grows empty. She is beginning to feel more deeply for life once again, and her new found compassion causes her great regret. But it may also inspire her. She wants satisfaction and begins to discover the joy which can be found through feeling for others and experiencing the oneness of life. All Pisceans passing through the second/third-stage transition re-discover their own spontaneity. Therefore this individual is likely to experience a spontaneous release of past behavior patterns. Great kindness suddenly emerges. Inspired by a new vision of life, this individual now uses her natural charisma to uplift and encourage others. If she has been negatively dominating, she now discovers that she possesses a natural capacity for balanced leadership.

Pisceans who have sought dependence upon others during second stage now find themselves trapped in a prison of their own making. Their lifestyle is not their own, and they feel a great need to explore beyond the secure and limited world which has been created by others. This individual may fear that she will die of boredom. Or she may be subject to the oppression of others. Abused and dominated she must make a break for freedom. The cannibals have invaded her desert island. To attain freedom, she must recognize her security needs. Admitting one's own tendency towards dependency is a bit hard on the ego. But once she is able to do so, she can begin looking for true security. When life destroyed her during first stage, she developed the attitude that the world was a dangerous place. This is especially so if she had chosen to end her lifetimes violently. Now she must learn to depend upon the Ultimate, to trust and float in the water where the cannibals cannot go. When she knows where her true support comes from she will have attained a form of freedom which she can share with others.

The Piscean who has chosen to dramatize her life as a response to second stage may now find that absolutely everything has been blown completely out of proportion. Her true emotions are surfacing and she reacts in an extremely volcanic manner. She may get herself and others into a lot of trouble, and does not see reality clearly. She has been used to living a Quixotic existence, tilting at windmills, and now the archetypal mind is beginning to show itself to her. She has powerful visions, but at first she has a great deal of difficulty integrating them with reality. Eventually she makes too big a mistake. He hurts herself or others in some traumatic manner which causes an awakening. At first she may fall more deeply into a morass of pain and suffering than might any other Piscean. Once she pulls herself out of that response, realizing it to be a dead end, she finds that she has become a very practical and powerful visionary.

If Pisces has been overly aggressive during second stage, she may now find the resulting alienation and loneliness too great a burden to bear. She realizes that she has chased everyone away, and is tired of fighting. To find her way out of this dead end, she begins the slow process of learning to care for herself and others once again.

The addictive Piscean here finds that her body simply can no longer withstand the assault. We all carry body karma, and tend to enter each lifetime with the constitution which we have earned from our pasts. Addictive behavior weakens the system, and if it is indulged in for too many lifetimes, we earn an inherently weak constitution. Second/third-stage Pisceans often reach the point where they must battle their addictions just to survive. The paradox for all second/third-stage Pisceans is that the behavior which once was a survival mechanism, now threatens that very survival in some manner. Pisces also finds that addictive behavior interferes with her search for enlightenment. It may be a hard battle, and she may often fall off her horse, because until she truly understands her own emotions and comprehends the reason why we all suffer, life will just be too painful to face unaided. Eventually she will triumph. And when she does, she will be that much better equipped to help others. She can help to save those who, as she herself did, wish to drown.

The practical Piscean may also begin to feel that her life has become too narrow by this stage. Life is more than survival, it is also a matter of personal satisfaction. She wakes up one day and wonders how she could have missed so much that life has to offer. Increasingly dissatisfied, she becomes a seeker. She may find herself prey to incomprehensible mood swings as the buried aspects of herself begin to emerge. Gradually she begins to understand how she has limited herself and which spiritual principles she can use to truly make a difference in her life. She can begin to take risks which she never would have thought possible before, because she has learned that life is not as dangerous as she might have once believed. She never loses what is best about her innate practicality. Instead she learns to fulfill herself through embracing a larger life and thereby becomes capable of instructing the masses. Her philosophy is practical and reasonable and this makes her heard by those who might otherwise not have an opportunity to benefit from the gifts which all Pisceans come to bestow.

The Piscean who has chosen to look at life through rose-colored glasses during second stage may now find that she can no longer ignore the troubles of the world. They may land on her doorstep. She may berate herself for having been so willfully naive. Eventually, she attempts to help someone who truly suffers, and so begins to receive the Divine understanding which will assist her in this process and which will ultimately lead to third stage.

Eventually, even when she is in her moments of despair, Pisces understands what is really going on. At last she has plumbed the depths of her inner pain. It has been her guide to the ultimate plan of human existence. Now her inspiration is unconquerable. Her natural charisma causes the truth to shine as it expresses itself through her. She reverses her polarities. Instead of passively absorbing the pain which exists around her, she learns to project her hope, inspiration and knowledge into world-healing —uplifting and assisting others with her vision. She is now at third stage.

Third Stage

Many third-stage Pisceans are highly creative people. Inspired by a new vision of life, their new found understanding must flow forth. They are caring and compassionate, and in their presence you always feel accepted and understood. An old symbol for Pisces is the whale. I feel that this is an appropriate symbol for third-stage Pisces, but I also believe that the dolphin describes the character of this individual aptly. Having learned to trust in the laws of life, this individual does not just float on the great sea of consciousness, she literally dances on the water.

Spontaneously creative and innovative, this individual seems to find completely new ways to transmit her inspiration to others. She trusts that her inner creative source will never let her down, and is always able to pull the appropriate knowledge and insights from the great ocean of being. She surprises herself almost as often as she surprises others. While this individual may have great intensity and presence, she is also capable of being quiet and serene. Even when she is not explaining the purpose of life, others are calmed and uplifted by her presence.

While she is intuitive and compassionate, she no longer absorbs the pain of others and cannot be made to feel responsible for their suffering. She knows the path which they must walk and why. She is there to lend a hand, but realizes that she can carry no-one with her to their final destination. Her purpose is to creatively demonstrate to others what their destination is, and that they will inevitably reach it.

Third-stage Pisceans have great courage. They completely trust themselves and their own feelings, and are capable of dealing with emotional situations no one else could ever face. They greet life with quiet wisdom, and while dependent upon no one, are capable of experiencing great intimacy—for they live a life of constant surrender to the Source from which we stem. They have at last discovered their true strength as individuals.

Pisces at the Crossroads
First/Third-Stage Transition

It is not necessary for a first-stage Pisces to have an early demise. I have not written this chapter to scare anyone, but to help to illuminate certain life patterns, and hopefully present some keys which will enhance the lives of my readers. A Piscean who seems to be heading for the difficulties of first stage can overcome their challenges in much the same way that a Pisces in the second/third-stage transition must. All they require is an opportunity to take a more objective look at their own lives, and the courage to trust in their purpose long enough to receive a new form of understanding which will allow them to make the transition into third stage and begin their true work upon the Earth.

While the transition into third stage can begin at any time, the crossroads usually presents itself after the individual has already spent several lifetimes in first stage. This individual generally finds herself leading a rather chaotic and destructive life. She may feel that her life is not truly her own, and longs for a way out of her seemingly impossible difficulties.

She sees everything that is wrong with the world and finds that it overwhelms her. She wants to change it all, but realizing she cannot, feels useless and inferior. She may begin to find herself trapped in some of the defense mechanisms or forms of compensation that seek to embrace her from second stage. If she is addictive or erratic, she knows that this behavior is only making matters worse, but she feels that she cannot help herself. If she compensates by seeking external security, she begins to feel panicked, for she knows that the form of illusory security which she is tempted to embrace will ultimately sap her freedom. Those choosing to feel superior to others or act overly rational or aggressive, secretly know in their heart of hearts that they are fooling themselves.

At the same time, their health may be suffering, they may experience strong suicidal urges, or may find themselves increasingly surrounded by or involved with violent types of people. Somewhere this all has to stop, but they do not know how or where. At this point they must remember what is truly important to them. What do they really stand for? What do they believe in? If they are about to reach the end of the line anyway, perhaps this is the time to let go of everything except these inner commitments which really represent their reason for coming here in the first place. They should not concern themselves with how their mission is going to be completed. They should simply trust in the power of this purpose to give them enough inspiration to face the future. The way there is unknown, but with trust and patience it can be discovered. You can only float when you stop struggling and let go.

Pisceans are very emotionally reactive. They can react to their life situations with despair, which will ultimately be their undoing if they remain in the first stage. Or they can react with resentment and a desire to conquer or get even with the world, thereby passing into the second stage. Alternatively they can forget all of this, realize that life really is one great mystery, and that they have yet to discover the answers which must somehow be there (after all they have nothing to lose) and react with awe, becoming inspired once again by the ideals which have always driven them.

If they have been able to let go for a moment, they will not only find themselves re-inspired, they will also have touched upon the quiet within. They know that there is some sort of wisdom silently waiting inside of them. Now they must dedicate themselves to listening to it. In time they find that this source within themselves explains things to them. They are given a reprieve from the destructive forces without and within, as life begins to send them messages and opportunities to use their natural intuitive abilities to understand the way in which the world truly functions.

Suddenly life is an adventure. They have never lost their ability to feel. They have never lost their passion. Now they apply this same feeling and passion to the discovery of the mysteries of life. As they find, they share, in a very pure and undiluted manner. "Here is the beauty. Here is the meaning. Here is the gift I have come to give."

If you think that you may be close to an individual who seems to express the traits of a first-stage Pisces, or who appears to be at the crossroads and may be considering suicide, encourage them to seek professional help.

Do not try to make them feel guilty for how they are feeling. Give them encouragement and try to believe in them. While they may appear to be suffering from their own personal problems alone, this is not the entire story. They truly feel weighed down by the world—even when they no longer realize that this is an important part of their problem. They want to contribute and feel that they cannot, so don't put further pressure on them. Try to help them to find a way to understand the underlying spiritual laws of life—how things function and where all of this is leading to. If they become involved enough in the inspiration which this form of understanding can provide, they will forget all about their personal problems. Try to show them that you care, and that you understand how deeply they care for life as well. If you can, show them that they matter.

If there was a first-stage Pisces in your life who you could not save, please do not feel responsible. We are all ultimately the guardians of our own fate. Because we are all immortal, those you have loved are never lost. Nor has your loved one ultimately failed. Every experience deepens our understanding and our capacity to care. They shall return one day to share with you and with others the understanding which they have gained. It took great courage to choose the path of this final sign of the zodiac. Their inherent strength will one day triumph.

Childhood Conditions and Relationship Patterns

Because Pisces is a water sign, and the element of water corresponds to the emotional nature, Pisceans generally tend to be more strongly influenced by their mother than by their father. Because Pisce's compassion forms one of her primary motivations for choosing to be born upon the Earth, she is often attracted to her mother at a time when her mother is experiencing great difficulty in her life. Pisces's mother may be generally unhappy and emotionally unstable, or may experience unusual difficulties during the early childhood of this individual. If her mother is generally overly emotional and rather unstable, she is very likely to inherit her tendencies. She may emulate her as she overreacts to life and blows things out of proportion.

In early first stage she is likely to have a very close and loving relationship with her mother. Her mother's sensitivity is very highly developed and may not always be used to her best advantage. However she deeply cares about life and inspires her child to do likewise. She grows up seeing her suffer and feels great empathy for her which she expresses towards many of the individuals whom she later encounters. As first stage progresses the relationship with the mother tends to deteriorate. Her mother is less stable as an individual, inclined to suffer more, and may be more self-centered. She is incapable of creating a stable childhood for her off-spring, and may demand a great deal from her, perhaps wanting her to take care of her or causing her to feel responsible for her suffering. It was her intention to help her, and she subconsciously always remembers her initial motivations. This causes her to feel very helpless and frustrated when she is unable to do so.

Pisces' relationship with her father is generally not strong. In early first stage he may be present and is likely to be an optimistic and inspiring individual, though possibly not an extremely deep thinker. He represents Pisces' initial hopeful idealism, which he encourages his child to pursue. However, he may not be a strong individual, and may not understand the actual risks which the Piscean may be willing to take in her attempts to assist others.

As first stage progresses, the influence of the father weakens. His function is to encourage his child to succeed in the world, but if he is absent, unrealistic or weak, he does not really help to promote the success of his child's life mission. By late first stage the father may be largely absent during this individual's childhood. If he is present his relationship with his child may be unclear, confused and lacking in true warmth and intimacy.

As Pisces prepares to enter second stage she may respond to her mother's character traits in a way which will ultimately provide her with the defense mechanisms which she feels she will need in order to survive. If her mother tries to put on a brave front, Pisces may develop aggressive tendencies. If her mother is overly emotional Pisces may emulate her tendencies and over-dramatize her life. Or Pisces may choose to take an excessively rational approach to life, viewing her parents as foolish individuals, and perhaps developing an attitude of superiority. The child whose mother is overly manipulative may choose to attain power in the world and may misuse her innate charismatic abilities. If Pisces' mother offers her protection from the big bad world, perhaps even long past the time when she should have attained independence, this will likely pave the way for Pisces to develop a dependent streak. If the family copes with their problems through addictive tendencies, Pisces will be quite happy to join them in the process. The final, and perhaps the most desirable alternative, occurs when Pisces looks at the chaos which surrounds her, and, realizing that her mother is far too self involved, comes to understand that she may have to go it alone. This response is likely to create the practical Pisces, who is still capable of feeling for others, but learns to set limits upon this tendency and begin the process of learning to master the concrete and material aspects of reality. Alternatively it may create the 'see-no-evil' sort of second-stage Pisces, who refuses to see the darkness which surrounds her, choosing instead to see the world through rose-colored spectacles.

The mother of a second-stage Pisces senses that her child is somehow different, and finds this knowledge somewhat disquieting. She is disturbed when her child displays her intuitive tendencies, and has a hard time coping with her emotional qualities. She herself may still be emotionally self-indulgent, but there is much which she is hiding from herself, and when others display their emotions she feels extremely uncomfortable. She may not nurture her child well, and encourages her to suppress much of her true self. If she withdraws too much from her child, this may also cause her to over-emphasize her intellect. The overly dramatic sort of Piscean may become involved in a great deal of conflict with her mother and may rebel against her authority, as she feels that her true self is not being accepted. This early attitude of rebellion may carry over into later years, causing her to develop a highly volcanic and erratic lifestyle.

Pisces' mother may have an aggressive and dominating approach to life which may develop a defensive, resentful or vengeful tendency in her offspring. Pisces' father generally remains distant, passive or uninvolved in his child's upbringing throughout second stage, unless other aspects exist to counteract this tendency. Sometimes when he is present, he is rather aggressive and erratic. He may also be the calm in the eye of the storm — someone who is quietly involved with his own projects, and whose cool and competent approach to life Pisces admires and seeks to emulate. If Pisces' relationship with her mother is difficult, she may turn to her father as a source of support, and choose to develop a similar approach to life in order to cope.

During second/third stage the family pattern may remain the same, and will help to provide the individual with further motivation to master the transition. Alternatively, a soul born into the second/third-stage transition may find that things are beginning to improve. Her mother is often inclined to be an empathic and caring individual who encourages her to be more comfortable with her emotions. However, she herself is only able to cope with a certain degree of emotion, and she may find herself with little personal support and assistance when her powerful emotional nature and ability to feel for life begin to surface. Shee feels loved and supported, but may also feel misunderstood and let down when she attempts to make the progress which she senses is necessary.

During second/third stage the father may also begin to come into greater prominence. He may begin (or continue) to possess certain traits which his child admires. He may have a certain level of spiritual or philosophical understanding which fascinates Pisces, but the distance in their relationship may prevent him from doing all that he might. Alternatively his understanding may be only partially formed, and he may also feel threatened once his child begins to go further into the unknown than he himself may have had the courage to do. Pisces may feel a secret sympathy for her father and feel that they share common values, but she always ends up going further than her father might have, and this may promote a certain amount of conflict in their relationship.

In third-stage Pisces may still choose to be born to a mother who is suffering in some way. However, the mother may be coming to the end of her difficulties, and her child discovers that she can finally be of some assistance. Her mother will speak of her as having been the tiny source of inspiration who helped her through one of the most difficult periods of her life. Alternatively the Piscean may be born to a mother whose life brings her much satisfaction, primarily as a result of her personal attitude and philosophy. She is very sensitive, caring and compassionate, and very much at home in the world and with her own emotions. Through her the third-stage Piscean reaffirms her ability to trust. She also experiences a much longed for closeness with her father, which is very rewarding for both of them. Her father is a philosophical thinker, with a great capacity to understand the abstract concepts of life, and the two may enjoy a lifelong intellectual and philosophical bond of communion.

Pisceans in first stage may be difficult for others to relate to or understand. In early first stage they may succeed in attracting a mate who can understand their tendency to feel for life as deeply as they do. This person may be wiser than they are, but may suffer the frustration of being unable to reach their troubled partner. Pisces may also choose a partner partly out of compassion for the difficulties which she may be experiencing. They may support and assist their partner, all the while suffering for them, having found that their burdens have been increased, rather than relieved as a result of the partnership they have chosen. They may also choose a troubled or erratic partner who is abusive and incapable of understanding their naturally intuitive and empathic tendencies.

It is not uncommon for first-stage Piscean women to be attracted to violent men. They are attracted to their apparent strength, as well as to their suffering, and may enjoy the dangers inherent in such a relationship—because after all, Pisces don't really want to be here anyway. Obviously this kind of situation is very much like the moth seeking out the flame, and should be urgently reconsidered. If the individual who is attracted to a very destructive partner can begin to question her motivations, perhaps the crossroads can be met in a positive manner.

The second-stage individual has difficulty trusting life and may therefore have difficulty trusting a partner or becoming intimate with others. Alternatively she may seek someone who will protect and care for her, providing the refuge which she is seeking.

Female Pisceans are likely to emulate their mother in relationships and to strive for dominance. This is particularly likely if they tended to attract abusive relationships during first stage. They may feel victimized by their partners, and yet play many subtle control games. They may be emotional whirlwinds, impossible to get close to because of the chaotic and irrational nature of their feelings. If they seek refuge and support from their partners, they may use their powerful charisma to gain control, but may then be inclined to disparage their mate for being so weak. They are like compelling sirens who want to be pampered as queens, and who see their own weaknesses and insecurities reflected in a partner whom they gradually come to despise.

If they still feel guilty for having failed to contribute to the world, they may choose to take a submissive role, perhaps marrying more for security than for love. They put up with whatever abuse may be a part of the contract they have entered into, because secretly they hate themselves and feel that they must pay for having used another individual just to attain personal security.

The female Piscean may distrust men because they are unknown quantities. Her father may have been absent or let her down, and she has usually been taught that men are weaker than women. The male Piscean may distrust women because of the incredible power which his mother may have had over him. At the same time it is possible that she acted in a destructive manner toward him or failed to fulfill his emotional needs. His need for women and the power they are capable of having over him may terrify him. He may compensate by being cold or controlling. He may play endless games in an attempt to guarantee the security of the relationship, until finally his partner gives up in perplexity. He may be cruel or dominating, or may neglect his partner or refuse relationships altogether in an attempt to prove that he does not need women. He may tell himself and others that they are inferior.

Or he may cling to his partner and develop an obsessive need for women. Second-stage Pisceans of either sex can be addicted to romance, using it as an escape from the difficulties which surround them. The second-stage male may also choose a strong woman to depend upon, acting very much like his dependent female counterpart. If his partner grows tired of his dependency, he may return home to mom.

In general, second-stage Pisceans are fearful of intimacy and inclined towards dependency. However, it is possible for them to experience romantic fulfillment. They may choose to be the strong partner in a relationship, and this role may enhance their self-worth as individuals. The practical Pisces may choose a partner with whom she can build a solid material life built upon an equal foundation. Their life together may sometimes lack spice, but Pisces will have the satisfaction of a life well and soundly lived. The sensitive, romantic Piscean with the rose-colored glasses may be able to find a partner who shares her ideals, and together the two can create an oasis to wait out the storms of second stage.

Third-stage Pisceans are fearless lovers. They inspire and believe in their mates, who hold them in awe. They can surrender fully to their emotions, passing confidently through the dark waters of the relationship, while playfully enhancing the times spent rolling along upon the quieter waves. Magical, powerful, wise and timeless, the oldest soul of the zodiac is an eternally joyful, youthful lover.

Famous Pisceans

First Stage: Frederick Chopin, Kurt Cobain (was approaching the crossroads).
Second Stage: Jean Harlow, Sharon Stone, Bobby Fisher, Joseph Mengele.
Second/Third Stage: Albert Einstein, Rudolph Nureyev, Elizabeth Taylor, George Harrison, Mikhail Gorbachev.
Third Stage: Dr. Seuss, Buffy Sainte-Marie, Helen Nearing, Edgar Cayce, Rudolph Steiner.

CONCLUSION

Figure 3 provides a summary of the stages of development of the 12 signs. This might be useful if you have found the detailed information in the earlier chapters a bit overwhelming. It may also be of value if you would like to look up friends and family at a glance.

Before we close I would like to share some more information I have found to be of value. First of all, I have already observed that each individual is likely to view the world through the perspective presented by their own unique stage of development. In addition, the later stages of development are usually invisible to those who are progressing through the earlier stages. This means that to a first-stage individual the world is a simple first-stage kind of place. Life is very straight-forward. You go out, you get what you need. End of story. To second-stage individuals life is dangerous and overwhelming. Safety is often found through denial. What you don't see won't hurt you. They are aware that some lucky people seem to have it made (first stage), but other than that, real life is serious and difficult.

To second/third-stage individuals there are three kinds of people in the world; the rather shallow inhabitants of first stage, those individuals in second stage who seem to hide from the truth, and those who have realized that the only way to survive is to open your eyes and grapple with that truth, as difficult as it may be. They hope that somehow, someday this will mean that life will improve. Third-stage individuals have solved many of their personal riddles and watch this greater pageant of life unfold around them. They are inclined to understand and accept everyone. But some of the earlier stages are not very compatible with one another.

There may be some envy between first and second-stage individuals, but generally they are capable of getting along with one another. The real problem occurs when second stage turns into second/third stage. To second-stage individuals, second/third-stage individuals look pretty crazy. They are digging up everything that should remain buried in order to ensure our survival. They concern themselves with dangerous spiritual and psychological

PURPOSE	To embody Divine Truth.	To teach and embody right lifestyle.	To serve human evolution, through his understanding of the underlying structure and function of reality.	To uplift and inspire humanity.
FIRST STAGE	Has natural, instinctive trust in life and Divinity. Is criticized for his attitude. Wonders why others suffer while he does not.	Experience of cultural immersion. Absorbs values of a harmonious or well-ordered society.	Achieves position of financial or political power by right of birth or sweat of brow. Attempts to change society on practical level.	Not of this world. Extremely empathic and emotionally oriented. Absorbs the suffering of others. Pain becomes too much. Escapes through suicide, illness, or violent death.
1ST/2ND STAGE TRANSITION	Criticism damages self-worth. Feels responsibility to aid others. Decides to search for the truth which will vindicate him and allow him to help others.	Encounters a corrupt society. May be traumatized by its effect on his culture. Compassion for those who suffer as a result of the corruption of their society draws him into a new world.	Changes he has attempted to institute not permanent. Loses heart in his struggle with corruption.	Tired of being destroyed, his goal changes from a desire to make a contribution, to a decision to ensure personal survival. Self-worth may be low because he has not helped others.
SECOND STAGE	Frantically seeking truth, easy prey for extreme dogmas and philosophies. May do violence to mind, body or emotions in an attempt to squeeze into mold. Later may conform or rebel in extreme manner, psychologically imbalanced.	Tries to change the world. May refuse marriage and family, due to dangers of his role. Later realizes futility or difficulty of his undertaking, rebels frantically or conforms fearfully.	Reacts to corruption. "If you can't beat them you might as well join them." Alternatively may refuse high positions and rebel, become servile, or work with people one on one. Feels he has failed.	Protects sensitivity through intellect, aggression, addiction, escapism, dependency, or the attainment of worldly power. Controlling, fearful of surrender; or views life through rose-colored glasses.
KEYS TO MASTER 2ND/3RD STAGE TRANSITION	Listens to inner voice. Learns love is the highest truth. Regains natural self. Integrates knowledge gathered in previous lifetimes.	Releases attachment to corrupt society. Moves literally or symbolically from city to country. Builds foundations of a new society.	Rediscovers visionary capacity. Learns all real change is inner. Begins to share visions with others in transformative manner.	Learns to use natural intuitive ability to comprehend Universal Truths. Knowing why people suffer creates emotional rebirth.
THIRD STAGE	Teaches people non-dogmatic spiritual truths. Draws from many sources. May inherit spiritual lineage. Natural joy returns.	Joyfully building a new world as the old world crumbles. Is joined by his tribe. Able to create fulfilling partnership and family life.	Sees internal structure of the Universe. Shares vision with groups and individuals at last facilitating desired transformation.	Inspired visionary. Creatively uplifts people. Frees them with his knowledge of meaning. Great emotional courage.

philosophies. They don't conform, and they are inclined to abandon their friends and families, and act very irresponsibly. Those in second stage often think that second/third-stage individuals are fools. While first-stage people might think that second/third-stage individuals are a little silly, they generally leave well enough alone.

To those in the transition, second-stage individuals also look crazy and a little dangerous at times. They seem to cling to illusions which are destroying them. They need to wake up! They seem intent on pulling their second/third-stage companions backwards. Those in second/third stage often think that second-stage individuals are fools. It is easy to see that in another time those in second stage would be burning those in second/third stage as witches or heretics. Yet both stages are necessary, and important, and neither type of individual is 'wrong'.

An important law of life is that like attracts like. This means that most of the people in your life are close to your own stage of development. Because the second/third-stage transition takes a relatively short time spiritually speaking (several decades, as opposed to several centuries spent in each stage), you are likely to have close ties with many souls in second stage when you first enter the transition into third stage. Obviously conflict is likely to result.

The most common pattern in families is for the children to always be slightly ahead of their parents. This is by no means always the case, for I have seen families which contain a good mixture of all three stages, but it is common enough to comment upon. Early first-stage parents have late first-stage children, who have early second-stage children. Early second stage begets late second-stage or second/third-stage, while late second-stage parents often spawn second/third-stage offspring (much to their dismay). Second/third-stage children have third-stage children who, in turn, beget late third stage or early first-stage children, beginning the cycle over again. If you think of the early childhood conditions of each of the stages, this pattern makes sense.

This means that if you enter second/third-stage somewhere between childhood and the age of fifty, it is a good bet that you are going to experience a great deal of conflict with your family. Your parents and perhaps your brothers and sisters as well, are likely to be in second stage, and you will be doing the unheard of! Some people at the end of second stage cling to their position very tightly and can be forces to be reckoned with. They are certain that you are wrong and crazy, and may attempt to manipulate you into conforming to their life philosophy while you are tentatively exploring this new and necessary, but highly challenging territory.

Life becomes more complicated when those friends and family who are getting very close to the transition themselves begin to instinctively sense that you are on to something. They often become quite envious, but won't admit this fact to themselves or to anyone else. Instead they may attack. Their intentions are not really as bad as they seem, they are merely victims of themselves. These same people may criticize you one day, and need your help the next. They want you to take them with you, but they are unwilling to actually face the truth about themselves and their lives and instead want you to pick them up and carry them. Obviously this is impossible.

Many people in second/third stage find that as a result of these difficulties they must break ties with their family and others in their lives, at least temporarily. This is not an easy thing to do. Once you begin to break away, everybody senses that you are ahead of them. They come to believe that they really need you and that you are abandoning them. One lesson that we all must learn as we pass through second/third stage is that each individual has to do it himself, and that each must also be free to live his own life even if that means 'being foolish enough to remain in second stage'. While you still feel responsible for others, you may be tempted to remain entangled with them in the hopes that you will be able to make them see reason. Eventually you get knocked around enough to see that this just doesn't work. One day you realize that trying to make people change goes against Universal Law. This is part of the positive detachment that is a facet of spiritual evolution.

Sometimes the only way to help those you must leave behind is to go forward yourself. Then you will have that much more to contribute to humanity as a whole, including your friends and family. Individuals who must leave their family behind during second/third stage often return once they have reached the third stage, to be received with honors. Somehow their family instinctively understands that the journey has been worthwhile after all. Third-stage individuals are not easy to manipulate and no longer need to be presented with the same life challenges and difficulties. In addition, many members of their family are by then ready to move forward themselves.

Another common situation occurs when an individual passing through the second/third stage falls in love with another individual who is at the end of second stage and may be contemplating the transition. Many of the same factors are at work here. There can be a strong soul tie, since the two are close to the same stage of development and may have been traveling together for some time. But the difference in their present perspectives creates a huge gulf between the two of them. Initially the attraction is mutual, and late second stage is entranced with the possibilities present by second/third. The second/third-stage individual can see all of the potentials of his second-stage partner and he wants to help her bypass the illusions of second stage and move forward.

Love is a powerful, magnetic emotion but the entry into the second/third-stage transition is a terrifying experience. No one wants to be pulled uncontrollably into a nightmare, and this is how it feels to second stage. The second-stage partner may develop ambivalent feelings towards her second/third-stage partner. He is just uncovering all of his most vulnerable and neurotic emotions and is very vulnerable to rejection. He is trying not to hide things from himself anymore, and is discovering a whole new capacity for intimacy which he longs to share with his soul mate. This may frighten her as well, for she is used to the safety of her barriers. He is motivated to try and force her through the transition. She will likely bolt and run. Second/third stage may end up with a broken heart, at the very time when it is most difficult to deal with one. But he will learn not to interfere with the free will of others. Years or lifetimes later, under a different dynamic, this relationship may be able to succeed, but first she must be set free to approach the transition in her own time and in her own way.

This same pattern may occur between first/second-stage and second/third stage, if the second/third-stage individual is choosing to be a gatekeeper for the first/second or first/third-stage individual. The decay of the relationship will likely be slower in this case, if the individual in first stage chooses the path of least resistance into second. If the individual in second/third stage has learned to leave well enough alone, the relationship may succeed, as he will be more inclined to be attracted to an individual who will succeed in mastering the first/third-stage transition. This can be a very dynamic and creative combination.

I have mentioned before that souls approaching the possibility of making the transition between first and third stage often attract a second/third or third-stage individual to assist them in this process. While this individual can often be a lover, mate or friend, he or she may also be a parent. This happens often enough to mention. While a third-stage individual usually has the wisdom to cope with the challenges which this situation represents, it can be more difficult during second/third stage. Another parent, a sibling or a close friend of the child's may be inclined to encourage his entry into second stage. The parent can only hold the alternative, understanding that his or her child is still a free entity with a will of his own. As a parent he may not be able to reach his child right away, but may be an invaluable resource later in life. If you are in a situation such as this it is important to offer your child support and encouragement. Learn all you can about his or her sign(s), and trust in the wisdom of his soul to guide him in the direction that is best for him.

Second/third-stage individuals may also have a tendency to look down on second-stage individuals and, having recently passed through (at least most of) that transition myself, I hope that my work has not reflected this bias. In addition, astrologers in this society are more likely to see people experiencing serious personal problems who do not always represent the general population. These factors may affect their research. In our practice, we astrologers are more likely to see older souls who have gotten themselves into bigger messes during second stage, since the lower you fall, the higher you can rise. In describing third stage I have been more inclined to describe the traits possessed by the older soul in that phase of development, since older souls are more likely to be reading this book. Younger souls can sometimes make the transition in a more instinctive manner, and may not be inclined to be introspective at all. They move slowly and spontaneously towards third stage, and express a more simplified version of its ultimate potential.

To compensate for these potential biases and omissions I would like to end by listing the positive characteristics of second stage within each sign, as well as the traits of the younger souls in third stage:

Constructive Responses to Second Stage

ARIES: Caring and generous souls; positive individuals in the second stage of Aries are capable of giving unfailing support to those they love or to the causes with which they are involved. They still may not know their limits, but those they care about, who are many, certainly know that they are loved.

They are accepting of almost everyone, appreciate the individuality of others, and are unlikely to ever say that one's ideas are crazy or stupid. They are usually looking after several other people of the two-footed or four-footed variety, as they roll on through life in their own humble and unique way, balancing their great menagerie with their own unique brand of (some might call it dis)organization. If they love you, they are your own best audience. Never a dull moment.

TAURUS: Here is a soul whose heartbreak never appears to get them down. They have a great spirit of adventure and use their misadventures of the heart as fuel for their powerful creative ventures. Their creativity is inclined to be unique, and perhaps a little dark around the edges (Salvador Dali came from this mold—which easily leads into the transition). This kind of soul can be in love with the unattainable for years, yet never lose their basic good nature.

Alternatively their need to build a dependable base in the world may turn them into financial geniuses. While the soul waits for the transition into the final stage of its development, the personality learns to be practical. Her practical approach to the material world ultimately spills over into her personal life, and she learns (usually) not to be taken for a ride in her relationships. While she may occasionally be lonely, the challenges of her career keep her quite busy and leave very little room for despondency.

GEMINI: Loyal and dedicated, some of the kindest people you will ever meet are second-stage Gemini's. They revere other people and are always ready to share with or support them in any manner possible. They are capable of undergoing much hardship to assist or care for those they love. Their humility is touching.

Also found in second stage are those who never lose touch with their futuristic ideals. They can work tirelessly for a cause whose time will not come until after their own lives have passed. Possessing great personal integrity, they fight the good fight, honoring each individual's right to be unique.

CANCER: These individuals never lose touch with their sensitivity or their power to care. Once their friend, you are a friend for life. Despite the fears, conflicts and difficulties which assail them, they still dedicate themselves to caring unconditionally for their families. Quietly unconventional, they may possess many unique talents and qualities which find expression in the quiet moments of their private life.

Those who are not active in creating their own family may find creative and unique ways to channel their energy while the soul waits for the transition where all questions will be answered.

LEO: "If you want something done, ask someone who is too busy to do it." This individual is actually capable of being in two places at once! Many second-stage Leos are unfailingly dedicated to their families, and to the multitude of causes which they support. They may occasionally burn out, but are soon back on their feet, and never lose their basic optimism. They can be the most dedicated employee their boss ever had the privilege of hiring. If they are instead inclined to be non-conformists, hang on for the ride of your life! They will never surrender! Absolutely unique and outlandish, they will defend their cause until death if need be, so great is the power of their convictions.

VIRGO: Humble and well organized, this individual is the salt of the Earth. A dedicated craftsmen, she quietly goes about life in her own thorough and efficient manner. If she has been hurt or abandoned by others, she will seldom show it, and is unlikely ever to complain. She knows that we must all pull our own weight in life, and is usually dedicated to her career. She excels in business, science, engineering, or any vocation which will allow her to work with her hands or be close to nature. She often possesses a great affinity for all living things.

LIBRA: You couldn't ask for a more dedicated mate. From different backgrounds, with different interests, maybe even different values, you were nonetheless strongly attracted to each other. He completely won you over. Always the first one to make up after a fight, your Libra is there with his or her winning smile, constantly coming up with a new creative or humorous way to get your attention. He never fails to forgive and forget. Each day is a brand new adventure which the two of you will face together forever. (Well.....maybe.....yeah, I guess so......Of course!)

SCORPIO: Here is an individual whose kindness and ability to care come from a deep understanding of what it means to suffer. She has not led an easy life, but she would be the last person to ever mention the difficulties she has actually experienced—unless it could help someone else. She is a survivor, and she shows those around him that they can do it too. No matter what happens, she always gets out of bed in the morning. She will never lose her strength, her spirit or her ability to care.

SAGITTARIUS: While you may occasionally have to put up with one lecture too many from your dear Sagittarian, you really don't mind, because you always know how much you are loved by this individual. He does not choose to hide his dedication. In addition, you can always rely upon his basic integrity. He always does the right thing. The more conservative Sagittarian builds a sound life on every level.

If you have the privilege of being close to a positive

and adventurous Sagittarian in late second stage, you are in for the most amazing journeys of your life. This individual can break the sound barrier, and take you with him. He is the very embodiment of worldly freedom. Unique experiences become the daily norm.

CAPRICORN: The Statue of Liberty must be a positively oriented second-stage Capricorn:

> Give me your tired, your poor,
> Your huddled masses yearning to breathe free.
> The wretched refuse of your teeming shore.
> Send these the homeless, tempest-tost to me,
> I lift my lamp beside the golden door.

(poem by Emma Lazarus, inscribed on a plaque at the entrance to the Statue of Liberty.)

At the heart of the Capricornian soul is a deep love for humanity. This individual has not yet reached personal enlightenment, but she always has time for you. She helps others often in the simplest or most mundane way, occasionally in a profound material or emotional manner. Often in humble circumstances, she has a quiet dignity and a respect for all people, whatever their station in life may be.

My grandmother was this kind of second-stage Capricorn. She lived alone with her six children in Hell's Kitchen in New York during the depression. Her first/second-stage Piscean husband had gone back home to Mom. She worked long hours to support her children. My mother remembers coming home from school one day to find her in the kitchen teaching English to two Chinese immigrants for free. (She was the daughter who inspired my great grandfather to pass from the first to the third stage of Aries — see the appropriate chapter.)

AQUARIUS: Of course the courage and dedication of the early second-stage Aquarian is beyond reproach. This individual will sacrifice all to better the lot of humanity. As his ardor cools in late second stage, his soul's capacity to dedicate itself to the tribal unit of which he is a part may express itself towards the family which he may create. As a rebellious Aquarian, he is creative and free spirited, expressing great loyalty to those who are also a part of his gypsy band.

If he takes the more conservative route, you can always rely upon his great practicality. A good resource person, he may not always agree with the way society is being run, but he will certainly be able to teach you how to use its rules to your best advantage. He is a good provider for those he loves.

PISCES: I have already mentioned the practical Piscean, who in addition to his wisdom concerning the ways of the world, also often possesses a calm spirit and a gentle quality of compassion. "God grant me the serenity to accept the things I cannot change, the courage to change the things I can, and the wisdom to know the difference." (Dr. Reinhold Niebuhr) This is his prayer.

There is also the gentle soul who lives inwardly in a world where kindness and justice are always triumphant. She may seem somewhat naive, but she is certainly charming. If you stay with her long enough, you just might begin to believe in the possibility of a better world. She is caring and creative, bringing the world of the faeries with her into this one. She may see the world through rose-colored glasses, but she also seems to lead a charmed life, and in her presence, you may do so as well.

The Young Soul in Third Stage

ARIES: A young soul in the third stage of Aries may not be a mystic, but he is certain to be a master of some specific art or skill. He might be good at whatever he does. His attitude towards himself is well-balanced. He is a disciplined individual, and often takes an innocent joy in himself which could never be considered the least bit offensive.

TAURUS: This individual possesses the innocent joy and unconditional love of first stage. Once again creative and strongly bound to the natural world, she is as loving towards herself as she is towards others, and is able to attract fulfilling partnerships.

GEMINI: Vulnerability is his strength. He is lovable and unique, and slightly ahead of his time. His trust in life and himself, coupled with his honesty and integrity as an individual, win him many friends.

CANCER: This individual works tirelessly for the good of her community. Religion may inspire her.

LEO: A playful soul who lives to create. He is caught up in enthusiasm for the experience of life, and his enthusiasm is often quite contagious.

VIRGO: This individual trusts herself. She can live independently and yet share deeply. She is in harmony with her body, and feels no need to question how she has become who she is.

LIBRA: Works to amend and perfect the structure of his society. Diplomatic, yet unbending and powerfully assertive when necessary.

SCORPIO: Lives from a simple, often conventional structure of faith, experiencing no need to question the mechanics of the operation. Accepting and non-judgmental towards herself and others.

SAGITTARIUS: Has learned to be himself without needing to explain his actions to anyone. May understand and express the basic tenets of several spiritual or philosophical systems in a non-dogmatic manner.

CAPRICORN: Perhaps an artist, engineer or healer on a physical level, her greatest joy is to see how things function from the inside out. If others can be inspired by her vision, so much the better, but she feels no drive to change the world or to achieve wealth and fame. She simply wants to 'know' and to 'see'.

AQUARIUS: This individual has learned to approach life with a positive attitude. While he is no great social scientist, he still knows what constitutes a positive lifestyle. In the process of living the life which brings him the greatest satisfaction, he may unwittingly teach others how they can improve their lives as well.

PISCES: Without remembering how, this individual has learned to trust life. She overcomes his problems as if by magic, as her unconscious confidence in the greater whole and her non-resistance to life create quiet miracles in their own right. Optimistic and inspired by life, she has flashes of psychic vision which she uses to assist others. Her quiet joy eventually proves quite contagious.

QUESTIONS AND ANSWERS

Q. *After reading this book, I am convinced that I am a late second/third-stage Libra. Many of the people I know appear to be in the first or second stage of their respective signs. Does this mean that I am more spiritually evolved than they are?*

A. One of the dangers of the theory presented in this book is that it may be misused as a form of spiritual one-upmanship. It is important to remember that almost all of us must pass through many signs — perhaps even completing each of the twelve signs more than once — before reaching perfection as human beings. The three stages of the signs may be likened to the three semesters of a school year. If you are in the third semester of the first grade, and someone else is in the first semester of the fifth, you could hardly claim to be ahead of that individual. It is not always easy to determine the level of spiritual development of a given individual.

Those who are passing through first or second stage with a great deal of awareness of spiritual concepts, and an ability to be objective about their life situations are likely to be very old souls, even if they possess certain flaws of character which tend to frustrate those in later stages of development. It is also possible for a very young soul to reach and complete third stage with very little conscious understanding of the process in which they are involved. First-stage people 'appear' to be behind second-stage people and second-stage people seem to be behind those in third stage, but in reality it is very difficult to determine who possesses the greater level of soul development. Relationships between an older soul at an earlier stage of development and a younger soul in one of the later stages can be enormously illuminating for all concerned.

Above and beyond all this, it is important to remember that spiritual growth and self-development is not a race. Nor are those at later stages of development in any way superior to those who have recently set foot upon the great road of life.

Q. *I am a Leo. What sign am I most compatible with?*

A. I hate to burst everyone's bubble, but the idea that those of a specific Sun sign are more compatible with certain Sun signs and less compatible with other Sun signs was largely invented to sell magazines andbooks! The best way to determine the dynamics of a given relationship is to compare the unique charts of the two individuals involved. This is usually done not to say yes or no to a specific relationship (although there are some situations where an obvious, strong compatibility or incompatibility is apparent), but to help the individuals concerned to better understand their relationship and each other.

No sign is really more inherently compatible with one sign than with another. However, on a general basis you would be better off asking what <u>stage</u> you are most compatible with. Generally speaking the most harmonious and compatible relationships are between individuals of the same stage of development. However there are always plenty of exceptions to this rule. Volume two of the New Astrology Series outlines the common dynamics with tend to exist between individuals of every sign and stage.

Q. *My Sun is in Aries, my Moon is in Capricorn, and I have Scorpio rising (i.e a Scorpio Ascendant). Does this mean that the sections relating to Scorpio and Capricorn will also apply to me? And what about the other planets in my chart?*

A. The Sun is the center of the solar system. It is the source of life energy for all beings upon the Earth, and all of the planets revolve in orbit around it. Because of this, the Sun's position in the birth chart represents the central spiritual theme of the individual. No other planet* in the chart can be viewed from the same perspective. The Moon, the Ascendant and all of the other eight planets each have their own individual meanings and functions which will be explained, for beginner and expert alike, in future volumes of this series.

However this does not mean that you will not be influenced by some of the other archetypes presented in this book. If we look at the symbolism of the Moon, we see that it reflects the light of the Sun onto the Earth. Because the light rays must first strike the Moon's surface before being relayed to Earth, it could be said that the light which reaches us from the moon is older than that which emanates directly from the Sun. In addition, the Moon seems to stand watch over the Earth, guiding the rhythms of life on the planet below.

According to certain esoteric sources, the position of the Moon in the natal chart usually indicates the sign position of the Sun in a previous cycle of incarnations. Having tested this theory with many people, I am inclined to believe it to be correct. In addition, I have noticed that most people will tend to relive the patterns of the Moon sign as they pass through the various stages of their Sun sign. In other words, since you are an Aries with the Moon in Capricorn, you will experience many of the same kinds of experiences as a first-stage Capricorn, as you pass through the first stage of Aries. In second-stage Aries, your life will also take on subtle tones of the second stage of Capricorn, and so on. Combining the meanings of the Sun and Moon signs can often result in startlingly accurate forms of character analysis.

In addition, an individual's oldest and most enduring personal conflicts can often be traced to the first stage or first/second-stage transition of the Moon sign, which seems to always seek to draw us back into our ancient past. Although the Moon can be our undoing, it can also be our salvation. Because we have mastered the Moon sign once, it is easier to do so again. As we step forward with the

*For simplicity's sake astrologers generally use the term 'planets' when referring to the Sun and the Moon, as well as the other eight planets which accompany our Earth in the Solar System. Of course we know that they are not really planets, but it is an old traditional term and a means of simplifying our language.

Moon sign, the process of doing so can give us a bird's eye view of the Sun, making it ultimately easier to solve the riddles presented to us by this central theme. This subject will be covered in greater detail when the Moon is explored in a future volume of this series. Your Ascendant and all or most of your other planets are interpreted according to a different system than the one presented in this book, and will also be discussed in future volumes. You may find that some of the childhood conditions described under your ascending sign may apply to you in a general manner. If you combine the childhood influences of Aries, Capricorn and Scorpio (your Sun, Moon and Ascendant) you may find that a very accurate picture of your early life may emerge.

Q. *I was born on July 25th, on the cusp of Cancer and Leo. Does this mean that I should read the information given under both signs?*

A. In recent years the mistaken idea that the cusp between two signs can last anywhere from several days to a week at most has been circulated. In reality the true cusp of the sign (otherwise known as the 29th degree) lasts for a little less than 24 hours. Therefore you are not on the cusp. You are a true Leo, and only the information given for that sign will apply to you.

If you are born very close to the end of the sign, or find that some astrology books list your birthday under one sign, while others list you under another, then you may be on the cusp of the two signs. A competent astrologer should be able to tell you easily whether or not you are on the cusp, as the times and dates are slightly different every year. An accurate time and place of birth may be required. Many people who are not actually on the cusp of two signs may believe that they are because they have many character traits of both signs. When this occurs it is usually because the planets Venus or Mercury or both are in the neighboring sign. These planets also influence character and are always very close to the Sun. When I first became interested in astrology I mistakenly believed that I was on the cusp. In reality I have Mercury, Venus and the Moon in the neighboring sign, so their influence is very strong.

Q. *I am very interested in finding out more about my previous lives. Is there a way that I could do this, or anything I could do to stimulate my memories?*

A. In our society, even if we accept the possibility of reincarnation we tend to believe that it is very difficult to remember other lifetimes and that this kind of recall must be very rare. In reality it is actually not that difficult. All memories, whether stemming from a past life or the present life, are not stored in the brain but in the soul. The brain is simply the receiving station for our memories. This may sound like a startling idea, but it is well known that science has not yet 'discovered' exactly where in the brain our memories are stored. It is known that electrical stimulation of the brain's surface will cause someone to recall certain memories, but no concrete proof that memory is actually stored on the brain's surface has been found. It is also known that certain brain injuries lead to memory 'loss', but once the brain has recovered, as it can from many injuries, the memories return. Where did they go? If we understand the brain as a transmitter of memories, the answer falls into place. In reality we can never lose anything. We just occasionally misplace it.

If this is the case, then why are we not born with the ability to automatically remember our previous lifetimes? The answer is that we often are, but because our early memories are not accepted by our culture these recollections tend to fade. In addition, the subconscious seems to have a protective mechanism which usually keeps much of our past memory rather hidden so that it does not interfere with the process of building the present personality. The exception to this rule occurs when the need to come to terms with past traumas is so powerful that it is able to override this protective mechanism. Certain aspects in the birthchart (to be discussed in a future volume) indicate that the individual is still being strongly influenced by certain past experiences. In this case the memory may emerge in the form of phobias, nightmares, longings or compulsions, or the individual may have full spontaneous recall at some point. An excellent book which describes this process is "Across Time and Death: A Mother's Search For Her Past

Life Children" by Jenny Cockell, a story of a woman who remembered the children she had left behind as a result of an early death in a lifetime which ended twenty years before she was born. It describes her successful search for her children from that lifetime, many of whom were still alive and in their 60s and 70s when she found them.

If you are interested in recalling previous lifetimes, there are certain steps which you can take. The same mechanism which tends to prevent easy access to past life memories can ultimately assist you in this process. This is because its purpose is to help to build, promote and integrate the present lifetime's personality. At first this requires that certain memories remain latent. However it is often valuable to recall one's soul history during certain phases of development, usually during the second/third-stage transition. If this process is of value to the present lifetime's personality this same subconscious mechanism will eventually assist you in recalling past life memories. If you have a strong interest in the subject, this is usually a sign that you are ready to begin recalling past experiences. Alert your subconscious through your interest. Spend some time thinking about and studying the subject.

Study history in a general manner and look at different cultures. Are there any specific times or places which seem to always evoke a certain reaction from you? Do you feel strongly attracted to a certain place or time in history? Do you almost know what it must have been like then? Do any places or periods evoke a strong unexplainable aversion or feeling of fear? These are likely indicators that you may have been there. A humorous example of this sort of thing occurred whenever my mother and I used to watch Western movies together. The cowboys and Indians would be fighting. Just as the cowboys were about to lose, the cavalry would come over the hillside. My mother would always say, "Oh goody, here comes the cavalry", as she admired their uniforms and felt great pride.

I would say, "Damn! Here comes the cavalry again!"

Pick a certain place or time which seems to provoke a reaction, and start with the assumption that you may have been there. Ask yourself questions. If I had been there who might I have been? Was I male or female? What part of society do I feel most comfortable in? Where did I belong? Was this a happy or unhappy lifetime? Why was it so? Sometimes it helps to put your questions into present tense. Who am I? Take note of any impressions which you might perceive. Many times our memories come as very subtle impressions at first. The subconscious gives us little bits of imagery and ideas to see how we deal with them, and to allow us time to integrate the information and prepare for the time when we will receive the full impact of the memory. At first many people wonder if it is not all their imagination, but at a later time the memories return with such force and emotional impact that they cannot be denied.

Many people walk around haunted by half-remembered traumas, wondering if they are being self-indulgent, trying to get attention (even though they usually keep these memories to themselves), or if their impressions can be explained as a result of their present life experiences. For example, I once had a client who was having miscarriages and difficulty in conceiving even though she very much wanted to start a family. She said she remembered seeing her children being killed in front of her because she had been a witch in a previous lifetime (her Sun was in Cancer). But then she said that perhaps she was making it all up because she was a witch in this lifetime. I replied that was possible, but another explanation might be that she had simply returned to the same path in this lifetime.

Patience is important. You may not be ready to remember everything all at once. Your first memory might consist only of vague images. Months or even years later the full impact may emerge. It may be useful to get together with close friends and relatives who are also interested in the subject. Anyone whom you have been close to, almost from the moment you first met, is likely to have also been close to you in other times. We travel in packs, and we can help each other to remember the past. Is there a time or a place that both you and your friend(s) feel a great affinity or aversion for? Sometimes we can look at one another and say "I could see you as this type of person." You might reply that you have always identified with that particular role or form of cultural experience, and this may cause you to reconsider something which had previously seemed too obvious or rather unimportant.

Sometimes our past-life memories are very traumatic and

we need a lot of support while we are remembering. You may find close friends useful for this, or you may wish to seek a competent therapist. There are good past-life therapists out there, although they are not always easy to find. Sometimes psychiatrists also use certain techniques related to past life recall, or you may wish to seek assistance from a reputable practitioner of the alternative healing arts such as Reiki or the Radiance Technique, et al. Past life therapists work in different ways—some through bodywork, since our body is in constant contact with the subconscious and is therefore in constant reaction to what is stored there.

Another technique involves using key phrases. Is there a key phrase which you constantly seem to use when experiencing certain problems that you believe may be related to past lives? This phrase is repeated while in a relaxed state, often causing memories to emerge. Hypnosis is the first thing most people think of when considering past-life recall. However, it is not the first thing which I would recommend. Some people have good results with it, but others are not good subjects. Some may find the memories which emerge too traumatic. It is usually better to try and access the subconscious while remaining in a conscious state. Your own intuitive feelings are usually a good guide as to which avenue to pursue.

How can you tell if you may have some traumatic memories? Repetitive nightmares, phobias or irrational behavior with no known explanation in the present lifetime may be an indication. I have had clients whose charts indicated that they were still strongly influenced by a traumatic previous lifetime experience and who admitted to questioning their own sanity as a result of the phobias and irrational actions which seemed to haunt them. Although I cannot always see specific past-life events, in these cases I have often been able to, and these clients ended up agreeing with me that it was a miracle that they did not have more reactions than they did. Remembering or understanding what happened and why often sets us free.

This book is also a good key to the past. Identify your stage of development and you will have a good clue to the types of experiences which you have encountered in previous lifetimes. If you are a second/third-stage Virgo for instance, and feel a strong affinity for a particular historical era perhaps three or four hundred years ago when you were in first stage, you already know that you were probably in a position of privilege or led a very protected life. This may help you to zero in on some more specific details. Another interesting book which may be helpful is "Astrology and Your Past Lives" by Jeanne Avery. This gives some very interesting details of regression experiences undergone by her clients. She lists the types of experiences of people with specific aspects in their charts. (This is a drawback if you do not yet know what the planetary aspects are in your birthchart and, yes, you guessed it, we will be learning to find these out in a future volume.) She also gives a past-life recall technique similar to those which I have listed above.

Q. *Do we always stay the same sign for several lifetimes in a row before moving on to another, or can we be one sign in one life and another in the next, jumping back and forth before completing a sign?*

A. From work with myself and others I have found that we do usually stay in one sign until we have completed it. I do not believe that this must be the case. The soul does not perceive time the way that the personality does, and our present life experience is often more strongly related to lifetimes which have occurred a very long time ago than it is to lifetimes which have occurred recently. This may be because we can have several different signs on the go at the same time, just like someone may be knitting a sweater while a half-finished pair of mittens and a hat sit in the knitting basket beside him. If you are in the middle of a sign in this lifetime, it is likely that you were the same sign in the previous lifetime, but this is not invariably the case.

Q. *Is it possible for someone to complete all three stages in one lifetime? Until my early twenties I acted very much like your description of the first stage of my sign, until my thirties I seemed like I was in second stage, and now I seem to be in the third stage.*

A. I have never seen it myself, but I suppose it would be possible for a very advanced soul to complete a sign in just one lifetime. This would likely be rare. What I have seen happen, however, is what could be called a review of the ground covered so far. A soul born into late second/third stage or early third stage sometimes chooses to relive all of the stages which he or she has previously experienced during the early part of the present lifetime. This helps to tie it all together. In second/third stage or early third stage it is often valuable to recall previous lifetimes in order to understand the process which has led to the formation of the present personality structure. Instead of actually remembering past events and experiences, if you relive the past patterns in miniature, the same benefits often result. This is probably what you have done.

It is often difficult to be certain of the stage of development of a child, partly for this reason. Even children who are not in the very last stages of development of their Sun signs may express first-stage tendencies when very young, and progress to second or third stage as they mature.

Q. *Can you tell by looking at somebody's chart what stage they are at?*

A. Not with any certainty, no. There are some clues, but the best way to determine the stage of a given individual is through personal contact. This is why I always prefer to speak to my clients in person or on the phone, or to speak to someone who knows the person for whom the reading is being done.

Certain patterns are common to individuals of a given stage of a specific sign. For example, it is common for Scorpios in second stage to experience a great deal of rejection. If I look at a chart with Sun in Scorpio and there are many difficult aspects related to relationships and a cold or rejecting early life experience, this gives me a hint that the individual may be in second stage. However, they may have been born into second stage and are now in second/third or even third stage. The overall conditions of the birthchart can give some hints, but they are not 100% reliable.

Another indicator of the possible stage of development is the condition of the ruling planet. The ruling planet is the planet which rules the ascendant. It represents an individual's self-worth and personal identity. If this planet is in a sign and house in which it experiences difficulty, the individual is likely to be in second stage. If it is in a sign and house in which it thrives, he or she is probably in first or third stage. More complex or sophisticated aspects to a positively placed ruling planet usually indicate third stage, while a more simple configuration usually represents first stage.

Q. *I have Sun in Pisces and Moon in Libra. You mention that many times when someone has Sun in Pisces, this is their first sign. You have also stated that the Moon sign represents the Sun sign we were before we chose our present sign. What does my Moon sign represent? I also have a friend who has both the Sun and Moon in Capricorn. What does his Moon sign represent?*

A. Your Moon sign represents your most predominant impressions of your experiences prior to entering this world. Animals are also affected by astrological factors. For instance, if your previous set of incarnations was in the animal kingdom you may have had a very Libran sort of existence. Perhaps you were a member of some species which mates for life, or worked in a very co-operative relationship with a human owner. Perhaps you were a team animal. If you have another kind of soul origin you may still have had a parallel form of experience which is indicated by your Libran moon.

When people have the same Sun and Moon signs, this indicates one of two things. The first possibility is that the individual is repeating the sign. This does not mean that he failed last time, instead he may have passed through the same sign in a much earlier series of incarnations. It is therefore a completely different journey when one is an older soul with a much more sophisticated form of experience. Another alternative is that she has become so affected by the experiences of the present sign that these are the predominant experiences stored in the subconscious. It is usually something of a disadvantage to have both Sun and Moon in the same sign, as it is more difficult to have a balanced reaction to one's experiences. However, once the individual begins to master her sign, she then has the advantage of a much greater ability to concentrate upon her soul purpose.